COLONIAL MISSISSIPPI

COLONIAL MISSISSIPPI

· A Borrowed Land ·

Christian Pinnen and Charles Weeks

University Press of Mississippi for the Mississippi Historical Society
and the Mississippi Department of Archives and History / Jackson

Publication of this book was made possible
by a grant from the Phil Hardin Foundation.

The University Press of Mississippi is the scholarly publishing agency of
the Mississippi Institutions of Higher Learning: Alcorn State University,
Delta State University, Jackson State University, Mississippi State University,
Mississippi University for Women, Mississippi Valley State University,
University of Mississippi, and University of Southern Mississippi.

www.upress.state.ms.us

The University Press of Mississippi is a member
of the Association of University Presses.

First printing 2021
∞

Library of Congress Cataloging-in-Publication Data available

LCCN 2020051280
ISBN 9781496832702 (hardcover)
ISBN 9781496832894 (epub single)
ISBN 9781496832887 (epub institutional)
ISBN 9781496832900 (pdf single)
ISBN 9781496832917 (pdf institutional)

British Library Cataloging-in-Publication Data available

CONTENTS

COLONIAL MISSISSIPPI

INTRODUCTION

"You are in a borrowed land," the Chickasaw chief Taskietoka told the Spanish commissioner to the Chickasaws and Choctaws, Juan Delavillebeuvre, in a 1793 letter. Delavillebeuvre was attempting to enlist the support of the Choctaws in an effort to end an ongoing conflict between some Chickasaws and Creeks despite opposition from another Chickasaw chief, Piomingo. More important, Delavillebeuvre wanted to facilitate a meeting of representatives of the major Native American groups in the region to create some kind of confederation to include the Spanish. The goal was to provide a mechanism to resolve conflicts peacefully and create an effective deterrent to perceived threats from the newly independent United States. Taskietoka had strongly supported the creation of such a confederation during a 1792 meeting in New Orleans with the newly appointed Spanish governor-general of Louisiana, François Louis Héctor de Carondelet.[1]

A group of Creek Indians had used similar words thirty years earlier at the end of the French and Indian War (1754–63), which resulted in the transfer of what there was of a French empire in North America to Britain and Spain.[2] John Stuart, the British superintendent of Indian affairs in the trans-Appalachian southern district created in 1763, reported to his superior that according to intelligence from the "Creek Nation," the "French Faction in that country" had expressed much distress at the news of the "removal" of the French from Mobile and Alabama forts and that "lands now possessed by the French must revert" to the Creeks because they had never been "ceded but only Lent." Although the earlier issues differed from those causing some dissension between Chickasaws and Spanish in 1793, both were political, with the word *land*—whether described as "borrowed" or "lent" or perhaps in a broader sense "shared" or "storied"—used to affirm presence and power.[3]

We use the phrase *borrowed land* and its many variations to frame the discussion for a better understanding of a "colonial Mississippi" because it appropriately characterizes the region as one in which Europeans consistently had to acknowledge the power of the indigenous people in the region. Before

3

it became a territory of the new United States in 1798 and a state nineteen years later, Mississippi existed only as part of a larger forested and rolling land crossed by rivers and streams that had long been the homeland of those whom European newcomers and their descendants generally came to refer to as First Peoples, Indians, Native Americans, or Amerindians. These Native peoples remained the most numerous group in the region until the second half of the eighteenth century, when the balance shifted to people of European and African origin. By 1800, the area had become very much a diverse, multiethnic, hybrid, or "Creole" world, and ongoing negotiations on many levels and in many different ways characterized life in this world.[4]

Taskietoka thus seems to have used *borrowed* to tell the Spanish commissioner that the Chickasaws did not welcome intrusion into these ongoing disputes that often resulted in violence. Rather, the Spanish should understand their role as limited. Taskietoka, sometimes referred to in documents as the "king" of the Chickasaws, came to be regarded as a leader of a faction that saw the Spanish as more supportive of Chickasaw interests. By using *borrowed* in a more ample sense, it can help us understand some of the many ways people viewed and represented land, landscape, and one another during the period of interaction, interdependency, and exchange between 1500 and 1800.[5]

Chapter 1 offers a brief review of the Native North American world as it was when newcomers from Europe and Africa began to arrive on Caribbean islands such as Hispaniola, Cuba, and Puerto Rico in the wake of Columbus's first voyage west from Spain in 1492.[6] Over the next century, European settlements moved to mainland North America. In 1513, Juan Ponce de León, a veteran of Columbus's second voyage, in 1493, set out from Puerto Rico on a voyage to the north to search for an island of Bimini. That trip initiated a period of exploration and discovery that extended to the entire Gulf Coast and beyond.[7] Beginning in 1519, Cuban-based Hernán Cortés led expeditions consisting of Spaniards, a large number of indigenous allies, and some Africans that triggered the collapse of the Aztec empire centered in what is now Mexico. The Spanish replaced it with a region verbally and cartographically described as Nueva España (New Spain). Discoveries of gold and silver whetted their and others' appetites for more.[8]

We then give attention to a period of initial and marginal contacts in the sixteenth century by the Spanish in "La Florida," which they had defined as stretching from the Florida peninsula to the west along the northern shore of what we now know as the Gulf of Mexico. Contacts between Europeans and Native Americans continued in this area during much of the seventeenth century, and we focus on the Soto expedition that began in the late 1530s and penetrated what became Mississippi. Native people encountered Europeans for the first time, and the newcomers left behind a human landscape that quickly changed. The Mississippian chiefdoms that existed at the time of the Soto expedition no longer existed—with the notable exception of the Natchez—as the French began to settle the region. A second Spanish attempt two decades later found a much-altered Native American world.

Chapter 2 explores French activities that began with a settlement along Biloxi Bay in 1699 to initiate a period of sustained contact between European newcomers and natives. The French, British, and Spanish contended with one another, sought support from Native groups, and brought enslaved Africans to serve as workers with the goal of establishing colonies as parts of larger empires. These efforts continued until the second decade of the nineteenth century, when another power motivated by aspirations for expansion—the United States—came onto the scene. While our sources predominantly stem from the European administrations that governed the region over the next century, those administrations never truly dominated the region. Native American people were certainly players on at least equal terms, and enslaved Africans sought independence and freedom in ways that shaped the responses of the colonial powers.

As the French endeavored to create a sustained and profitable presence on the Gulf Coast and in the lower Mississippi Valley, they encountered immense difficulties. In addition to the problems associated with marshaling the financial and demographic resources needed to run a colony as large as Louisiana, the French discovered that building their imperial dreams on funds generated through protocapitalist stock companies and the ensuing booms and busts of speculative bubbles hamstrung the development at every turn. Louisiana frequently changed economic trustees and settlers did not always come voluntarily, with the result that the colony lingered on the edge of French Atlantic possessions. However, these issues meant that the Europeans who came—and the enslaved Africans they kidnapped—were diverse and polyglot, and they intermingled with an equally diverse group of Native Americans in the area.

Trouble abounded. Imperial rivalries, wars, ineffective diplomacy with the Native Americans, and growing racial tensions undermined any progress made by the French administrators. In the Natchez country in particular, successive moments of crisis eventually led the Natchez people to join forces with enslaved Africans to oust the French in 1729. However, the Natchez eventually succumbed to a combined force of French and other Native allies and were forced to flee to allies around the region. The French settlement project never recovered from the financial losses and the damaged image of the colony.

Chapter 3 turns to the British period, when even the world's most powerful empire could not muster enough resources to succeed in the region. The conclusion of the French and Indian War brought Great Britain to the pinnacle of its territorial expansion. However, it also marked the beginning of the end of its empire in what is now the United States. The 1763 Treaty of Paris nominally gave Great Britain control of North America from the Atlantic coast to the Mississippi River, but Native American power beyond the Appalachian Mountains was unbroken, and westward expansion quickly became too expensive. Hence, West Florida lingered at the edge of the British empire.

Tension with Spain, which received New Orleans and land west of the Mississippi River from France in 1762, was initially of less concern. Most important, the British had to find diplomatic means to retain the allegiance of Native peoples in the area and to secure the loyalty of groups that had developed generally good relations with the French. A peaceful region was necessary to attract settlers, many of whom were veterans of the French and Indian War. But they came slowly, and economic success eluded the British in West Florida. The promise of the soil did draw people to the region, but the instability of the area—in particular with the onset of the American Revolution—did not bode well for the future. Indeed, a 1778 raid by former Natchez resident James Willing brought the fighting to Natchez, and when Spain joined the war on the side of the French a year later, the British episode in West Florida ended with as little fanfare as it had begun.

Chapter 4 picks up the story of colonial Mississippi in the Spanish period. During the American Revolution, the Spanish had occupied British posts along the Gulf Coast and north along the Mississippi River. Beginning in 1779, Spanish holdings in North America were enlarged, and many of the settlers were Anglo-American. Encouraged by a generally tolerant Spanish religious policy and generous land grants, they continued to arrive in the area, at times proving an irksome presence to the Iberians. Coupled with expansionary schemes by individual states of the struggling American republic, local Anglo-Americans continued to follow their own ideas about the future of the region.

The Spanish were often challenged by complex diplomatic negotiations with the newly independent United States, which did not have a strong federal government until 1789. Hence, sustaining good relations with Native Americans and individual states required frequent meetings that often involved hundreds or even thousands of people. Treaties had to be negotiated and gifts provided. Indian rivalries and a need for trade goods also presented challenges for the Spanish, as they had for the French and British before.

Spain retained a Natchez district as part of the Province of West Florida only until 1798. Although a 1795 treaty gave the region north of the Thirty-First Parallel to the United States, Spain did not vacate the region until three years later. This caused some consternation and commotion among the people in Natchez and the surrounding Indian nations, as trade agreements and power structures hung in the balance. Even the considerable linguistic and diplomatic skills of Natchez's governor, Manuel Gayoso de Lemos, were challenged to maintain peace and deliver the district to the Americans. The area to the south remained in Spanish hands, at least marginally.

Chapter 5 explores the history of the Mississippi Gulf Coast. Many descendants of the original French settlers remained in the region, and family and place-names reflecting these origins are still evident today. With the addition of British, Anglo-American, and Atlantic African people, the nominally Spanish region assumed a polyglot and multiethnic character. In addition, the local Native groups, in particular the Creeks, required the Spanish to sustain a careful diplomacy among all people. Yet Americans, either in official capacity or simply as adventurers, continued to undercut Spanish government efforts.

If local affairs were bad, international affairs were much worse for the Spanish empire. Napoleon Bonaparte's invasion of Spain forced the Spanish government to operate through local juntas for much of the first two decades of the nineteenth century, leading to independence movements in Spanish America. Napoleon ceded all of Louisiana to the United States in 1803 after he had failed to suppress the independence movement of formerly enslaved Haitians in Saint-Domingue, further weakening Spain's position in the Gulf. By 1810, West Florida was no longer under its control, and nine years later, Spain finally gave up both East and West Florida to the United States under the Adams-Onís Treaty. By then, Spain's once extensive empire was crumbling everywhere, and Mississippi was in American hands.

Chapter 6 investigates the transitions of the region's settlers, Natives, and political institutions after 1798. Before Mississippi could reach statehood, much of the land had to be wrested from the hands of Native peoples, notably the Choctaws and Chickasaws. Multiple treaties seized land from the respective Native people. Driven by the booming cotton market and not deterred by the War of 1812 and economic declines, enslavers from the east coast poured into Mississippi, buying large tracts of land at inflated prices and laying the groundwork for the cotton empire, which would dominate Mississippi's economy and help fund the nation's westward expansion. Finally, chapter 7 summarizes some of the ways Mississippi's colonial past has been remembered, recovered, and represented since 1800, highlighting the most important collections of documents both in the state and abroad.

CHAPTER ONE

La Florida and Mississippi

Early European Contacts and Native Responses

In the spring of 1541, Native Mississippian warriors attacked a Spanish expeditionary force led by Hernando de Soto in the northern part of modern-day Mississippi. The local Indians almost ended the longest *entrada* (expedition) of Iberians into the North American Southeast, attacking a group of some 350 European explorers, soldiers, and adventurers (roughly half the original number), who managed to stave off annihilation by the Chicaza but nevertheless lost almost all of their food, some weapons, and other supplies.[1]

This period of initial but not sustained contact between Spaniards and Mississippian peoples of the Southeast had begun two decades earlier with Ponce de León. Though the Spanish devoted substantial resources and manpower to the region they baptized La Florida, the results were disappointing. La Florida never even remotely rivaled the colonies in Mexico, Peru, or the Caribbean. Europeans' efforts to find wealth and status through conquest across the Southeast were thwarted by Native people and nature.

The Soto expedition inflicted environmental changes on the Mississippian culture and the North American Southeast. Mississippian people were adversely affected by the presence of the European conquistadores, yet warfare and violence were not unusual to the Natives. Although Soto and his people caused upheaval, they ultimately moved on. But unwanted visitors such as deadly pathogens remained and exacerbated the transformations of both nature and humanity that were already underway.[2] While Soto and his followers did not stay, the pathogens and social changes begun by the *entrada* did.

This chapter explores the effect of Soto's army on the people and environment of the region as well as the first French settlement initiatives on the Gulf

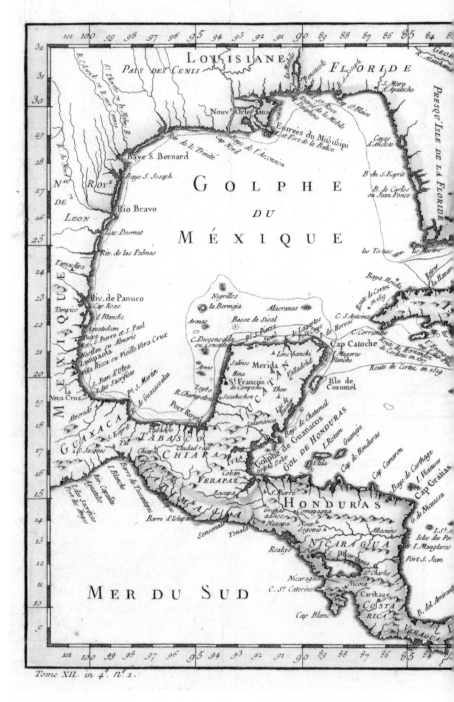

Jacques-Nicolas Bellin, *Map of the Gulf of Mexico and the American Islands*, 1754.
This detailed map visually represents some significant first contacts among peoples
from Europe, Africa, and America. It shows some routes taken by early explorers
as Juan Ponce de León and Hernán Cortéz. Courtesy of the Archives and Research
Services Divisions, Mississippi Department of Archives and History, Jackson.

CARTE DU
GOLPHE DU MÉXIQUE
ET DES
ISLES DE L'AMÉRIQUE.

Pour servir à l'Histoire Générale des Voyages.
Par M. Bellin Ing.ʳ de la Marine 1754.

Echelle
Lieues Marines de France.

Coast. It also places Soto's expedition in its historic context both in the larger Atlantic world and in a long line of previous marginal encounters between Spaniards and Native Americans along the Gulf Coast. Finally, it traces the transformations that subsequently occurred within the indigenous landscapes.[3] Contact with European people, animals, and microbes permanently altered the Natives' culture and society and even nature so much so that Spaniard Tristán de Luna y Arellano, who traveled to the region in 1559, could not reconcile what he found with the land and the people described by his predecessors in the Soto campaign.[4] The initial contacts between French and Natives in the century after the Spanish expeditions in the region provide a stark contrast. The French were more willing to interact with local people via trade and diplomacy rather than violence and thus were able to sustain contact as long as Natives believed that the presence of the foreigners was beneficial.

Mississippian Cultures

Archaeologists and historians have used the term *Mississippian* to describe this region from about 900 to 1700. The area was characterized by the presence of chiefdoms or regional polities where one leader ruled over subordinate villages, small farms, hunting grounds, fishing spots, mines, and salt licks tied together in a variety of ways. Divided into elites and commoners who cultivated sub-stantial areas of land stretching along river valleys, many of these chiefdoms had large town centers.[5]

The largest chiefdom was Cahokia, in present-day Illinois east of St. Louis, Missouri, and characterized by Ronald Wright as a "full-blown city with several hundred mounds and pyramids." With as many as forty thousand inhabitants in the thirteenth century, it was "populous as the London or Paris of that time."[6]Although Cahokia had been abandoned well before Europeans began to arrive in the region, it and other similar urban centers had an ongoing influence on Native or indigenous peoples and even on those Europeans who encountered the architectural ruins.[7]

Farther south, similar chiefdoms and mound sites emerged during this time at such locations as Moundville in present-day Alabama, Etowah in Georgia, Apalachee in the Florida panhandle, Emerald Mound at the southern end of what is now the Natchez Trace Parkway, and Winterville in the Yazoo–Mississippi Delta basin region just north of Greenville, Mississippi. As in Cahokia, many of these settlements had both large and small mounds as a defining physical feature. Agriculture centered increasingly on the cultivation of squash, beans, and especially corn, which developed a rich mythology, as a subsistence base to support a rising population and the emergence of kin-based societies. In addition to streams and rivers, an elaborate trail system connected communities and facilitated the spread of the Mississippian culture. Over time, these independent Native polities made the region increasingly a bordered, owned, or "storied land," as European newcomers later noted. Chiefdoms often fought for control over resources and people, but because warfare endangered the agricultural centers, Mississippians were careful to keep campaigns and casualties to a minimum.[8]

By the end of the sixteenth century, however, a devolution back to kinship-centered polities had begun. Much of this world, with the notable exception of the Natchez country, evolved toward confederations characterized by decentralized authority, allowing for greater flexibility in resisting external control and possible diminution of ethnic variety and identity.[9]

European Beginnings

In early October 1492, Christopher Columbus and his fellow mariners arrived on an island in the Bahamas east of the Florida peninsula.[10] Because of what followed—the opening up of the Americas to European exploration and exploitation involving encounters between people from Europe, Africa, and America and the accompanying biological, ecological, and cultural exchanges that followed—one historian has characterized Columbus's arrival as having as much influence on the planet as did the retreat of the continental glaciers.[11] In that context, historical anthropologist Samuel Wilson has used the term *mutual rediscovery* to focus more explicitly on the Native side of the encounters begun by Columbus.[12]

Columbus was born in Genoa into a world characterized by a blend of commerce, incipient capitalism, exploration, and religious fervor. In the fifteenth century, changes in thinking about geography aided by a revival of interest in Ptolemy and in the work of such people as astronomer and mathematician Paolo Toscanelli led many to conclude that it would be possible to reach Asia by sailing west. With the help of his cartographer brother, Bartholomew, Christopher Columbus, who had become a skillful navigator, eagerly absorbed much of this research and thinking, and in 1484 he began approaching patrons seeking backing for an Atlantic crossing. After failing to secure support from both the Portuguese and the French kings, he finally persuaded an Aragonese treasury official closely associated with Fernando and Isabella of Spain to put together a financial consortium to underwrite the cost of the voyage. In addition, Columbus received a *capitulación* (concession) from Isabella providing a legal framework for the voyage that brought him to America in October 1492.[13]

That year had begun auspiciously for Christian militants on both sides of the Pyrenees with the somewhat disorderly conclusion of the centuries-long Reconquista (Reconquest), the effort to end Moorish and African Muslim occupation of the Iberian Peninsula. In 1469, the king of Aragón, Fernando, had married the queen of Castilla, Isabella, establishing the dynastic basis for a kingdom of Spain.[14] In late December 1491, Abu I-Quim al-Muhli signed treaties that surrendered Granada to the Roman Catholic kingdom of Castile, and on January 2, 1492, the flag of Castile and a Christian cross were raised on the tower of the Alhambra, an Islamic palace in Granada.[15] Columbus's achievement later in the year enhanced the status of the monarchy and the prospects for a new kingdom of Spain. Columbus's voyages and the expeditions that followed linked the Reconquista—the religious crusade that had defined so much of Spanish culture during the Middle Ages—with the more secular processes of state-building and commercial precapitalism of the Renaissance. For many, "Gold, Glory, and God" remained watchwords and motivations.[16]

Spain extended the feudal principles inherent in the *capitulaciones* granted to Columbus and others to America with the sanction of the Roman Catholic Church. The papal bulls of 1493 and the Treaty of Tordesillas with Portugal divided the non-Christian world between Spain and Portugal.[17] Neither France nor other emerging powers in Europe with aspirations for empire paid much attention to the papal bulls or the treaty. Reacting to news of Columbus's trips, Henry VII of England authorized a 1496 expedition by another Italian, Giovanni Caboto, who had come to England and assumed the name John Cabot, to explore coastal North America. Twelve years later, the king authorized another trip by Cabot's son, Sebastian, to try to find a northerly passage to Asia. Those voyages continued a series of explorations that had begun in 1480 from Bristol in western England.[18]

French king Francis I also began to challenge both Spanish and Portuguese colonial aspirations. After the 1522 return of the remnants of a Spanish-sponsored expedition led by Ferdinand Magellan that had circumnavigated the globe, Francis backed an effort by yet another Italian, the Florentine Giovanni da Verrazzano, to explore the east coast of North America, an area already known to Basque, Breton, and Norman fishermen, seamen, and merchants. Francis also hoped to find an all-water route to the Pacific Ocean and thereby diminish the prestige and power that seemed to be accruing to Spain. In a report submitted after his 1523–24 voyage, Verrazzano claimed to have found a one-mile-wide isthmus extending for some two hundred miles beyond on the other side of which lay an eastern sea that went "around the tip of India, China, and Cathay." That report proved incorrect, but this trip and successive journeys laid the basis for the name Nova Galicia (New France) to be attached to what became the North American heartland of a French empire in the Americas. Toward that end, Francis I persuaded Pope Clement V to revise the bulls of the 1490s in 1535, thereby limiting Spanish and Portuguese claims. This revision, which provided that a state could claim possession of territory and a monopoly on its trade only by means of actual occupation, established the basis for a new concept of colonialism eventually accepted by all European powers.[19] European states then began to compete with each other for possessions in the New World that would both yield commercial success and increase rulers' glory, goals that necessitated excursions and explorations to lay claim to "virgin" land that of course was not virgin at all.

Early Spanish *Entradas*

In the early sixteenth century, the Spanish were the first European explorers to reach the lower Mississippi Valley. Their expeditions utilized both land and sea routes to spread Spanish influence, but unlike later English settlers in North America, who extended their reach from east to west, the Spaniards began in Cuba and later Mexico and worked their way north. Spanish settlement thus runs counter to the nineteenth-century idea of westward expansion.[20] These would-be conquerors encountered varying degrees of Native American resistance and cooperation as well as environmental challenges. In the short run, these hurdles diminished the Spaniards' interest in settling along the Gulf Coast, but in the long term, these factors contributed to the displacement of entire Mississippian cultures and led to the emergence of new groups that later played major roles in the history of Mississippi. The Choctaws, Chickasaws, and Creeks, just to name a few, all sprang from the Mississippian chiefdoms whose collapses were accelerated if not caused by Spanish contact.[21] In modern-day Mississippi, the Natchez are the only people whose chiefdom continued the Mississippian tradition.[22]

Many of the Europeans, particularly the leaders of the expeditions, had years of experience in the Americas. While Hernán Cortés, Francisco Pizarro, and the other men who now crowd the history books detailing the European "discovery" of the Americas never set foot in Mississippi, they nevertheless played an important role, submitting reports that served as blueprints for later conquistadores. The expeditions of Ponce de León (1513 and 1521 to Florida), Cortés (1519–21 to Mexico), and Pizarro (1531–41 to Peru), among others, provided future leaders with experience that they used in subsequent efforts to find wealth and glory in the Americas.[23]

Even though the Spanish did not establish a sustained presence in the area until the middle of the eighteenth century, they significantly altered the trajectory of the early history of Mississippi in numerous ways. Following Columbus's first encounters with American people, Cortés, the conquistador who claimed some of Meso-America for Spain in 1521, laid the foundation of the rapid expansion of land and riches for the Spanish Crown under Charles V in the New World.[24] Cortés's expedition and the resulting wealth drew more conquistadores to the New World, including Pizarro.[25]

Establishing the viceroyalty (vice-kingship) of Nueva España in 1535 with Mexico as an administrative center, the Spaniards sought to expand their influence and to further exploit the resources of the New World. In North America, they initially sought one particular resource before turning to silver and gold: slaves. The Native populations who were worked to death in Caribbean and Mexican mines and fields and fell to new European diseases had to be replenished, and the region north of New Spain, in particular Florida, seemed well suited to provide new captives for the required labor.[26]

Utilizing their military mentality and training as well as what they had learned in previous conquest of the Atlantic Azores and Maldives, the Spanish generally attempted to subjugate the Native peoples of the Americas and turn their new colonies into production units of considerable wealth.[27] Long-established cultural traditions of the Reconquista taught hidalgos—an entire class of Spanish nobles dependent on the warrior trade—to enhance their social standing through conquest. Bound to ideas of honor, bravery, and duty, these hidalgos wasted little time in bringing their methods to the New World in pursuit of their mission of continuing what had begun on the Iberian Peninsula in the Americas.[28]

Rather than track straight north from Mexico into the area that is now Arizona, Texas, and New Mexico, the Spanish began to explore the Gulf Coast region, usually using Cuba as a base of operations. The search for enslaved labor rather than for the Fountain of Youth led Ponce de León to "discover" Florida in 1513.[29] Preceding both Cortés and Pizarro, Ponce de León had originally come to the New World with Columbus's second fleet and became the first governor of what is now Puerto Rico.[30] After receiving permission from the Crown to establish a settlement on what he believed to be an island that he named Florida after landing there on Easter Feast day, Ponce de León died in a skirmish with local Indians in 1520 and never completed his mission. In 1517 and 1518, his first pilot, Antonio de Alaminos, explored and mapped the Gulf Coast from the Yucatán Peninsula to the Pánuco River. Alonso Álvarez de Pineda then filled in the gaps between Charlotte Harbor and the Pánuco River in 1519.[31] In 1521, Lucas Vásquez de Ayllón journeyed to the Gulf Coast for slaves, and he returned three years later to pursue a plan for settlement.[32] Neither mission succeeded, but his reports planted legends of wealth in the popular descriptions of the Gulf Coast, mostly based on reports of a legendary city, Chicora. Pineda's maps guided the Narváez expedition, in which four hundred people, including some women and Africans, traveled from Spain to Florida, arriving in February 1528.[33] Narváez's voyage included the Andalusian royal treasurer, Álvar Núñez Cabeza de Vaca, who was one of only four survivors of the expedition. After eight years of Native captivity, wandering throughout the Gulf Coast and North American Southwest, Cabeza de Vaca and his fellow survivors returned to Mexico City in 1534 and reported their experiences. Cabeza de Vaca recorded stories he had heard about a city of fabulous wealth, tales that motivated other conquistadores to follow in the Narváez expedition's footsteps in attempts to find the legendary city. Instead of another Incan or Aztec empire with vast amounts of gold and silver, however, they found only indigenous cultures rich in food crops.[34]

Poor nobles such as Cortés, Pizarro, and even Soto may have been particularly eager to find wealth: all three came from Extremadura, one of the economically weakest regions in Spain.[35] Yet their shared culture and mentality ran deeper than their personal connections. Both written and oral reports of conquistadores' exploits circulated in Spanish government circles, and when enough wealth was on the line, Spaniards were not averse to combining their efforts.[36] Historian Paul Hoffman argues that Ayllón's tale of Chicora, with its promised sylvan, agricultural, human, and mineral wealth, and Verrazano's tale of an isthmus in North America at about thirty-seven degrees north led a generation of European explorers and colonizers in the second half of the sixteenth century to search the southeastern coast for the new Andalusia and a way to the Orient. Soto both utilized the stories of the men preceding him and inspired other Spaniards to try again.[37]

Hernando de Soto

What Soto and the other conquistadores sought in their *entradas* were ways to expand their power and along with it their social standing and wealth in Spain. Soto not only entered into a *capitulación* with the Spanish king to explore the Southeast but also secured the right to claim vast amounts of wealth if he could both find and extract it from the region. He and the other *adelantados* were primarily interested in anything that could be monetized: slaves and gold and silver bullion. The Crown would receive one-tenth of any gold extracted from the possessions Soto hoped to conquer, a share that would rise to one-fifth over the years, but the rest would fall to the *adelantado* who extracted the wealth and became de facto governor for the Crown.[38] However, the *capitulación* also required Soto to explore the entire area granted to him by the king and bring

Catholicism to the Natives.[39] Had he survived, Soto would have become governor and captain general of Cuba, received grants from any new land claimed for Spain, held the right to extract labor from the Natives living on his possessions in the New World, and been able to import (duty-free) fifty enslaved Africans—one-third of them female—to work these assets.[40] All in all, Soto stood to make an enormous amount of money from his trek, although he had to bear the initial cost of the expedition. The fact that Soto was also required to bring along missionaries to convert the Natives to the Roman Catholic faith may have been important to Spain's Charles V, but it was not a priority for Soto. Surviving sources do not reveal any sustained efforts by the European intruders to introduce Mississippians to Christianity, even though Soto at times used the purported might of God and Christian symbols to convince Mississippian chieftains that he had otherworldly powers.[41]

Soto, then, had clear expectations when he landed on the west coast of Florida. He was closely connected to many of the *adelantados* who had come before him, and he equipped his expedition to the best of his abilities, an effort that included gathering all available intelligence and maps to guide him. Now, he simply wanted to execute his plan and reap the resulting fame and fortune. Of course, much of his plan was based on assumptions of European and Christian superiority over the Native cultures and beliefs. Not surprisingly, however, those Natives had different ideas and did not comply with his plan, ultimately forcing Soto's men to abandon the *entrada*. However, this proved to be a pyrrhic victory for the Mississippian societies.

Soto's arrival marked an important turning point in the history of the region. With the destruction of the Mississippian societies' ancestral culture, religion, and language, they evacuated their mounds and formed new, still-powerful, but much more decentralized confederacies that came to dominate the area. The Natchez were one of the last surviving Mississippian peoples, continuing to exist as a chiefdom until their displacement at the hands of the French in the 1730s.[42] European participants in Soto's *entrada* created the first written records of the Mississippians' culture, thereby providing historians with a rare glimpse into the Native way of life. Spanish records demonstrate that the Mississippian chieftains were frequently at war with one another, and Soto's appearance drastically accelerated existing cycles of violence and conflict.[43]

The Beginnings of Soto's *Entrada*

Soto's journey through the Southeast began in 1539 on the west coast of Florida, around modern-day Tampa Bay.[44] The conquistador landed somewhere in that area with nine ships carrying roughly 700 men and some women, heavy armor, and several hundred heads of livestock, including 237 horses and several hundred pigs.[45] This number does not include the Indian servants and captives Soto later added to his small army as it marched through the woodlands and swamps. By 1542, when the remnants of Soto's expedition returned to Mexico, fewer than three hundred survived.[46] Little is known about the participants in Soto's *entrada* with the exception of a few survivors who wrote accounts of the journey.[47] We do know, however, that Soto and his men were motivated to find the rumored riches of the southeastern Natives, a story that had been perpetuated by Cabeza de Vaca's well-publicized accounts of his time in Indian captivity. To that end, Soto tried to enlist Cabeza de Vaca for the expedition: he apparently signed on initially but then latter declined.[48]

As characterized by biographer David Ewing Duncan, Soto was a man possessed, driven by a desire for fame even more than fortune.[49] He had already accumulated enormous wealth through his service in the conquests of Panama, Nicaragua, and especially Peru under Pizarro. Nevertheless, he needed the promise of wealth to lure people to join his dangerous mission. Experienced in subjugating and exploiting Native people in the New World, he focused only on his goals, with no concern for loss of life, either among the Indians or among his own men.[50]

The first people Soto encountered were the Apalaches at their capital, Anhaica. After moving north, he wintered at what is now Tallahassee.[51] In March 1540, he made his way into modern-day South Carolina to see whether the rumored wealth of the Cofitachequi would serve the ends and means of his army. But Soto already faced a significant problem. As throughout his entire mission, the *entrada* struggled with a sense of direction and place. The maps from early missions sketched the coastline but had little to no detail on the interior. Meandering through the American Southeast, he had to rely on indigenous guides, who were usually captured Natives and were often boys or women, who were perceived as more pliable than grown men. The captives also served as hostages, guaranteeing Soto safe passage through the area. Yet each guide had knowledge only of the area within a few days' of travel of his or her home, leaving Soto and his small army without reliable orientation for much of the journey.[52] The Spaniards had to trust their captives to point them generally in the direction that would result in the best outcome for the Europeans. That trust rarely proved well placed.

Although Soto's men were experienced sailors and could easily orient themselves at sea using the stars, they were much less equipped to determine their exact location on densely forested land. A Native guide from a particular group could steer the Iberians away from that group's villages and of their own people, and instead, point the Europeans toward rival peoples, regardless of whether they were located in the direction that Soto intended to travel. And the conquistador was unlikely to realize that he had been misled.[53]

Toward the Mississippi River

From Cofitachequi, Soto and his *entrada* turned northwest toward North Carolina, then west into Tennessee and then back south through northern Georgia into Alabama toward the Gulf of Mexico as they decided that the looming Blue Ridge Mountains were not good grounds on which to support the group. On the march, Soto traversed the territories of the Coças, Ulibahalis, Tascalusas, and other Native groups. Soto and his men were not inclined to build cultural bridges, and reports of brutality, ferociousness, and tactics preceded them to Mabila, their next stop. At Mabila on October 18, 1540, a number of Native people—the Tascalusas the largest group among them—prepared an ambush that almost completely devastated the expedition, killing men and horses and taking weapons. After his haphazard escape Soto had to decide whether to try to rendezvous with Francisco Maldonado, who had brought ships and supplies into the Gulf of Mexico at Achuse, or to continue to the west without Native guides. Soto opted for the latter course, still hoping to find another Incan empire in America and perhaps fearing that his tired, defeated men would choose to return to Mexico or Cuba if they had a chance to do so.[54]

After nine days during which Soto's own scouting parties did their best to find a route that would take them to villages that could be raided for food stores, the *entrada* captured another guide—a chief, Apafalaya. Through "many bad passages and swamps and cold rivers," the chief led the Spaniards to the region under the control of the Chicaza, in modern-day Mississippi.[55]

The march remained hazardous for both Soto's men and the people they encountered. Native resistance rose to a level that intimidated the soldiers, and Soto was forced to acknowledge that his perceived superiority was waning. As his troops succumbed to wounds or sickness, Soto turned to tactics other than pure oppression. To protect his mission and extend the range of his expedition, he began to exchange military favors with local chieftains. He would ally himself with a chieftain and attack his rivals, thereby obtaining food and shelter for the members of the *entrada* . In so doing, Soto unknowingly entered into the Mississippian world in which chiefdoms competed with one another for agricultural wealth and spiritual power.[56]

Mississippian people did not live in a utopian world. Towns were in a state of constant competition for revered objects that had tremendous cultural if not monetary value. The chief or village with trading connections to rare items secured power by trading these items with subordinate chiefs and their villages. Inferior chiefs and villages also could trade with the Spaniards, gaining access to valuable goods that enabled these former subalterns to rise to power. Thus, despite the disastrous long-term effects of Soto's *entrada*, some Mississippian people saw him as useful and at least initially benefited from his presence. Major chiefdoms fell, smaller chiefdoms rose, and new alliances between competing powers reorganized the political landscape. In addition, the lower Mississippi Valley experienced enormous environmental change as the Little Ice Age drastically changed the climate and the growth patterns of the crops on which the Mississippian cultures relied.[57]

Soto operated under standard European military strategies, enhanced by his experience fighting Native people in South America prior to his *entrada* into the Southeast. The core of his military strategy and his survival was to live off of the land and the people he encountered. As the failure of multiple other Spanish expeditions traveling north from Mexico attests, Soto was fortunate that his small army encountered the Mississippian culture. The cultural and social traits of the Mississippians allowed Soto and his men to sustain their march. Many other indigenous cultures would not have been able to provide the necessary support, forcing Soto to abort his mission. As was often the case with Amerindian-European contact, the Native culture initially sustained European settlement or "conquest," but the indigenous contributions were not properly valued or understood by the would-be conquerors, and their subsequent actions contributed immensely to the destruction of Native peoples.[58]

Chicaza

The people that Soto and his men encountered in modern-day northern Mississippi were the ancestors of more familiar Native people, the Chickasaws and to an extent the Choctaws. However, the Chicaza differed from the Chickasaws in many ways. A Mississippian people, the Chicaza chiefdom appears not to have been particularly complex or powerful; rather, the chieftains maintained their power by virtue of their ability to "marshal a cohesive defense against outside attacks and to facilitate food storage and protection by offering a safe place to store surplus foods at the palisaded mound centers." The Chicaza, led by their chief, also named Chicaza, knew of Soto's impending arrival and of his military prowess, and they understood the threat he posed. They also knew about his recent defeat at Mabila and about his troops' deficiencies in food and support. The Chicaza sought to block Soto's march into their territory, gathering on December 14, 1540, on the Tombigbee River, probably around present-day Columbus, Mississippi.[59]

When Soto arrived, he encountered a substantial force of Chicaza warriors on the bluffs across the river. According to Robbie Ethridge, "War staffs blew in the wintry wind. Indian men armed and dressed for war shouted at the Spaniards from the bluff tops. Although the Spaniards would not have been able to understand the warriors without a translator, after two years of experience with Southern Indians, they would by now have recognized their gestures, dress, and harangues as unmistakably hostile."[60] The Chicaza were not willing to let Soto's men into their territory.

For three days, Soto and his men were trapped on their side of the river while the Chicaza warriors kept watch. When Soto sent a messenger to the *mico* (leader of the Chicaza), the waiting warriors quickly killed him. This act should have sent a clear message, but after two years in the American Southeast, Soto was not about to simply walk away. On December 16, 1540, Soto deployed a few of his troops to the north to scout a second river crossing and readied a canoe to cross the river. The Natives discovered his plan and abandoned their position, a common indigenous tactic. Soto then advanced on the town of Chicaza, which was fortified through palisades but had been abandoned by its people in anticipation of Soto's violence. The Spanish wintered in the town during 1540–41, while the regular inhabitants dispersed to surrounding towns in northeast Mississippi.[61]

Soto subsequently built a cautious alliance with the Chicaza, who offered the Spaniards some of their rations over the winter. The Chicaza chief informed Soto that another chieftain, Miculasa, formerly subordinate to Chicaza, was withholding tribute, and Chicaza asked Soto for a formal military alliance to punish Miculasa and restore Chicaza's authority. A combined force of about two hundred warriors, including thirty Spanish horsemen, traveled to Miculasa's village but found it abandoned and burned it to the ground. Miculasa quickly capitulated.[62]

Soto and his chroniclers ignored their heavy losses and interpreted their successes as a sign of their martial, religious, and cultural superiority. The Chicaza, in turn, exploited this worldview to their benefit. As Joseph Hall argues, "Spaniards remained interlopers in a region where the world was still best understood, honored, and regulated in the town square or atop the temple mound."[63] Soto never understood the potential pitfalls that accompanied his journey into the diplomatic and political entanglements of the Mississippians.

Archaeologists and historians have learned much from Soto's expedition and the available archeological record about the area the Chicaza likely inherited. The area had only three major population centers, as the fact that chief Chicaza introduced Soto to only two subordinate chiefs attests. Accounts of conversations with the Chicaza indicate that most of the competing polities of the era were impressive but much farther away, meaning that to support and feed his troops, Soto had little choice but to strike up a friendly relationship with the Chicaza and work toward common goals.[64]

But in the spring of 1541, Soto again misjudged his position vis-à-vis the Chicaza. By March, the Chicaza were no longer willing to bear the burden of the conquistador's demands for food, women, and enslaved laborers. One of Soto's chroniclers, Luys Hernández de Biedma, recorded that "some Indians . . . under the pretense of being at peace, came to see the manner in which we slept, and how we guarded ourselves." The Chicaza then sneaked three hundred warriors into the Europeans' camp with "some little jars in which they brought fire, in order not to be noticed or seen."[65] The Chicaza set Soto's camp ablaze, and panicked men ran out of their tents naked and without their weapons; horses either fled or died through the flames in their stables.[66]

Soto himself survived by saddling a horse, grabbing a lance, and feigning a cavalry attack against the horseless Natives. He skewered the first warrior who crossed his path but was thrown off his horse by the impact. Although that warrior was the only Chicaza casualty, the attack, the masses of horses, and the general chaos confused the Native warriors, who may have thought that a cavalry assault was imminent. In a development that the Spaniards attributed to "a great mystery of God," the attackers vanished into the night, having cost Soto's army most of its clothing and weapons and fifty-seven horses and saddles. The Indians also killed eleven Spaniards and took more than four hundred of Soto's pigs as prizes. Though the soldiers expected the Chicaza to return quickly to finish the job, a week passed before they mustered another attack. This time, Soto and his men were ready, killing many of the Native warriors. Nevertheless, the Spaniards were further weakened.[67]

Onward to the Father of Waters

Still unwilling to give up on his quest for another Peru, Soto made plans to leave the region controlled by the Chicaza and venture further into the unknown. He sought to give his troops two months to rest but his stores were dwindling, his pigs were gone, and he lacked the power to force the Chicaza to support the *entrada*. Hearing that another wealthy Indian empire lay further west, Soto's ragtag, tired, wounded, and demoralized band set out once more.[68]

While following a well-trodden path through the north Mississippi wilderness, Hernández de Biedma recounted, "something happened to us that they

Map of the Soto Expedition, 1543. This is the earliest visual representation of the disastrous Soto expedition of 1539–43 and was created with help from some survivors. Although it lacks a line showing a clear route, it is remarkable for its detailed pictures and place-names. For a full discussion of accounts of that expedition with some attention to this map, see Charles B. Moore, "Documentos Menos Conocidos," esp. 138–40. Courtesy of the Archives and Research Services Divisions, Mississippi Department of Archives and History, Jackson.

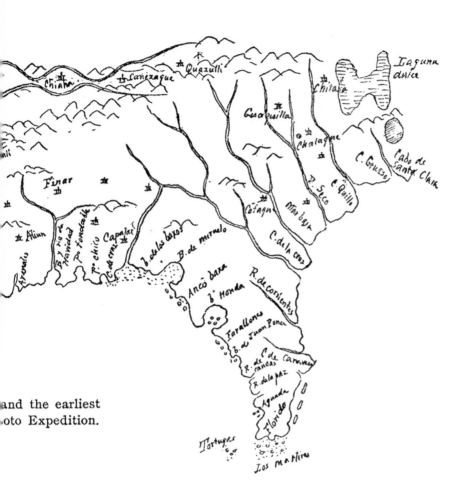

Chiato

Canezague

Quazulli

Chitala

Laguna dulce

Guacauilla

Chalaque

Finar

C. Grueso

Cabo de Santa Clara

Aliun

B. de Navidad

Pº tondali

Pº chico

C. de cruz

Capalai

R. Seco

R. Quillo

Celagne

Maraga

Arenales

B. de las baxos

B. de miruelo

C. de la cruz

Ancó baxa

R. de corientes

bº Honda

Farallones

B. de Juan Ponce

R. de cancas

C. de Canoveral

R. de la paz

Aguada

Florida

and the earliest
oto Expedition.

Tortugas

los martires

say has never happened in the Indies, which was that in the middle of the road where we were to pass, without having food to defend nor women to guard there, but rather only to prove themselves against us, they made a very strong barricade of poles . . . and about three hundred Indians placed themselves there, with determination to die before they relinquished it."[69] The Natives had clearly gotten the news that Soto's army was vulnerable. Though the Spaniards prevailed, they suffered further casualties and had made no progress in obtaining supplies. Moreover, the situation worsened over the next few days, as woods, swamps, and bogs made travel increasingly difficult.[70]

On May 8, however, possibly near the modern town of Walls, Mississippi, the Iberians found a Mississippian people they called Quizquiz, who had corn in storage as well as in the fields. The men were not in town, and Soto's men attacked the first village and took three hundred women hostages as well as "hides and blankets," which provided much-needed replacements for the clothing lost in the fire.[71] The people of Quizquiz surrendered without a fight in exchange for the hostages and then suggested that Soto move further west to the next, even larger town with more provisions for the army. There, Soto and his men first laid eyes on what became known as the Mississippi River and began to deal with the problem of crossing it and avoiding more casualties.[72]

As they constructed boats, another Mississippian people, the Aquixo, appeared in a highly organized fleet, menacing Soto's men with bows and arrows. Rather than being intimidated by the watching Aquixo, however, the Spaniards were enticed by the display of military might, discipline, and craftsmanship, which seemed to indicate that they had finally found the next Incan empire. Soto's Iberians crossed the river on June 17 and 18, avoiding the hostile armada by crossing at night.[73]

An Unremarkable Ending

Soto then continued his journey through what became Louisiana, Arkansas, and Texas but did not find anything approaching a second Incan empire. He found plenty of Mississippian people, most of whom treated Soto as a hostile. His men grew weary, his supplies became depleted, and his will finally broke. In 1542, Soto ordered his men to return east. However, Soto did not make it back across the Father of Waters. Weakened by three grueling years in the wilderness of the Southeast and soundly defeated not as much by the people but by the region, Soto succumbed to a fever that slowly drained his life away until he drew his last breath on May 21. His men remained surrounded by the Quigualtum, one of most powerful Mississippian peoples they had encountered, on the Arkansas side of the Mississippi River. After several more months of wandering the roughly three hundred surviving Spaniards built floats and headed down the Mississippi. Along the way, the Quigualtum did their best to discourage the Spanish from returning by showering them with a barrage of arrows launched from flotillas of expertly navigated canoes. The Quigualtum were supported by another powerful group further south, most likely the Natchez. On September 10, 1543, the survivors finally arrived in Mexico.[74]

Tristán de Luna y Arellano

Despite the Natives' efforts, the Spanish remained undeterred, and in August 1559, Tristán de Luna y Arellano sailed into Pensacola Bay to establish a settlement. Luna was a veteran of the Francisco Coronado expedition that had explored modern-day New Mexico around the same time that Soto was in the Southeast. That expedition, too, had failed in locating the desired riches. Luna's expedition arrived in Pensacola Bay after two months of travel with fifteen hundred people, among them Natives from Mexico, five hundred soldiers, and settlers as well as clergy. The goal of this expedition was to establish an outpost, Santa Maria de Ochuse, that would then serve as a key part of a chain linking the Gulf Coast to the Atlantic coast. This audacious undertaking sought to expand Spanish power and check a possible French advance into the region.[75]

Just a month after their arrival, a hurricane struck, sinking seven ships, drowning many of the colonists who had yet to disembark, and ruining most of the provisions. Desperate for food, Luna sent three expeditions to seek provisions from Native Americans with a more extensive farming culture than the groups on the Gulf Coast. One expedition discovered the town of Nanipacana, not far from where Mabila had been. The men who located the town had been part of Soto's *entrada*, but they found a land much changed.[76]

Luna then ordered his colonists north to make camp in the Natives' town. In the spring of 1560, however, the Natives, who certainly knew how Spaniards expressed their gratitude, harvested their crops, took their supplies, and fled. In April, Luna sent another expedition farther north to find the town of Coosa. The men encountered many smaller villages and their fields along the way, but the people there had fled with their stores. The expedition turned back toward Pensacola, only to find that the officers had rebelled and that the settlers from Nanipacana had returned. Luna recognized that he had failed, and in early 1561, the settlers picked up and returned to Cuba.[77]

Another century passed before Europeans made another attempt to settle on the Gulf Coast, but European contact had already made its mark. As Ethridge notes, "the archeological and documentary evidence attests to the disappearance of Native polities, movements of people into tightly compacted and heavily fortified towns, a dramatic loss of life, multiple migrations and splintering of groups, the coalescence of some groups, the disappearance of many, and an overall decline in artistic life."[78] Soto's *entrada* contributed in numerous ways to these changes. The devastation in his wake caused many of the Native people to reorganize the way they lived—for example, by changing their villages from open layouts on top or around mounds to smaller, easier-to-defend, fortified towns. New residential patterns, in turn, altered the way the Indians engaged in diplomacy, as they now preferred smaller groups to the larger Mississippian tradition of settlement. Diseases also wrecked the larger population centers, and the growing number of sick people threatened villages' survival by causing shortages of agricultural workers.[79] Despite the trauma that must have accompanied the transformation of everyday life, people in the region also adapted to change. The exchange of gifts remained an important part of the Native culture as confederacies developed, and despite their best efforts, Europeans were unable to transition the Natives away from gift-giving to a full-fledged capitalist system.[80]

Overall, Soto's arrival probably accelerated if not started a downward spiral for the Mississippian cultures. His violent *entrada*, combined with the stress placed on the local agriculture by the Little Ice Age and the subsequent changes, certainly altered Mississippian culture in a way that later European explorers could not recognize. Even though the fall and rise of chiefdoms had always been a part of the Mississippian culture, it had never before hit so many neighboring people at roughly the same time. As a result, with a few exceptions, including the Natchez, when the French settled the Gulf Coast, they found not the wealthy and powerful polities of the Mississippians but smaller, poorer, and weaker peoples who had formed loose confederacies. Despite the changes that had occurred, issues of cultural understanding remained a problem.[81] The Natives remained very much in control of the region militarily, but their position weakened as the eighteenth century progressed.

French Beginnings

In the late seventeenth century, the French and English brought to the Mississippi Gulf Coast a new set of economic and social values related to a market economy that valued private ownership of land and people. In addition, the French brought Christianity. In response to pressure and enticements from the English in the Carolinas, Native groups—particularly the former Chicaza, now

Chickasaws—preyed on one another, capturing slaves for shipment and sale to plantations in the West Indies. That practice continued into the eighteenth century, when African slavery introduced by Europeans became increasingly important and spread to the west to infect what became Mississippi.[82]

Taking captives was a normal part of warfare among Native Americans, as it had been for Europeans and others. But Native warfare differed somewhat in the sense that it was often linked to lack of kinship association. Groups that lacked such ties waged war, and captives faced a range of possibilities, among them adoption, death, and servitude. For Native Americans, the opposite of slavery was not freedom but kinship. That difference did not deter a blending of slaveries as practiced by both Natives and newcomers in what came to be called New France in the seventeenth century. Furthermore, as historian Allan Gallay points out, "the scale of slavery altered considerably when Europeans arrived and organized an international slave trade in American Indians that led to the decimation of large groups and depopulation of large areas."[83]

In contrast to their counterparts in Spain, Portugal, and the Netherlands, French public officials tended to see their country's European interests as more important than its colonial possessions.[84] Furthermore, beginning in 1562, France fell into a period that has been described as "an advanced state of decomposition" brought about by about forty years of civil war rooted in the Protestant Reformation. That conflict did not end until the 1590s, when the new king, Henry IV, abjured his Protestantism and embraced Catholicism. He did, however, issue the Edict of Nantes in 1598, thereby offering a degree of tolerance to the French Protestants, the Huguenots.[85]

What followed in North America was the identification of Québec as a suitable location for a colony and the placement there by Samuel de Champlain and others in 1608 of the symbol of royal or state authority, the fleur-de-lis. That followed establishment three years earlier of a settlement at Port Royal in Acadia. However, no sense of permanence existed until the middle of the century thanks to challenges from a diverse lot of French traders, Dutch and English competitors, and their Indian allies as well as from continued weakness in France. The English moved into the Hudson Bay region to the north but eventually offered more challenge from the south, along with the Dutch, who established a trading post at what is now Albany, New York. At least in a symbolic sense, the establishment of another English colony, Jamestown in what is now Virginia, in 1607 provided an omen for both French and Spanish imperial aspirations in North America.[86]

Early English colonial ventures at first differed from those of other European powers. Many came about through the device of the joint-stock company, which had served well for financing trading voyages. In 1606, King James I chartered the Virginia Company, leading to the establishment of Jamestown on the Powhatan River, close to Indian country. These first waves of English colonization in America generated a massive literature that ranged from letters home by "nearly illiterate servants to the official propaganda of colonizing companies."[87] France and other countries eventually adopted the joint-stock company as an important if not preferred or only way to establish and maintain colonies and benefit the state.[88]

Henry IV died in 1610 and was succeeded by Louis XIII, who acquired as his principal minister Jean-Armand du Plessis, Cardinal de Richelieu. He was resolved to break Spanish power and saw mercantilism—collaboration between private and state economic interests—as a means of strengthening France and believed that government-sponsored and -chartered companies could help reach that goal. In addition, Richelieu and others saw an important role for the church in this endeavor and turned toward Jesuit and Récollect priests to establish mission villages, colleges, and hospitals in Canada as well as the Caribbean.[89]

Richelieu died in 1642, and Louis XIII followed a year later. He was succeeded by Louis XIV, then only five years old. Louis XIV assumed his royal duties and responsibilities in 1661 and remained head of state until his death in 1715. Jean Baptiste Colbert, Louis XIV's chief administrative officer, was a strong advocate of mercantilism who believed that successful and powerful nation-states required well-regulated colonies.[90] Colbert initially thought that goal could best be achieved by limiting New France to just the St. Lawrence Valley.[91]

Others in New France, however, had different ideas that caused Colbert to modify his thinking. These people included hunters—*coureurs des bois* (independently minded and unlicensed fur traders)—and their Indian partners as well as missionaries eager for converts, government officials, and a governor, Louis de Baude, the Comte de Frontenac, who arrived in 1673. Frontenac caught the fur fever and secured, along with his protégé, René-Robert, Cavelièr de La Salle, a monopoly on the western and southern fur trade.[92] Samuel de Champlain, Jean Talon, and two Le Moyne brothers, Iberville and Bienville, used their "exceptional vision and energy" to expand the foundation for a French empire in North America.[93]

Jesuit priest Jacques Marquette, surveyor and cartographer Louis Jolliet, and five others launched a 1673 expedition that began in the Straits of Mackinac, reached the Mississippi, and traveled downriver to some Quapaw villages near the mouth of the Arkansas River. After learning from the Quapaws that the Mississippi flowed into the Gulf of Mexico, Frontenac turned to the experienced and knowledgeable La Salle, who had worked closely with Talon and Frontenac, to explore the region further. In 1682 La Salle undertook an exploration of the lower Mississippi Valley and its peoples that began at the confluence of the Mississippi and Illinois Rivers and continued all the way to the gulf. Along the way, the explorers encountered various Native groups, including the Natchez.[94]

On April 9, 1682, somewhere in the vicinity of present-day Venice, Louisiana, La Salle and his group nailed to a tree what Jean-Baptiste Minet described as "three copper fleurs-de-lys made from a cauldron" and then made a cross, which they planted in the ground with an inscription on a lead plate: "Took possession of this land in the name of Louis XIV, King of France and Navarre." The group then sang a Te Deum and fired three volleys.[95] La Salle named the river Colbert after the king's principal minister. French maps that followed, however, sometimes referred to it as Fleuve Saint Louis. Ultimately, however, the Ojibwa name Mississippi prevailed. In the hope of securing support for a return expedition to establish a port or post at the mouth of the river, La Salle wrote to Colbert that all had been done for "the glory of our King" and to spread the "presence of the Gospel" among more "numerous docile and settled nations" than those "in other parts of America." La Salle suggested that the French could imitate Spanish missionary methods in Florida and Paraguay as well as those practiced by the English in New England.[96]

No doubt flattered to have a river named after him, Colbert saw the potential of a port or post at the mouth of the river from which the French, with the help of Indians, could "harass the Spaniards in those regions from which they derive all their wealth, even invade 'New Biscay' (Nueva Vizcaya) in Mexico and seize mines there."[97] After returning to France in 1683, La Salle obtained Louis XIV's support to establish such a post at what many Spanish geographers believed was the mouth of the Río del Espíritu Santo that Alonso Álvarez de Pineda had "discovered" and named during a 1519 trip to the northern Gulf of Mexico.[98] La Salle sailed from France to establish the settlement in 1684, but poor maps and navigational equipment led him to miss the Mississippi River delta and land about four hundred miles to the west at Matagorda Bay in February 1685. He erected a fort, St. Louis, on an extension of the bay and continued overland in search of the river's mouth. His men then mutinied and killed him.[99]

Despite the failure of La Salle's colony, the French continued to claim the Gulf Coast, including what is now Texas. But the Spanish had come to view the entire Gulf as a "Spanish sea" and were unnerved not only by La Salle's explorations but also by events in the Caribbean, where the English, French, and the Dutch had made settlements. Spain sought to contest the French "encroachment" by launching five sea voyages and six land expeditions from the Florida Keys to Tampico.[100] La Salle's trips down the Mississippi and along the Gulf Coast attracted enough interest in France to initiate a time of sustained contact with the region and the people living there, and in 1699, Iberville founded what

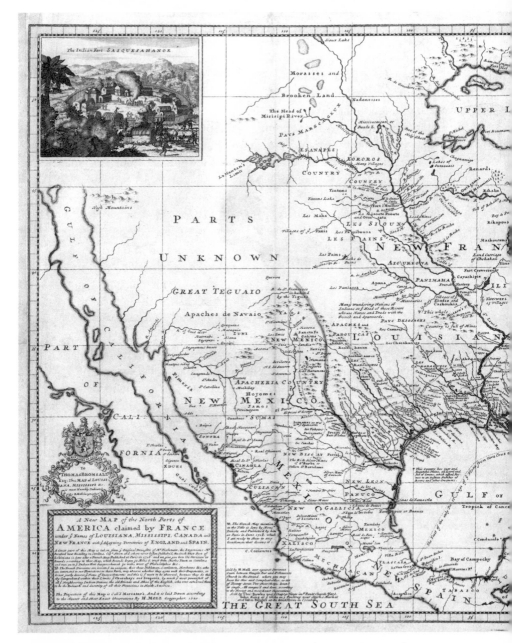

Herman Moll, *America Claimed by France . . .* , 1720. Perhaps of Dutch origin, Moll came to England in 1678 and remained there for most of the rest of his life, working as a mapmaker and publisher. The map's full title is *A New Map of the North Parts of America Claimed by France under ye Name of Louisiana, Canada, and New France with ye Adjoining Territories of England and Spain: to Thomas Bromsall, esq., This map of Louisiana, Mississipi & c. is most humbly dedicated."* Courtesy of the Archives and Research Services Divisions, Mississippi Department of Archives and History, Jackson.

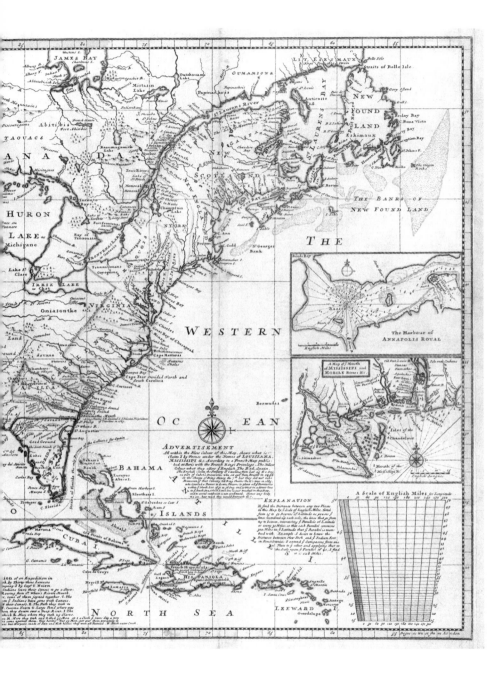

became the first successful French settlement in Louisiana. In the words of Robert S. Weddle, "In straining at a gnat—La Salle's colony—Spain had swallowed a camel—Iberville."[101]

Nevertheless, the French failed to establish a permanent colonial or imperial presence in the Gulf, as did the English and eventually the Spanish. Many Europeans who came to the area were not focused on issues of colony or empire and instead stayed and mingled with the land and its people. Enslaved Africans often escaped from their bondage. The stories of some of these people and the rich ethnic legacy they bequeathed to Mississippi and the surrounding region are at least as and perhaps more important as the geopolitical history.

CHAPTER TWO

L'Espérance de Mississippi

The French in Mississippi, 1699–1763

"L'Espérance de Mississippi" (The Hope of Mississippi) is the title the baroque composer Georg Philipp Telemann attached to a movement of his overture and suite "La Bourse" (The Stock Exchange). The score carries the date of 1720, a time when Telemann was living in a building in Frankfurt that housed a stock exchange. He apparently could not escape being aware of the manic enthusiasm many people of the time—perhaps himself among them—felt for acquiring shares of stock in the Company of the West, which Scottish financier John Law had established three years earlier. More popularly known as the Mississippi Company, it had assumed for-profit operations of the colony that had come into existence after La Salle's 1682 trip down the Mississippi River and his claim of the entire region drained by the river and its tributaries for his king, Louis XIV, and naming it in his honor. Law convinced the French regent that this profit would help solve the country's financial problems as well as promote settlement and development of the colony. Those who acquired shares would also benefit. The company acquired ownership of other stock companies and in 1719 was renamed the Company of the Indies. Its shares prompted "a frenzy of speculation," but by 1720, it became clear that the company could not pay dividends, and the Mississippi Bubble burst, making investments a veritable *d'ésespérance de Mississippi* (despair of Mississippi) for those who held shares.[1]

But hope required much more than just ownership of shares of stock in a company. La Salle and his group had placed two objects along the Mississippi River—the fleur-de-lis and the cross, symbols respectively of the French state and the Roman Catholic Church—to claim the region for his king and promote support for a permanent French presence. Toward that end, another

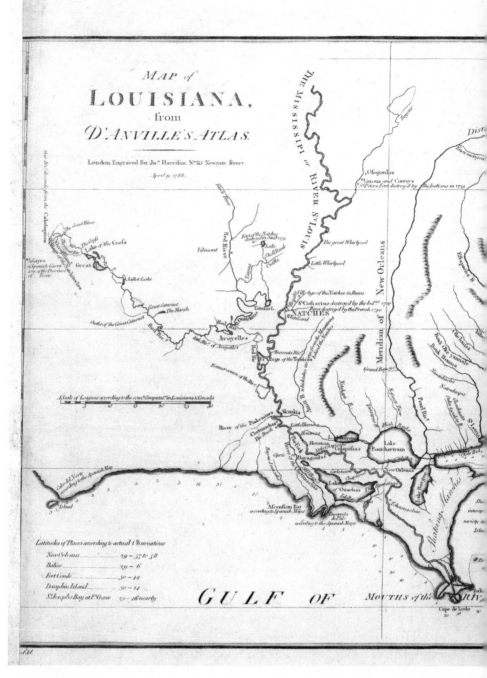

Map of Louisiana from D'Annville's Atlas (London, 1788). This detailed map shows Louisiana from the upper reaches of the Red River, including the "Village of the Natchitoches" in the west, to the Apalachicola River on the east and north to include the "Tchicachas," "Upper Louisiana" and "a bit of Illinois." Courtesy of the Archives and Research Services Divisions, Mississippi Department of Archives and History, Jackson.

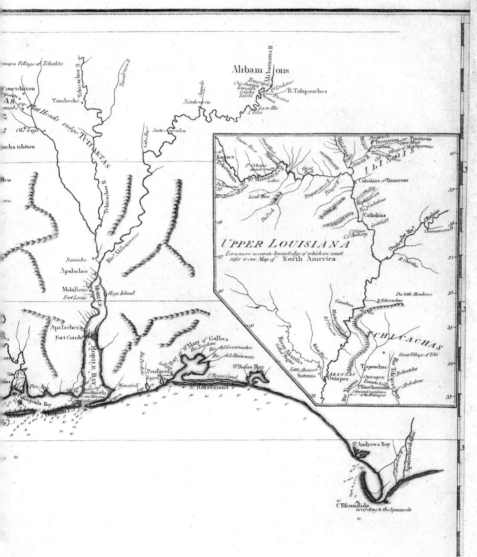

object came to assume much more meaning and significance: the calumet.² It and its associated ceremonies had long been important for people the French and other Europeans encountered in the region and who remained for a long time its most numerous residents.³

Some scholars contend that the French promoted the ceremonial use of the calumet after coming to understand its importance to Native peoples in Canada and Louisiana. The Roman Catholic Church used the calumet when converting Natives. Indeed, the word itself may come from the medieval French word *chalemel* and later *chalumeau*, which signified a reed, cane, or pipe.⁴ La Salle and his men found the calumet in use among a number of groups, including the Natchez. Smoking the pipe as part of ceremonies of greeting that at times lasted as long as three days reminded European newcomers that they needed to see the land as a shared or borrowed space. They also learned that these ceremonies could sometimes connect with war.⁵

Calumet ceremonies continued long after La Salle had passed from the scene, as numerous popular accounts attest.⁶ French composer Jean-Philippe Rameau attended a 1725 performance by two Louisiana Indians in Paris; subsequently wrote a dance for harpsichord, "Les Sauvages"; and then used the music in a major opera-ballet, *Les Indes Galantes,* that was performed more than sixty times in Paris between 1735 and 1737. The work concludes in the grove of a forest in America where a ceremony of the "Great Pipe of Peace" is celebrated. About to sign a peace treaty between his nation and the French and the Spanish, an Indian chief, Adario, worries that the leaders of both groups have designs on his beloved Zima. Happily, she chooses him, and the work concludes amicably with the singing of "Forêts-Paisibles" (Peaceful Forests) and the "Danse du Grand Calumet de la Paix."⁷

Varied Views of America

Other people saw America in different ways. Since the sixteenth century, French monarchs and their advisers had understood colonies and empire as necessary for the health for the state and the expansion of its power, though some, particularly Louis XIV, also believed that colonial ventures at times needed to be subordinated to the dreams of European continental hegemony. As a consequence, royal support for such projects as La Salle's attempt to establish a post along the Gulf Coast at Matagorda Bay proved inadequate and may account for their failure.⁸

Regardless of the European concerns of monarchs and their advisers, traders and trappers in La Louisiane, many of whom had lengthy experience working with

An advertisement for a March 1736 performance in Paris of Rameau's opera-ballet *Les Indes Galantes* (*The Amorous Indies*). This ad was one of many documents used by the Opéra National de Paris to promote its fall 2019 revival of the work at the Opéra Bastille.

Natives in Canada, sustained a presence that "safeguarded the right of French occupation." Scientists and intellectuals represented a second group of important stakeholders. Most notable are Jacques-Nicolas Bellin, appointed chief cartographer of the French navy in 1721 at the age of eighteen, and geographers Claude and Guillaume Delisle, who wanted more information about the region and more specifically the location of the mouth of the Mississippi River. Religious orders associated with the Roman Catholic Church, particularly the Jesuits and the Seminary of Foreign Missions, saw new opportunities in any effort to sustain and expand what La Salle had begun.⁹

Others promoted the French enterprise in the lower Mississippi Valley by sustaining and embellishing memories of La Salle and what he had accomplished. Minister of the Marine Jean-Baptiste Antoine Colbert, the Marquis of Seignelay and the son of Jean-Baptiste Colbert, continued his father's efforts to promote colonies and empire, using La Salle's account to argue that a principal object of the trip had been to find a place for a permanent settlement on the Gulf of Mexico. Such a settlement would prevent "foreigners"—not only the Spanish but particularly the English—from outmaneuvering the French in the Mississippi basin and potentially contribute to the demise of England's Canadian ventures centered along the St. Lawrence River. Such a settlement would also serve as base for operations should hostilities break out between the Spanish and the French.¹⁰

Parisian lawyer Gabriel Arnoud became a strong advocate of a proposal put forth by Alexandre de Rémonville, an old friend of La Salle with knowledge of the Mississippi region, in a December 1697 memorandum: the creation of a joint stock company to establish a colony in "the estuary of the Mississippi" to deter the English and take advantage of what Rémonville described as a "country that abounds in everything necessary for the conveniences of life." He noted in some detail the area's potential to provide such "conveniences." It produced two crops of maize each year, had "a great abundance of wild cattle," and offered a "great variety of grapes" that "make excellent wines." It had also had much potential for a valuable trade in "furs and peltry" as well as numerous white mulberry trees and a climate like that of Italy and parts of India, meaning that it was ripe for the production of silk. The proposed company initially failed to secure support from either investors or the king but finally came into being in 1700 as the Company of the Sioux following Pierre-Charles Le Sueur's exploration of the Minnesota River Valley.¹¹

Henri de Tonti, who accompanied La Salle during his 1682 trip down the Mississippi River, became an especially effective advocate and major factor in the establishment of what he and others hoped would be a permanent French presence in the Mississippi region. A fur trader, Tonti became something of a legend among Indians in North America because of the iron hook that took the place of his right hand after it had been mutilated by a grenade. He argued vigorously that La Salle's enterprise should be completed so that French commerce and institutions could be extended to the Mississippi Valley and France could secure a more effective defense against England.¹² In 1687, survivors of the La Salle expedition traveling along the Arkansas River found a palisaded house Tonti had built the preceding year that he hoped would evolve into a permanent French post and community. With alterations in location, the Arkansas Post was thus born.[13]

Iberville and Fort Maurepas on Biloxi Bay

Those views and actions resonated with such key people as Louis XIV's minister of the navy in charge of colonial affairs, Louis Phélypeaux de Pontchartrain, and his son, Jérôme Phélypeaux de Maurepas, who in 1699 succeeded his father as minister of the navy, serving until 1715. In 1698, a year after the conclusion of the War of the League of Augsburg, in which France opposed England, Spain, and the Dutch Republic along with other powers, Louis Pontchartrain appointed Pierre Le Moyne d'Iberville, a French Canadian who had distinguished himself during that war, to head an expedition to complete the establishment of a French military post and settlement at or close to the mouth of the Mississippi River. Iberville sailed from France in late 1698 with an expedition that included his nineteen-year-old brother, Jean-Baptiste Le Moyne de Bienville.[14]

Eighteen-year-old André Pénicaut, a "literate ship's carpenter and chronicler," also accompanied Iberville and recorded experiences and observations in a journal that has been described as "the best sustained piece of literature pertaining to French dominion in early Louisiana."[15] It and Iberville's journals describe in detail the 1699 establishment of a settlement on Biloxi Bay, which received its name from the Native Americans living in the area, and the construction of Fort Maurepas, which Iberville named in honor of the Comte de Pontchartrain. The Spanish had learned of the French plans to establish a post on the Gulf Coast and in late 1698 had moved quickly to secure a site along Pensacola Bay.[16] The French settlers encountered such Native groups as the Biloxis, the Pascagoulas, the Chicachas, the Mobiliens, and the Oumas (Houmas), all of whom came to play more valuable roles on behalf of the French than did forts. Pénicault's, Iberville's, and others' accounts of these encounters compelled a revision of the generalized European view of Amerindians as no more than "wild people of the forests."[17]

Encounters with Natives

These encounters, especially the initial ones, often centered on the ceremonies associated with the calumet. Iberville's first exploration took him along the coast and west of Massacre Island, which he named after finding the remains of fifty or sixty people there. Iberville and Bienville also met some Bayagoula and Mougoulascha Indians who lived on the Mississippi River and had come east to hunt. The two groups had a pleasant exchange during which they communicated by signs, and the Natives not only embraced Bienville many times but presented the French party with some tobacco and an evening meal. According to Iberville, after the meal, they smoked an iron calumet that he had made "in the shape of a ship with the white flag adorned with fleurs-de-lis and ornamented with glass beads," signifying a union between the Natives and the French.[18] A similar encounter occurred in 1700, during Iberville's second excursion, when a group that included Pénicault traveled west to the Mississippi and upriver to the Natchez. Pénicault described them as "the most civilized nation" of all the "savages" and noted that they "sang their calumet of peace, which lasted three days, after which we departed laden with game and poultry." Pénicault also reported that the Biloxis, too, came with their chiefs to sing "their calumet of peace, as all the nations do," suggesting that Native peoples attached at least as much importance to public rituals and ceremonies as did the French.[19]

Pénicault's descriptions of many similar encounters also include comments about complexion and other physical differences. As the French felled trees to build houses and the fort, "some savages" watched from a distance and "were surprised at our clothes and the color of our faces." "They kept gazing at us, astonished at seeing white skinned people, some heavily bearded, some bald headed," a sharp contrast to the Biloxis, "who have very tawny skin and heavy black hair which they groom very carefully." Iberville insisted that they come and meet him and his men and offered them food and drink, which they refused, "either because these things were not to their taste or because they were still afraid."[20] In time, both Natives and Euro-Americans came to include references to complexion and other physical differences as a way to rationalize behavior by creating, in the words of historian Nancy Shoemaker, "new identities for themselves based on the fiction of irresolute difference."[21] Creating those differences could often serve Native interests and facilitate cooperation and collaboration with the newcomers.

Sustaining Good Relations

Both Pénicault and Iberville recognized the need for interpreters fluent in local languages to facilitate "talking with Indians." Iberville became frustrated with a Recollect priest, Anastase Douay, who was unwilling to remain in Biloxi and deeply regretted the lack of a Jesuit missionary "who in a short time would know the language of this country."[22]

Continuing the French practice in Canada, Iberville brought six young boys with him in the belief that they could learn Native languages and become acculturated in Native ways more readily than older men. After an extended calumet ceremony at Natchez that included a "substantial present" from Iberville, he promised the chiefs that he would send a small French boy "to learn their language among them."[23] And in 1702, when some Chickasaws came to meet Iberville, they asked him to send them a French boy, "whom they would teach the savage language of their village." According to Pénicault, Iberville gave them one of the six boys, "little St. Michel," the fourteen-year-old son of the harbor master of Rochefort.[24] Indian leaders were eager to have French boys in their villages not only to learn languages but also to become kin through adoption and eventually marriage. They then would be in a position to serve as *fanimingos*, a type of chief who came from another tribe and served, especially among the Chickasaws and Choctaws, as an advocate for that group whenever war threatened to break out.[25] Squirrel King played that role for a band of Chickasaw families who moved to South Carolina in 1723 to take up residence among the English and came to be regarded as the "guardian of the English calumet."[26]

Forts and Communities

Forts played a key role in French plans to establish an empire in America and protect it against both English and Spanish threats.[27] They came to be seen, however, as more than just military structures. Rather, they were viewed as parts of larger communities that would include Native peoples and villages as a way to facilitate and sustain ongoing communication and exchange.[28] Begun over a decade after Maurepas, Fort St. Jean Baptiste des Natchitoches and the associated village, Natchitoches, provide an especially good example. In 1713, the newly appointed governor of Louisiana, Antoine de la Mothe, Sieur de Cadillac, eagerly responded to the opportunity to establish both a fort and a community along the Red River in western Louisiana and a base to develop trade with Spaniards in New Spain, even though Spanish law forbade such commerce. Cadillac ordered Louis Juchereau de St. Denis, who had accompanied Bienville on a March 1700 trip up the Red River and had served as commandant of the Biloxi post, to undertake that task. St. Denis persuaded a group of Natchitoches Indians living along Lake Pontchartrain to return to their former village site and help the French build a fort along the Red River in exchange for a regular supply of French goods. They found the site occupied by some Doustioni Indians, but St. Denis convinced the two

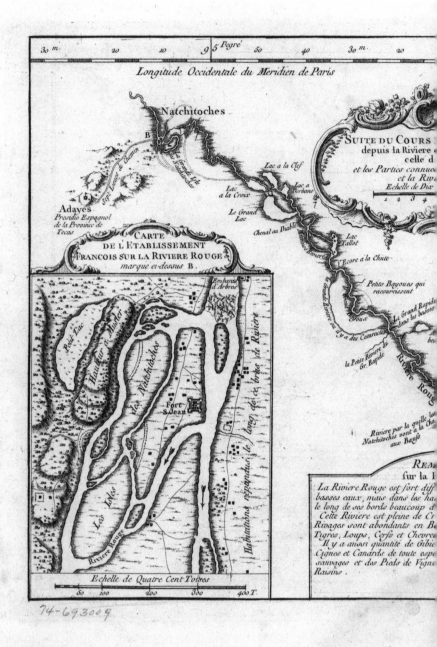

30 m.   **20**   **10**   **9** 5 Degré   **50**   **40**   **30** m.   **20**

Longitude Occidentale du Meridien de Paris

Natchitoches

B

La Grande fite Nakichitoches

Sept Lieues de chemin

Adayes
Presidio Espagnol
de la Province de
Tecas

Lac a la Clef

Lac
a la Croix

Lac a
Herbane

Le Grand
Lac

Chenal au Diable

SUITE DU COURS
depuis la Riviere
celle d
et les Parties connue
et la Riv
Echelle de Dix
1   2   3   4

Lac
Tallot

L'Ecore a la Chute

CARTE
DE L'ETABLISSEMENT
FRANCOIS SUR LA RIVIERE ROUGE
marque ci-dessus B.

Embarras
d'Arbres

Petit Lac

Hauteur St Michel

Les Natchitoches

Fort
S. Jean

Habitations repartues le long de ce bras de Riviere

Petites Bayoues qui
racourcissent

Le Grand Rapide
dans les basses

la Grande Riviere au il y a des Cataractes

la Petite Riviere du
Gr. Rapide

Riviere Rouge

Riviere par la quelle les
Natchitoches vont à la cha
aux Boeuf

Les Isles

Riviere Rouge

Echelle de Quatre Cent Toises

50   100   200   300   400 T.

REM
sur la l
La Riviere Rouge est fort diff
basses eaux, mais dans les ha
le long de ses bords beaucoup d
Cette Riviere est pleine de Cr
Rivages sont abondans en B
Tigres, Loups, Cerfs et Chevre
Il y a aussi quantité de gibie
Cignes et Canards de toute espe
sauvages et des Pieds de Vigne
Raisins.

74-693009

A Jacques-Nicolas Bellin map, probably done in the early eighteenth century, displaying the course of the Mississippi River, also identified here as the Fleuve St. Louis, from the mouth of the Iberville River in the south to the Yazoo River in the north. A major focus is the region from the mouth of the Red River south of "Fort Rosalie" (with a note about

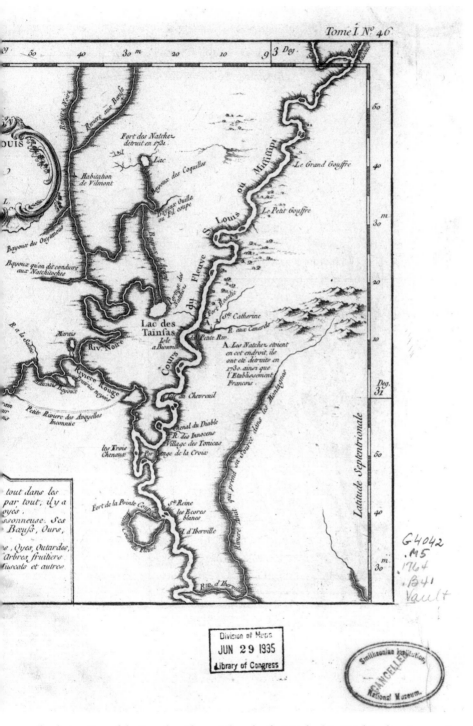

the destruction of the French settlement there by the Natchez) to Natchitoches. A separate enclosed map focuses on the region of Natchitoches, where the French established a fort and community in 1714. The map was published in 1764 in Paris. Courtesy of the Archives and Research Services Divisions, Mississippi Department of Archives and History, Jackson.

groups to live and work together. By 1714, the site had become a new French post with an associated community, and two years later a group of Yatasis joined. Sébastian Le Prestre, the Marquis de Vauban, Louis XIV's commissary general of fortifications and an especially influential adviser for Jérôme de Pontchartrain, believed strongly that such structures and their communities, including Indian villages, were a key to the success of a French empire in Canada, the Caribbean, and Louisiana.[29]

When the French established a fort among the Natchez in 1716, they seemed to prioritize developing and sustaining good relations with Native peoples. Historical geographer Donald Meinig's concepts of "discrete colonization areas" and "points of attachment" are useful for understanding this "shaping of America." According to historical archaeologist Jack D. Elliott Jr., "demographic distribution, spatial organization, and the continuities of the same through time" are far more important than simply a structure "politically defined" as a fort.[30] Louisiana at this time, as well as other parts of America, was experiencing, in the words of historian Colin Calloway, the emergence of "new worlds for all" defined and characterized perhaps more by "internal relationships forged by inhabitants" than "external linkages."[31]

Spanish and English Challenges: From Biloxi Bay to Mobile Bay

Pontchartrain and others in France saw both the Spanish and the English as offering not only challenges but also opportunities for the French on the Gulf Coast. When Iberville was returning from Natchez to Biloxi in early 1700, his group encountered an English ship "careened in a bend three leagues long" that came to be called Détour à l'Anglois (English Turn). Iberville chose to build a second French fort, the Fort de La Boulaye or Fort de Mississippi, south of that bend. The site proved unhealthy, lacking in fresh water, and subject to frequent flooding and hence not at all congenial for the development of any kind of settlement and community. Its fabrication was minimal and had only a few cannon for its defense. Bienville eventually assumed command of that post, and before leaving for France in 1702, Iberville advised his brother to move the fort upstream, nearer to Lake Pontchartrain.[32]

In late December 1701, however, Iberville had developed a plan to establish a fort and colony on Mobile Bay. Although Fort Maurepas on Biloxi Bay was, in the words of architectural historian Samuel Wilson Jr., "perhaps the best-designed and best-constructed fort built by the French in the Mississippi Valley," Iberville and others concluded that a principal post farther east was needed, closer to Spanish Pensacola and to various Indian groups, including the Mobile, under pressure from the English based in the Carolinas. In January 1702, the French began to move to a location north of Mobile Bay on the Mobile River.[33]

Relations between Spain and France had improved after Philip of Anjou, a grandson of Louis XIV, ascended to the Spanish throne in 1700. With the outbreak of the lengthy War of the Spanish Succession the following year, France and Spain found themselves united against England and other European powers. However, the Spanish commander at Pensacola informed Iberville that establishing the fort at Mobile would require permission from the Spanish viceroy in Mexico. Nevertheless, Spanish and French settlers in Pensacola and Biloxi were willing to help each other when supply ships failed to arrive or arrived late, and the commander asked the French to lend a ship to bring supplies from Veracruz.[34]

Iberville consequently dispatched people to Biloxi to begin transferring goods and equipment from Fort Maurepas to Massacre Island and ordered the construction of a warehouse there to serve as the port for the new post. Work on building both a town and a fort began along the west bank of the Mobile River upstream from its entrance into the bay. The new Fort Louis of Louisiana and town of Mobile briefly became in effect the capital of French Louisiana.[35]

Iberville and Bienville, who served as the post's commandant, liked the site because of its strategic location some distance up from the mouth of the Alabama River. In addition, the location was close to the Mobilian Indians and other Native groups experiencing increasing pressure and enticements from the English. The English were seeking Indian slaves and were eager to dislodge the French from the coast. But because Massacre Island lacked a fort or military installation, in the fall of 1710 it suffered a disastrous attack by English pirates from Jamaica.[36]

That event exacerbated the many other problems that had long plagued the fort and settlement at Mobile. Swampy ground led structures, including the fort, to deteriorate rapidly. Food was often in short supply, and the post had then to rely on Mobilian and Tohomé neighbors for corn and other staples. In 1708, D'Artaguette (Dartaguiette Diron), the post's young commissioner and second-in-command to Bienville, reported to Pontchartrain that "there is nothing so sad as the situation of this poor colony." Discharged Canadian soldiers sought to go to Pensacola rather than stay and help create settlement, and the English, especially those in South Carolina, had increasingly begun to recruit Native allies to attack French settlements. By the spring of 1712, more than three years had passed since a supply ship had arrived from France, the fort and other buildings had further deteriorated, and heavy rains had caused extensive flooding. Soldiers and settlers had become demoralized, and Bienville finally conceded that D'Artaguette was right: the town and fort should be moved south to the mouth of the Mobile River. Massacre Island was renamed Isle Dauphine (Dauphin Island) in honor of the young heir to the French throne, and the settlement and post became Port Dauphin.[37]

More Forts—and Diplomacy: Tonti's Mission to the Chickasaws

The French built additional forts over the next quarter century: Fort Toulouse, on the Coosa River near where it meets the Tallapoosa, in 1717; Fort St. Pierre, just north of Natchez on the Yazoo River in 1719; and Fort Tombecbé on the Tombigbee River in 1735–36. All those locations played vital roles in the ongoing French rivalry with the Spanish and the English and in maintaining close and good relations with Indian groups.[38]

In 1702, Iberville turned to Bienville to organize a major diplomatic initiative to try to end Chickasaw slave raids on their neighbors inspired by English traders. As a larger objective, Iberville hoped to create an alliance between the French and the Chickasaws that would include other Native groups, exclude the English, and provide peace for the entire region. Some Mobilians and Choctaws who had gone to Fort Maurepas to ask for help in their conflict with the Chickasaws encouraged that goal. Raids on the Choctaws, the most numerous Native group in the region by not only the Chickasaws but also the less numerous Abikhas (Conchaque) and Alabamas provided further incentive. Iberville hoped that his initiative to bring about a Pax Gallica would end such insecurity and violence.[39]

Bienville chose Tonti, a former associate and loyal supporter of La Salle, to lead the mission and provided him with ten men, a small quantity of gifts, guns, powder, and ammunition. Although initially reluctant to join the French in this risky incursion into Chickasaw Country, two Mobilians, two Tohomes, and a Choctaw joined the group. Beginning on February 8, the party traveled north to the Chickasaws. They persuaded five Chickasaw chiefs and three Chickasaw women to return with the group to Mobile, along the way encountering some Chickasaws and two English slavers with a captive Choctaw boy. Tonti secured the boy's release by agreeing to pay the Chickasaws what the slavers had offered. The group later met another Chickasaw slaving party that had just attacked a Choctaw town, killed three men, and captured all the women and children of one household. That encounter almost caused the Chickasaws accompanying Tonti to defect and return home, but Tonti persuaded them to remain.[40]

The group arrived in Mobile at the end of March 1702, just after Iberville. He and an associate had laid out the streets of the new town, and a fort as well as a chapel and some buildings had already been constructed. Gifts of all kinds were set out in the town's plaza, which served as a meeting place. With Bienville serving as an interpreter to the best of his ability, Iberville delivered an ultimatum to the Chickasaws: if they did not cease their raids on their neighbors and expel the English, the French would provide arms to the Choctaws and other groups so that they could wage war on the Chickasaws. After some negotiation, the Chickasaws agreed to cease hostilities, and the French pledged to pay the prices the Chickasaws set for trade goods. All smoked the calumet of peace, gifts were distributed, and the Chickasaws departed. The French also provided the Chickasaws with a boy to learn their language and serve as an interpreter. He had already acquired some linguistic skills as an interpreter for either the Bayagoulas or the Houmas, neighbors on the Mississippi River.[41]

Whatever Tonti's mission achieved proved limited, fragile, and temporary. Any kind of alliance primarily involved the Choctaws and the French. Some Mobile and other chiefs came to Mobile but apparently did little more than reconnoiter and assess the French potential to be better trade partners than the English. Other groups, notably those that composed a Creek confederacy, remained closer and too susceptible to increased English commercial and political influence and activity. In response to Iberville's objectives, made tangible by Tonti's mission, the English prepared a kind of counteroffensive, rendering a Pax Gallica for the region illusory, as was confirmed by the 1703 murders of some men Bienville sent to the Alabamas. That action prompted him to enlist the support of Choctaws, Pascagoulas, Tohomes, and Mobilians to create a force to retaliate.[42]

War: Issue of the Spanish Succession

Shortly after Iberville's Mobile meeting with the Chickasaw chiefs and others, the War of the Spanish Succession began. France and Spain were allies in the conflict, and it diminished their rivalry in the Gulf region, but it also negatively affected efforts to create a colony in keeping with Colbert's goals.[43]

Those effects were symbolized by the destruction of the two ferries Iberville brought on his first trip to the region—*La Précieuse*, which met its end at Dauphin Island in 1705, and *L'Espérance*, smashed by a 1707 hurricane.[44] Those losses and the lack of other ships severely restricted what could be carried to, from, and within the region, diminishing hope for the kind of Louisiana supported by Colbert, the Pontchartrains, and other officials. In the words of historian Marcel Giraud, "Left on its own, Louisiana seemed doomed to fail."[45]

Dumont de Montigny's artistic representation of the community of St. Pierre on the Yazoo River, probably done between 1748 and 1752. Dumont served at the fort here while he was also associated with the fort at Natchez between 1726 and 1728. Reproduction courtesy of the Newberry Library, Chicago. Courtesy of the Archives and Research Services Divisions, Mississippi Department of Archives and History, Jackson.

PLAN du fort des ya choux
concession de m.gr le Duc de
belle isle et associez derait 1729

explication des chiffres
1 maison du Capitaine Commené
2 cuisine
3 chapelle
4 mais. de l'aumonier
5 Logement des officiers
6 magazin
7 Cazernes
8 corps de garde
9 quartiers des ouvriers
10 rezervoir d'eau bonne a boire
11 M. de denoyers sergent
12 M. de vire sergent
13 baton de pavillon
14 debarquement
15 M. de poulain interprette
16 jardin de la concession
17 m. du chirurgien
18 batterie des canon
19 egoust
20 meuriers et bois

échelle de 300 pieds

Y A C H O U X

Other Challenges to the French Colonial Enterprise

War exacerbated the colony's many problems. Ships arrived less frequently, and when they did arrive, they often brought inadequate supplies. In addition, supplies were frequently diverted to satisfy the personal interests of administrators or naval personnel. Iberville and his brothers—Bienville, Joseph Le Moyne de Sérigny, and Antoine Le Moyne de Sérigny—were suspected of involvement in such activity. Ships for a major expedition Iberville organized in 1705 against two English islands in the West Indies were used to transport illicit goods for the benefit of local merchants.[46] About two years later, Pontchartrain learned that on the arrival of a ship, the *Aigle*, Bienville had used the king's crews and boats to transport goods belonging to him and to officers for sale to inhabitants at exorbitant prices.[47] Such activity, as even Bienville noted, led to a decline in morale among both civilians and military personnel. People often became dependent on Native groups or on the Spanish in Pensacola and Cuba. Many of the large number of Canadian hunters and trappers who had come south hoping to sell pelts just moved on to Indian country.[48]

Above all, the early colony failed to develop a solid demographic and economic base. Most of the few people in the region identified and described by historian Daniel Usner as "Canadian soldiers, sailors, and voyageurs" lacked both the willingness and the ability "to deforest the land and cultivate the soil." People in France expressed little interest in moving to vaguely known and remote Louisiana. Even Canada and Martinique, perhaps France's most valuable possession in the Americas at the time, failed to generate much enthusiasm.[49]

Some effort was expended in trying to get farmers to migrate so that the colony could become self-sufficient in food and maybe even cultivate commercial crops. La Salle's friend Alexandre de Rémonville saw the place as especially suited for mulberry trees for silk, grapes for wine, cattle, forest products, and even mineral resources. Others promoted tobacco, for which there was major demand, sugar, and cotton. Nevertheless, in 1704, only five inhabitants were engaged in farming. Wealthy merchants, too, had little interest. The French government opposed the creation in Louisiana of a system of seigneuries like those in Canada, meaning that it was far more attractive to stay in France and look forward to acquiring a seigneurial title and estate there. Louisiana had few European women, meaning that births were rare.[50] Of the 279 people counted in a 1708 "official census," 122, including 1 interpreter and 6 cabin boys, were part of the garrison. The balance included 24 "colonists, who have no assured concessions, which prevents the majority from beginning plantations"; 28 women; 25 children; and 80 "slaves both Indian men and women from different nations."[51]

All sorts of other possible sources of people received attention. Suggestions included pirates from Cartagena and elsewhere who had military talents that could be exploited and "young rogues" in prisons or correctional institutions, as well as the sons of gentlemen or of law officers whose parents sought to have them sent to the colonies for disciplinary reasons. The king, however, refused to send away such young men without their consent. "Libertines" and "unruly people" also did not meet his standards. Others advocated sending the foundling children who, according to Giraud, "filled the hospitals."[52] Nevertheless, by 1712, the colony had no more than four hundred non-Native inhabitants, many of whom came from outside France. Even those who were French-born lacked cohesion, coming from various regional backgrounds and speaking a number of different dialects.[53]

In late 1705, Pontchartrain reported to Bienville that the English had attacked and "almost destroyed" the Spanish colony among the Apalachees, causing many of the Apalachees, especially those who had become "Christians and Catholics," to take refuge near the Mobile fort. Shortly thereafter, Bienville wrote that the English and three thousand Indians had raided Choctaw villages the preceding autumn. Bienville also noted the need for colonists and "negroes to dig the ground with pickaxes."[54] In 1704, Pontchartrain reported to Bienville that a ship, the *Pélican*, would bring "twenty girls" from La Rochelle, France, to Louisiana "to be married to the Canadians and others who have made homes on the Mobile." The group also included a midwife, and Bienville later confirmed that the ship arrived and that the marriages took place.[55]

Pontchartrain generally maintained a positive view of Louisiana that reflected the current thinking of both Colbert and the king. Nevertheless, this perspective required that the colony "be able to subsist by itself in difficult times when the assistance from Europe may fail." Pontchartrain cited the English of Virginia, with their exemplary commercial skills and reputation, as a model and recommended that Bienville focus on the creation of tobacco plantations and land development.[56]

The king's view of the value of Louisiana, however, turned decidedly negative after 1710. Historian James Pritchard argues that Louis XIV and the regent who followed after his death in 1715 generally saw France's European continental interests as more important than its empire and "viewed colonialism as a form of adventurism leading to a weaker France." The private interests of the Le Moyne brothers, which led them to undertake illicit trade with the Spanish, exemplified the "adventurism" that weakened an absolutist model of colonialism and by 1730 made empire "elusive."[57]

A Company Solution? Antoine Crozat

During the peace negotiations leading to the Treaty of Utrecht, which ended the War of the Spanish Succession, the French king initially attempted to exchange

Louisiana for the Spanish part of the island of Hispaniola. He abandoned the idea after deciding that a French presence at the mouth of the Mississippi River seemed to have an enhanced strategic value. Because of the near bankruptcy of the French treasury, Pontchartrain and the king decided to focus on making Louisiana economically viable for both individuals and the government and turned to a company project that had been considered in 1710. In September 1712, the king granted Antoine Crozat, a wealthy French financier, a grandee of the tobacco monopoly, and a royal counselor and financial adviser, proprietary or monopoly rights to Louisiana until 1731.[58] First Crozat, then Scottish entrepreneur and financier John Law, and finally the Company of the Indies attempted to make Louisiana economically beneficial for themselves and others as well as the French government.[59]

Crozat's agreement gave him a monopoly on the colony's commerce and ownership of the mines and the lands he would acquire and improve to produce such commodities as silk, indigo, wool, and hides, but the arrangement lasted only until 1717. Although Crozat had experience and skill as a financier and some knowledge of colonies and colonial problems, he was a poor choice for a proprietor. He had interests in the Company of the Indies and served on the boards of directors of other companies. Although he gained some appreciation of Louisiana as more important than just a speculative venture, his interests tended to be limited to personal commercial exploitation. He initially imposed a 300 percent markup on goods imported into the colony, making them "prohibitively expensive" for both Indians and colonists. Populating the colony and building an empire were beyond his financial means. He was required to bring only two ships a year with some young men and women on each vessel and some goods and munitions for the king. He also made unwise choices for high government positions—in particular, Cadillac as governor and Jean Baptiste du Bois du Clos as commissioner (*commissaire ordonnateur*) in charge of finances. In addition, in the context of negotiations to end the war, Crozat's appointment had some negative international effects. Merchants in Holland and in Britain saw him as a threat to their commercial interests and found ways to express those views during peace negotiations.[60]

The French in Natchez

During Crozat's tenure as proprietor of Louisiana, the French established an enclave among the Natchez that included a trading post, the fort, and some concessions or plantations. In a political sense, Crozat's substantial markup on imported goods helped that initiative, for Cadillac, Bienville, and others had become aware of English traders' increased activity traders among Native groups, including the Natchez, as a consequence of the English ability to provide lower-cost goods. As early as 1713, however, Crozat may have recognized the need to establish a warehouse or commissary among the Natchez to help divert the trade in pelts from the English to the French. His earlier success in the tobacco trade may have also directed his attention to what had been identified as especially good land in the Natchez country for the cultivation of tobacco and other readily marketable crops. Despite Cadillac's unwillingness to provide military personnel from Mobile unless they could be replaced, Crozat persuaded two brothers to establish a Natchez commissary to trade furs with the Indians in early 1714. Later that year, when more extensive English fur trading along the Mississippi became known, Bienville was ordered to establish two additional forts, one farther north on the Wabash River and the other on the Natchez bluffs. Despite Cadillac's initial reluctance to support a fort at Natchez, Fort St. Jérôme, named for Jérôme Phélypeaux, the Comte de Pontchartrain, came into being on the Wabash, and Natchez's Fort Rosalie, named for either the comte's second wife or his daughter, followed in 1716.[61]

The new fort on the Natchez bluffs was built with Native help but was not much more than an "upright palisade made of 'stakes as thick as a leg' with four bastions, one at each corner." It stood on a "little mountain" that dominated the Mississippi River. One engineer noted that "it was possible to walk into the fort from any side with the greatest of ease." The buildings consisted of a guardhouse and barracks that were no more than "wretched huts." Still, at the time it was built, it was a significant accomplishment, and it seemed to ensure the French occupation of the area. A storehouse was restored and stocked with merchandise.[62] Crozat's successor, Law, focused on Natchez as an ideal region for plantation agriculture that would help him achieve his goal of making Louisiana France's most successful commercial tobacco producer.[63]

But from the outset, the post among the Natchez had its problems. In late 1715, four traders who had stopped at Natchez to hire some Natives to help them paddle upstream were murdered, allegedly by the Indians, who then helped themselves to the traders' merchandise. The French responded by dispatching a military force under Bienville that sought to establish itself on an island in the Mississippi River. Bienville, who had never been on good terms with Cadillac, believed that the murders had occurred because Cadillac refused to smoke the calumet with the Natchez and with other Natives further north. The Natchez attempted to resolve the issue by sending delegations with the calumet, but Bienville refused to smoke the pipe until the perpetrators of the murders had been brought to justice, and he held several Natchez, including at least three suns or chiefs, hostage in a makeshift jail. The affair, which became known as

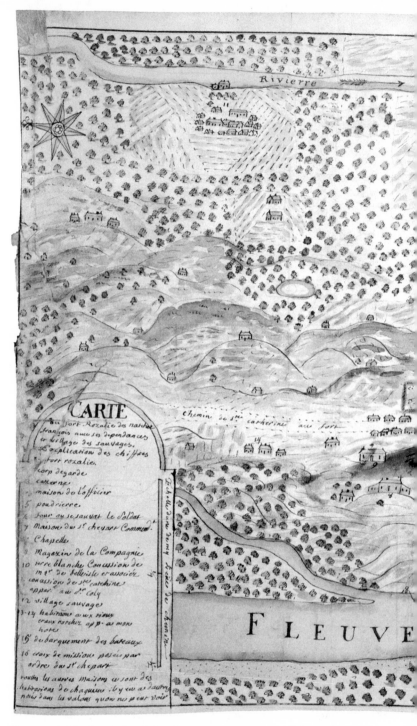

Dumont de Montigny's detailed and artistic representation of the community of Natchez, 1748–52. Montigny was assigned here from 1726 to 1728. Reproduction courtesy of the Newberry Library, Chicago. Courtesy of the Archives and Research Services Divisions, Mississippi Department of Archives and History, Jackson.

BLanche.

St. LOUIS

the First Natchez War, eventually ended after negotiations and the execution of some of the alleged perpetrators.[64]

From Crozat to Law

By 1717, Crozat decided to ask the regency to relieve him of what was turning out to be a costly privilege. Mineral wealth had proven a chimera, and settlers simply were uninterested in cultivating tobacco, sugar, indigo, mulberry trees, and even basic food commodities. Furthermore, residents of Louisiana disliked Crozat for what they saw as his profiting at their expense, and dual governance made life more difficult for him. Metropolitan authorities seemed to value Louisiana only for its strategic location and its potential to relieve France of its fiscal problems. Crozat recommended that some kind of effective company replace him, since the expenses were too great for any individual to bear. To support that request and recommendation, he provided an optimistic assessment of the colony's potential.[65]

In early 1717, the regency replaced Crozat with John Law, a Scottish financier who had come to France in 1714 to help Louis XIV resolve his country's financial problems and stayed on after the king's death. Despite some initial opposition, the French government, through its *conseil extraordinaire*, authorized him to establish a bank in 1716 and gave it essentially unlimited power to issue bank notes backed by gold and silver reserves. This paper currency stimulated commerce and helped the government out of its financial difficulties. Reconstituted in 1718 as the Banque Royale of France, the bank eventually merged with the Company of the West, which Law had organized and which received a twenty-five-year monopoly on Louisiana trade. Law served as the chief director of both the Company of the West and the bank. Law and two women, Françoise-Marie Farges, a *fourniseur* (contractor for the French army), and Catherine Barré, the wife of Antoine Chaumont, honorary secretary to the king, were the company's major shareholders. The monopoly grant also included ownership of lands and mines and the right to build fortifications and nominate directors for the company. Given its primary focus on the Mississippi Valley, the company was frequently referred to as the Mississippi Company, and by 1720, it had absorbed other companies and became the Company of the Indies, with a monopoly on all of France's trade outside Europe.[66]

Given Law's skill as a promoter of himself and his project and a very effective Europe-wide advertising campaign extolling Louisiana's mineral and agricultural potential, shares of company stock sold well, with prices rising.[67]

Law, of course, benefited. In addition, Law added assumed other titles and responsibilities: controller general and superintendent of general finance for France. He became in effect France's finance minister.[68]

A mania for acquiring shares in the Company of the West developed not only on the exchange in Paris but anywhere they were available, including the bourse in Frankfurt where Telemann was living in 1720. To meet demand, the company issued more shares than French bank notes or government debt could cover, and by January 1720, the scheme began to unravel. Inflation topped 20 percent. Stock prices declined, gradually at first and then sharply, falling from as high as ten thousand livres per share to two thousand livres. Sellers panicked, and by the end of the year, Law had lost control of the company and his career as France's financial savior was over.[69]

The Company/Colony Continues

For better or worse, however, the era of the company continued in Louisiana.[70] A reorganized Company of the Indies oversaw operation of what there was of a colony until 1731. Both Crozat and Law left legacies of sorts. Law had some success in attracting people from Europe and importing enslaved Africans to Louisiana with promoters and materials that extolled it as a place "filled with gold, silver, copper, and lead mines" and with a salubrious climate and "extremely pleasant soil." As many as four thousand Germans and Swiss crossed France to get to the port of Lorient, and just over 140 Swiss soldiers arrived at Biloxi in February 1721.[71] Few others successfully made the crossing, and those who did found nothing but difficulties. The settlers who settled on Law's concession on the Arkansas River, for example, found themselves abandoned when his enterprise collapsed in 1720. Bienville persuaded them not to return to Germany but instead to settle on a concession along the Mississippi River twenty or thirty miles north of New Orleans, an area that came to be known as the Côtes des Allemands (German Coast).[72] A few people from the Netherlands also migrated. Some people went as indentured servants, while others were forced to go—military deserters, vagabonds, mendicants, and dealers in contraband salt. Between 1719 and 1721, women were "scooped out of the orphanages, poorhouses, and maybe even the prisons of France, either by seduction, threats, or outright force," and sent to become brides, becoming known as *filles a la cassette* (cassette girls) because of the little bags in which they carried their clothes and other belongings.[73] By the early 1730s, the non-Amerindian population in Louisiana had topped four thousand.[74]

Beginnings of New Orleans

Crozat had observed as early as 1714 that "it is not right that there should be no post on the Mississippi River towards the sea, that of Natchez being sixty leagues away."[75] Others agreed, and a new post was established and named New Orleans after the Duke of Orleans, who was serving as the French regent. Iberville had noted the site during his first trip to Mississippi—it was the place where his men had made their portage to the river from the bay where their ships had anchored.[76] Bienville played a key role in the creation of New Orleans, urging that the colonial headquarters be moved to the Mississippi River. By the fall of 1717, a "store-keeper and cashier" had been appointed for a counting house at the new site, and the following June, Bienville reported that work was underway to establish the post and town.[77]

Opposition surfaced, however, and the project was delayed. Some company directors expressed concern about the cost of building levees to protect the city from flooding. Furthermore, in late 1720 and early 1721, the council decided to move what there was of a post at Old Biloxi to New Biloxi, name it Fort Louis, and rename the post at Mobile Fort Condé, causing a "ruin of their concessions" for many colonists and "a considerable expense for the colony."[78]

In 1722, a young Frenchman, Jean-François-Benjamin Dumont de Montigny, arrived in New Orleans and declared it "now capital of all the country," with "attractive" and "well-made buildings made all of brick or half timber and half brick" and streets "laid out perfectly straight." Bienville reported to the council the following year that New Orleans had become "the principal establishment of the colony."[79] In July 1729, another French newcomer, Marc-Antoine Caillot, a clerk for the Company of the Indies, found New Orleans "a very fine creation for the country."[80]

Two years earlier, a young Ursuline nun, Marie Madeleine Hachard, had arrived along with other nuns from Rouen, France, after a long and difficult journey. The women took up residence at a the temporary convent in New Orleans, and Hachard described the town as "very beautiful and well-constructed and regularly built."[81] She concluded, however, that the local economy was dysfunctional and, perhaps reflecting a sense of mission for herself and her colleagues, that there was a lack of regard for religion: "The devil here possesses a large empire."[82]

Opportunities—And Challenges: Toward the End of a French Natchez

The establishment of New Orleans as the de facto capital of "le Mississippi" can be seen as clear evidence of a shift in French interest from the Gulf Coast to the Mississippi River.[83] That change enhanced the status of Natchez, which in early 1722 became one of the nine parts of the colony of Louisiana.[84] That upgrade was sustained after 1763, when the British created a Natchez District within the British province of West Florida, and it retained a fair degree of autonomy under the Spanish after 1779 as part of a province of Louisiana within the Spanish viceroyalty of New Spain. The Spanish defined what there was of a town surrounding the fort within this district as a "city," and after 1798 the district came to comprise "the core area of the Mississippi Territory."[85]

Meinig's concepts of "points of attachment" and "discrete colonization areas" are useful for understanding the evolution of Natchez under the Company of the Indies.[86] George Edward Milne prefers to see the Natchez country as a jumble of places and diverse cultures that began with the liquidation of Law's enterprise and the arrival of significant numbers of people from Europe and Africa. Interaction among roughly two thousand Europeans, Africans, and Indians took place in an area smaller than a dozen square miles, making the Natchez country somewhat unique in American colonial history.[87]

The Company of the Indies initially seemed promising. It invested heavily in infrastructure, and for a time, Natchez became the center of tobacco production in the French Atlantic.[88] The Natchez, like many other Native groups, tended to be open to newcomers as long as they could be absorbed. In addition, the Natchez considered their chiefs to be suns, an idea that connected with Louis XIV's depiction of himself as the Sun King, entitled to absolute rule by divine right. Iberville declared the ruler of the Natchez "the most tyrannical Indian," and Jesuit chaplain Paul du Ru described the chief's manner as resembling that of "an ancient emperor."[89]

But these European newcomers generally had little interest in being absorbed. Beginning with the Crozat enterprise and continuing with Law's Mississippi Company, the arrival of European settlers had "a devastating effect" on the Natchez Indians.[90] By 1718, the Company of the West had granted extensive Louisiana concessions or plantations to upper-class Frenchmen but had failed to attract ordinary yeoman farmers. And those recruited or forced to serve as workers included vagrants, orphans, smugglers, prostitutes, and thieves.[91] It is in that context that the abbé Antoine-François Prévost (1697–1763) set his best-known story, *Manon Lescaut* (1731), about a love affair between a woman, Manon, and a chevalier, des Grieux. Manon is exiled to Louisiana because of her willingness to take lovers either to make ends meet to support their affair or to satisfy her desire for luxury, and both characters meet a tragic end there.[92]

Private land and private property exemplified by the company and the concessions it granted tended to clash with the more communal ways of life in the Natchez area. The first major concession was located along the "River of the Natchez," which was later named St. Catherine's Creek, after the wife of the *commissaire-ordonnateur*, Marc-Antoine Hubert, who arrived in 1717 but gave up the post in 1719 and moved to the Natchez country, where he had obtained a concession along the creek upstream from the Grand Village. He brought personal and trade goods and some sixty *domestiques*, about thirty of them enslaved Africans and Native Americans. The second concession, the Terre Blanche (White Earth) Concession, was established downstream from the Grand Village by a group of tobacco workers led by Monplaisir de la Guchay, who came with the same convoy that brought Hubert.[93]

In late 1719, further changes occurred quite independently of any consultation or diplomacy with the Native Natchez peoples. The St. Catherine concession, which, like the White Earth, acquired a village to house people, changed ownership when it passed to three men who had been involved with Law in France. They formed the Associates of St. Catherine and negotiated with the Company of the West for an agricultural concession, contracting with a manager to oversee the operation. They also secured permission from the company to purchase fifteen hundred enslaved Africans for shipment to the colony.[94] This permission, along with the 1724 adoption of a version of the Code Noir specifically designed for Louisiana, marked not only the beginning of Louisiana's experience with substantial numbers of African slaves but also, in the words of historian Jennifer Spear, "a transition from a status-based hierarchy to one rooted in race." Many of those enslaved became part of the Natchez Country.[95]

An important cause of the Second Natchez War, also known as the Village Crisis of 1722, centered on different perceptions of just what use or possession of land meant. According to most contemporary accounts, the affair began with a conflict between a sergeant of the garrison at the fort and some Natchez over a debt; ultimately, it came to expose other issues related to how two towns, Apple Village and the St. Catherine's concession "would construct and use space around them."[96] Several people were wounded or killed during the crisis, and as had been the case with the First Natchez War in 1716, the Natchez chief, the Tattooed Serpent (Serpent Piqué) took an active role in bringing about an end to the conflict.[97]

Hostilities resumed the following year with the Third Natchez War, which Milne calls Bienville's War. The conflict has been attributed to a variety of causes, including "renegade settlements" (the Natchez villages of the Apple Village, Jenzenaque, and the Gris or Grigra, which had previously come under the influence of the Chickasaws and English traders and slavers) and a free African who was living among the Natchez and encouraged them to turn against the French and their Indian allies.[98] Bienville led a force north and conducted a "scorched earth campaign" against some of the Native villages. The Tattooed Serpent again played a key role in resolving the conflict, an effort that included producing the head of the free African to satisfy Bienville. However, this settlement deepened the "fissures within the Natchez-Louisianan relationship," and the situation worsened with the death of the Tattooed Serpent in 1725 and that of his brother, the Great Sun, three years later. Bienville had developed good working relationships with both chiefs.[99]

The fissures deepened still further with the 1728 appointment of a man named Chépart as commandant of Fort Rosalie. Chépart had arrived in Louisiana in 1719 as a lieutenant and become a captain in 1723, the same year in which he was wounded in a duel in Natchez. Bienville and others found Chépart to be "a good, capable officer," and Louisiana governor Étienne Périer, who succeeded Bienville in 1728, apparently backed the appointment of Chépart as commandant in the belief that he could develop the agricultural potential of the Natchez Country.[100]

As commandant, Chépart garnered much more negative assessments. Indeed, he is frequently blamed for the events that culminated with the 1729 Franco-Natchez War. In the view of Marcel Giraud, Chépart imposed "a veritable tyranny" on the Natives and behaved with "dissolute" fashion in their villages," drinking heavily and displaying a short temper.[101] More significantly, his greed underscored what many Natives had come to see as a disregard for their conceptions of how land should be used.[102] Chépart sought to acquire part of the White Apple village for a plantation and set his sights on occupying the Grand Village.[103]

But casting Chépart as the sole villain of the tale is too simplistic. Many other events and conditions contributed to the outbreak of war in 1729, primarily by causing the Natchez to conclude that the French and other Europeans posed a threat to their values and their way of life. In particular, the Natchez saw private property in land, livestock, and people—Native as well as African—as alien. Maroons—Africans who had escaped—formed autonomous communities and added to growing discontent among the Native Americans. With their livestock and agricultural technology, the European newcomers tended to undermine an economy of exchange and gift-giving.[104]

In 1728, the Superior Council forbade marriage between Frenchmen or other white subjects of the king with "the Savages," thereby threatening the traditional Native practice of absorbing newcomers via marriage. All of these factors combined to create what Milne has characterized as "a united opposition to Louisiana," which had demonstrated its inability to respect indigenous standards of "civilized" behavior. In addition, after observing how Europeans differentiated themselves from Africans using the language of color, the Natchez adopted the practice to differentiate themselves from Europeans. By identifying themselves as red, they imitated what other Native peoples did in diplomatic exchanges, as happened in Charles Town during a conference sponsored by the South Carolina government in early 1726: "We are now all the Red People now met together," said a Cherokee chief, referring to his group as well as the Creeks in attendance.[105]

Despite some opposition among the Natchez, on November 28, 1729, Natchez warriors apparently known and trusted by inhabitants of Fort Rosalie used a pretext to get close to the settlement and then opened fire, killing almost all the white men and some women and children—a total of between 200 and 250 people.[106] Enslaved Africans were generally spared, possibly so that they could be sold or exchanged. In his report, Périer wrote, "The Natchez, pretending to be going hunting, fell upon the settlement at this post on the 28th of the past month between nine and ten o'clock in the morning, and massacred not only all the men who were at the fort in our village, but in addition attacked the concessions from which no one was able to escape. They kept the women, the children and the negroes. They captured the galley that I had sent there with goods and which was to bring the tobacco that I had gathered there."[107] Three months later, Périer's men found "nothing but a landscape of ruins."[108]

Just to the north along the Yazoo River, where the French had established Fort St. Pierre in 1719 and granted concessions, the Tioux, the Yazoos, and the Koroas joined the Natchez uprising, killing other settlers, including the garrison at the fort, which they also destroyed. Other Indian groups, particularly those close to New Orleans, the Houmas and Bayagoulas, remained loyal to the French, as did the Tunicas and a small group, the Ofogoulas.[109]

Périer described the November 1729 attack as a "massacre." The French commandant in Mobile, Diron d'Artaguette, also employed the word in a February 1730 report that primary blame on Chépart and suggested that incidents might have been avoided had the repeated warnings of Tattooed Arm, the wife of the Great Sun, and others been heeded.[110] Patricia Galloway has used equally strong language to describe the French reaction: "a genocidal retaliation."[111]

More D'ésespérance de Mississippi

Périer and others intended to eliminate the Natchez or at least those who had been responsible for the "massacre." Many survived, however—not in the Natchez Country but elsewhere. In so doing, they conveyed to the French and other Europeans the important fact that although the Natchez were a smaller group than the Chickasaws or the Choctaws and occupied a much smaller space, they could not be viewed as a single nation or nationality. Jesuit missionary Michel Baudouin recognized that diversity among a much larger group, the Choctaws, in 1732. He described them as a polity consisting of "forty-two villages" with a "Great Chief" possessing only limited power: "All the villages are so many little republics in which each one does as he likes." Many French governors and commandants may already have understood that the Chickasaws and Choctaws were organized this way, and French officials certainly were aware of the diversity among the non-Native community, which included peoples from Africa and from various parts of Europe.[112]

From the colonialist perspective, whatever "hope" there was for Mississippi, ended in 1729, if not even earlier. It did for Marc-Antoine Caillot, a recently arrived agent for the Company of the Indies who was in New Orleans when news of the events in the Natchez Country began to arrive. His career as a company agent in New Orleans turned out to be short as the conflict with the Natchez and the promise of more lucrative ventures elsewhere led the company to give up its concession, finding Louisiana to have been no more than a sequence of pipe dreams. In early 1731, the French colony reverted to the king of France and became a royal colony.[113]

Périer continued as governor until 1733. In response to growing anxiety in New Orleans and the immediate area, he strongly advised people to stay in or as close to the town as possible. He also sent a force of enslaved Africans a short distance down the Mississippi to eliminate a small Chaouacha village, even though its inhabitants had taken no part in the events in Natchez. And he sent Jean Paul de Le Sueur, a relative of Bienville's, and Swiss officer Joseph Christophe de Lusser to the Choctaws to enlist their support in a war against the Natchez. They had no difficulty doing so, since the Choctaws had fought a short war and seemed eager for any opportunity to enhance their power and influence.[114]

By joining a French detachment from Pointe Coupée, some Choctaws provided initial support. Although the Natchez had constructed two forts along St. Catherine's Creek and had studied French cannon technology with the assistance of formerly enslaved Africans, a French force joined by some five hundred Choctaws, fifteen enslaved Africans, and Tunica and Colapissa (Acolapissa) warriors besieged the Natchez. Choctaw chief Alibamon Mingo negotiated the release of some women, children, and African hostages, and most of the rest of the Natchez—with some enslaved African allies—escaped under cover of darkness on February 25–26, 1730.[115]

Not until the end of 1730 did Périer lead an expedition north to eliminate the Natchez. By that time, the largest group, including the Great Sun, had crossed the Mississippi and established themselves at a fort along the Black River, a tributary of the Red. Again with substantial help from Native groups, the French force found them there and established a siege. After extensive

negotiations, the Great Sun gave himself up as a hostage, resulting in the surrender of about thirty-five men and two hundred women. They, along with
the Great Sun and his family were taken to New Orleans and sold as slaves to
be shipped to Saint-Domingue. Those who managed to escape dispersed and
joined others in Chickasaw and Creek Country.[116]

Bienville returned to the post of governor in 1733. Like his predecessor,
Périer, Bienville concluded that the Chickasaws in particular were too closely
attached to the English, and he continued to provide a haven for some Natchez.
The Chickasaws had sent delegations with the calumet to try to find peace
with the Choctaws, Périer, and later Bienville, but those endeavors failed. In
this context, the Choctaws emerged as elusive or divided. One of their leaders, Soulouche Oumastabé (Red Shoe), provided early and major support for
the French, receiving a great medal as a reward. Other Choctaw chiefs were
outraged. Red Shoe became more elusive. The Choctaw chiefs engaged in
what Richard White characterizes as a "play-off" system in which they sought
to exchange their support for rewards in the form of medals, gifts, and trade
advantages. Europeans, too, sought to benefit by playing off Native chiefs and
their groups against one another. The English found particular value in the
use of liquor and credit. These efforts contributed to the ongoing conflict
between the Choctaws and the Chickasaws in the 1740s and 1750s as well as to
the emergence of significant internal fissures among the Choctaws. Western,
eastern, and southern divisions of towns emerged, and 1746 saw the start of a
virtual civil war that lasted four years.[117]

Bienville's war against the Chickasaws consisted of three campaigns he orga-
nized beginning in early 1736. The first, led by Pierre d'Artaguette, brother of Diron,
came down the Mississippi River from the Illinois Country and arrived at the
Chickasaw Bluffs on March 4 before marching overland to the Chickasaw village
of Ougoula Tchetoka, located in the northwestern part of what is now Tupelo.
The second, led by Bienville, began in Mobile and used the newly constructed
Fort Tombecbé as the base for a late May attack on the Chickasaw village of
Ackia. Both campaigns resulted in disaster for the French forces. Bienville then
waited until 1739 for his third attempt, departing New Orleans in November and
traveling up the Mississippi River to the new Fort Assumption on the Chickasaw
Bluffs. They planned to stay there until supplies and reinforcements arrived from
the north before marching overland along d'Artaguette's route to the Chickasaw
villages, but the supplies never arrived, and Bienville abandoned the effort and
arranged a peace with the Chickasaws in 1740.[118]

Although he was a skilled diplomat with a good understanding of tribal
power structures who had mastered the Choctaw-like Mobilian trade language,
Bienville was dismissed as governor and replaced by Pierre Vaudreuil, a Cana-

dian by birth, in 1743. He served until 1753, when Louis Kerlérec assumed the post, which he held for another decade. At the conclusion of the Seven Years' War (French and Indian War), in which the French and British again opposed each other, Jean-Jacques-Blaise d'Abbadie (1763–65) and Charles Philippe Aubry (1765–66) briefly served as governors or directors-general.[119]

For both Vaudreuil and Kerlérec, the ongoing presence and influence of the English among the Choctaws and Chickasaws continued to offer challenges and opportunities. The Chickasaws seemed to want peace. After learning of Vaudreuil's arrival, some chiefs sent him a message: that "all the red men of the North are your children and that for a long time you have been their chief; and that you have always kept peace among them." They went on to say that they no longer wished to attack the French and that providing them with such necessities as "coats, blankets, powder, vermilion or beads" might persuade them to assist the French.[120]

After a 1744 meeting in Mobile with twelve hundred Choctaws, Vaudreuil reported that furthering peace would require more and higher-quality gifts. He also noted that Chickasaws had sent him a message promising that if peace were secured, they would drive out the English, reinforcing the message by sending a white flag attached to a calumet. Red Shoe nevertheless remained a challenge, and Vaudreuil provided him with a gift but also reminded him that to continue receiving such gifts and retain his medal, he needed to refrain from attacking either Chickasaws or the English. Vaudreuil wanted the Choctaws to follow the Chickasaw example and maintain peace with the French. The governor found the Choctaws to be "docile Indians" who were "deeply attached to the French" but also echoed Baudouin's earlier assessment that "there was little subordination in the Choctaw nation and that the medal chiefs have only a little influence in it." "Each village has its own chief, who, with his many warriors, follows whatever course that seems good to him, so that they are so many small republics."[121]

Rather than improving, however, the dearth of trade goods subsequently intensified after a European war that had begun over the succession of Maria Theresa to the Austrian throne spread to America. With France facing off against England yet again, both the Choctaws and Chickasaws remained vulnerable to English influence, primarily from the Carolinas. Red Shoe manipulated English traders for supplies when the war interrupted French supplies, while other Native leaders and groups, especially the Alabamas, remained open to whoever could best serve their interests. Red Shoe also went further, ordering the assassination of three French traders. In response, the French demanded blood revenge—the death of Red Shoe—but the idea received support only from some Choctaws.[122]

The consequence was what has been characterized as a "civil war" among the Choctaws. One of the casualties was Red Shoe, who was killed by some French-allied Choctaws. The conflict finally ended in 1750 with Alibamon Mingo's promise that the Choctaws would cooperate in bringing to justice anyone who murdered a French person and in a French commitment to providing gifts.[123]

French officials had long recognized the colony's fragility and indeed, in the case of Kerlérec, its destitution. The French administration could not meet the trade or gift-giving expectations of Alibamon Mingo and other Native leaders, meaning that no cooperation was available to help deter the ongoing English challenge. Kerlérec, like his predecessors, lamented the lack of adequate troops. As a consequence, Mississippi remained "a land of Indian nations."[124]

In 1754, six years after the conclusion of the War of the Austrian Succession, the French, helped by Indian allies, attacked and defeated a small regiment that the governor of Virginia had sent to the forks of the Ohio River to contest the French claim to the area and thus promote English interests. Among the members of the defeated regiment was a young George Washington, who was keenly interested in acquiring land. The ensuing conflict, generally known as the French and Indian War, became part of another European and global conflict, the Seven Years' War.[125]

The war exacerbated the long-standing problems in French Louisiana—a dearth of settlers and enslaved workers to cultivate the land and insufficient goods to keep the Indians pacified. In December 1756, Kerlérec wrote, "All of my letters are filled with representations about the needs of this colony . . . today they are more pressing than ever."[126] The English took advantage of these weaknesses to enlarge their presence and influence among Indian groups including the Alabamas, Cherokees, and Choctaws. Kerlérec even allowed English trading ships into New Orleans, an action that led others to suggest that he was not governing lawfully.[127]

In late 1762, the French agreed to give all of what they claimed as Louisiana west of the Mississippi River, along with the island or peninsula of Orleans and its city, to the Spanish. The following year, the Treaty of Paris gave all of French Louisiana east of the river to the British.[128] D'Abbadie and Aubry oversaw a complex withdrawal, including managing the arrival of British officials and dealing with an uprising by opponents of Spanish rule. Also important to French officials was explaining the changes to Native American allies: Kerlérec had emphasized the need to recognize "the great number of nations that surround us, who have sacrificed their lives and their tranquility for the service of the French." The transition should be managed in such a way as to "perpetuate the French name among nations that we shall be very glad to recover and perhaps sooner than we think."[129]

Kerlérec also reported to his superiors that "Cherokees, Choctaws, and Alabamas, making together more than twelve thousand men," had objected to the treaty that ceded "their lands to England" on the grounds "that the French have no right to give them away and finally they know what they have to do when the time comes."[130] In July 1763, chiefs of several of the smaller nations—the Biloxis, Chitimachas, Houmas, Quapaws, and Natchez—as well as Choctaws came to New Orleans to meet with d'Abbadie and "sound out rumors circulating among them concerning the cession of fragments of Louisiana to England" and Spain. They stressed the point that the French did not own the land and had no right to cede it to another group.[131]

Indian unrest, along with ongoing intra-governmental problems, feuding between the Capuchin and Jesuit religious orders, and the anti-Spanish revolt, and the poor conditions plagued d'Abbadie for the balance of his term as director-general, during which his principal assignment was "the speedy and orderly transfer of Louisiana to England and Spain."[132] But from his perspective, the greatest difficulty was the English, who were "giving me . . . more trouble than the Indians." As he wrote exasperatedly in November 1763, "What a commission to have to deal with people intoxicated with their success who regard themselves as the masters of the world!"[133]

CHAPTER THREE

Masters of the World?

The British in Mississippi, 1763–1779

When Jean-Jacques-Blaise d'Abbadie used the words "masters of the world," he might have revealed more about himself than about the British officials who had begun arriving in late 1763 to replace the French. His assignment was a difficult one. Neither Indians nor European colonists had taken part in the complex negotiations related to the French government's decision to withdraw from continental North America, and both groups had to be accommodated or placated. Francophile Native leaders in particular, had to be persuaded to keep the peace and work with the British. D'Abbadie recorded in his journal frequent visits by Pascagoulas, Choctaws, Houmas, Tunicas, Chitimachas, Alibamons, and others. Disgruntled French residents had to be accommodated, a process that included relocating some of them west of the Mississippi River on land grants provided by the French government. And French military personnel had to be evacuated from their posts. D'Abbadie's health was poor, and he died in early February 1765 and was succeeded by Charles Philippe Aubry, who had been serving as commander of Louisiana's garrison.[1]

Initial Challenges for the British and Responses

Like their French predecessors, British officials struggled to balance their interests with the at-times divergent interests of the colonists.[2] They sought to increase order and peace while lowering costs and maximizing benefits. An October 1763 royal proclamation divided the additions to Britain's American empire into four new colonies: East Florida, West Florida, Quebec, and Grenada. The proclamation also set aside the region west of the Appalachian Mountains as a "Land Reserved for Indians" and limited private individuals' ability to purchase and settle on that land. This restriction served two purposes, both pacifying the Indians and preventing the challenges that such interior settlements potentially posed to English manufacturing interests. The northern boundary of both West and East Florida—from the Atlantic Coast to Mobile and Pensacola—was originally the Thirty-First Parallel but was modified in 1764 in part to satisfy what historian Robin Fabel describes as "expansionist entrepreneurs." British policy also sought the more immediate goal of suppressing an Indian uprising to the north known as Pontiac's War after the Ottawa war chief.[3]

Native Diplomacy

The 1763 proclamation divided Indian country into two districts, and John Stuart was appointed superintendent of Indian affairs for the southern district.[4] He arrived in Pensacola in October 1764 and chose a Frenchman, Chevalier Henri de Montault de Monbéraut, to serve as his assistant. Monbéraut, who had acquired substantial property in the area of Mobile, had indicated a desire to become a British subject and retain his holdings. His command of French and general linguistic skills enhanced his status among French inhabitants of the area. Those skills and his position as commandant of Fort Toulouse beginning in 1755 also helped him to gain a considerable reputation among the local Indians. For all of these reasons, he was a valuable deputy for Stuart during this time of transition.[5]

In the summer of 1763, British military forces established themselves in both Pensacola and Mobile. The Spanish evacuated Pensacola, leaving the newcomers to provide food and presents for visiting Indians. George Johnstone became the first governor of the newly created West Florida, and Pensacola became its capital.[6] In October, British forces headed by Robert Farmar arrived in Mobile, which had the largest number of remaining French inhabitants in the new West Florida, and found that d'Abbadie had called an Indian congress and that many Choctaws had already arrived to attend it. D'Abbadie instructed Farmar to take possession of the post and its dependencies when he deemed it appropriate but recommended waiting until after the congress. In November, between three thousand and five thousand Choctaws met, among them many chiefs ill-disposed toward the British as well as toward one another. Although relations between d'Abbadie and Farmar sometimes were difficult, the two collaborated in a speech to the Choctaws that sought to answer their concerns regarding the peace negotiations and settlement.[7]

Also in November 1763, Stuart held his first major meeting with the southern Indians in Augusta, Georgia. He had hoped to bring together representatives of all the major groups along with southern governors with the ambitious goal of "overcoming the unfriendly disposition of the different groups of nations that are to be invited" toward one another and bringing them under British jurisdiction. About eight hundred Cherokees and Chickasaws came, as did some Lower Creeks, a few Catawbas, and even fewer Choctaws. Two prominent Upper Creek chiefs, the Mortar and Emistisiguo, attended, and they confirmed what Stuart had already learned: some Creeks were greatly distressed by the French departure and that, as a consequence, "the lands now possessed by the French must revert to them having never been ceded but only Lent." The meeting produced an agreement, but, according to historian Steven Hahn, its importance was diminished by other Indian groups' belief that the Creeks had not only capitulated to the British too easily but also were greedy for land.[8]

Additional formal meetings occurred with the Chickasaws and Choctaws in Mobile during March and April 1765 and with the Creeks in Pensacola in late May and early June.[9] Most attending the Mobile meeting were Chickasaws, who were friendly toward the British. The Choctaws arrived late, and those who came represented only the eastern group. The chiefs among them were initially so anti-British that they refused to give up their French medals. After being introduced to the Choctaws and Chickasaws by Governor Johnstone as their "ancient friend," Monbéraut played a crucial role in persuading most of them to change their minds.[10]

From late May through most of June, Creeks came to Pensacola in response to a diplomatic mission Johnstone had sent to Creek Country shortly after his arrival in late 1764. With Mobile and Pensacola now in British hands, the Creeks had fewer options—or none at all—to play off competing imperial powers. The two men Johnstone dispatched lived among the Creeks until May 1765 and persuaded the Mortar and others to come to Pensacola, meet the governor, exchange their French medals for British, secure an agreement about boundaries, and discuss other matters meriting attention. Although the Creeks "proved obtuse," Monbéraut and Stuart helped forge an agreement with regard to a land cession. The Mortar, a northern Creeks headman, initially was not inclined to accept a medal from the British, having never found it necessary to have one from the French, but ultimately accepted the British offer.[11]

Other meetings followed as the British sought to sustain some degree of amicable and lasting relations with the various Native American leaders and villages. Additional major congresses took place in 1771–72 and 1777 in the context of the American Revolution. Stuart reported that 2,312 Choctaws and Chickasaws attended the weeklong gathering in Mobile, which lasted from the end of December 1771 to early January 1772. The principal Chickasaw speaker there emphasized how important it was for the British to "supply our wants." A few weeks earlier, British officials had met with the Creeks.[12] The 1777 meeting was even larger, with about 2,800 Choctaws and 40 Chickasaws present.[13]

Gifts retained their vital function in allowing Indian leaders to earn respect and support by demonstrating their generosity, while medals helped create a hierarchical network of large- and small-medal chiefs and gorget captains. In addition to boundaries and land use, other issues had to be discussed. Alcohol remained a problem, with the Choctaws in particular, "hunt[ing] for liquor." Unscrupulous traders sold or gifted alcohol to stimulate deerskin production and, in the words of anthropologist Anthony F. C. Wallace, "lubricate the wheels of commerce." During the 1770–71 Mobile meetings, one chief described alcohol as a great sea coming from Mobile and surrounding his nation's plantations and settlements. In 1778, Charles Stuart, deputy superintendent of Indian affairs in the southern district and cousin of John, reported that he had difficulty establishing a day for a meeting with Chickasaws and Choctaws because many of them were drunk: "Unless some effectual step is taken to put a stop to the immoderate importation of rum into the Indian country, and until his Excellency the Governor enforces the Proclamation respecting it, it will never be in the power of your officers to carry your instructions into execution." Related issues such as unlicensed and abusive traders, the need to establish and respect prices, and the presence of what were often described as "vagabonds" provided an ongoing leitmotif of these meetings and discussions.[14]

British West Florida

The 1763 proclamation's boundary for the trans-Appalachian region reserved for Native Americans soon began to be revised, a consequence of its improvised, tentative character.[15] Before leaving London to take up his post as West Florida's new governor, Johnstone petitioned the Board of Trade to move the line two hundred miles to the north, thereby encompassing more of the Mississippi Valley as well as the Alabama and Tombigbee Rivers above Mobile. In March 1764, the board, with later Privy Council confirmation, awarded Johnstone much of what he wanted, authorizing movement of the border north to the confluence of the Yazoo and Mississippi Rivers and east to the Chattahoochee River. West Florida consequently included the "lush riparian region around Natchez and Walnut Hills" as well as nearly 38,000 square miles of Indian villages and hunting lands.[16] The change seemed to end any prospect of the trans-Appalachian region east of the Mississippi River remaining a closed preserve for Native

American and fur trading interests. However, Native peoples found various ways to make the point that they needed to be consulted before any major settlements could occur on land that they considered theirs.[17]

Johnstone and other officials were much more interested in finding ways to lure people to West Florida.[18] Most of the few Spanish in Pensacola evacuated, but many French inhabitants of the Mobile area, including Monbéraut, chose to stay. Johnstone and other promoters attracted a handful of settlers by the mid-1760s, but a lull followed until the early 1770s, when Peter Chester became governor. He and others focused on the western part of the province along the Mississippi River, and the outbreak of the American Revolution in 1775 did not deter migration, at least initially. Between 1776 and 1779, Chester granted more than eighteen thousand acres of land between the Mississippi River and the Yazoo and Big Black Rivers, including fifteen thousand acres to British naval veterans of the Seven Years' War. Fabel has characterized 1772–79 as "boom years."[19]

Johnstone was an inveterate promoter who used his time in office to further not only the colony's interests but also his own, receiving a land grant of 100,000 acres. He encouraged migration, settlement, and investment by touting West Florida as the "emporium of the new world" and compared Pensacola to Venice, Italy. Along with others, he advocated the creation of an all-water link from the Mississippi River to the Gulf of Mexico that bypassed New Orleans (now part of Spanish Louisiana) via the Iberville River, which in some places was choked with logs and other debris, and Lakes Maurepas and Pontchartrain. Such an enterprise, he believed, would stimulate commerce on the Mississippi River and even with Spanish America. The idea was nevertheless abandoned in 1768.[20] Because military authorities had concluded the value of the province had been exaggerated and that posts on the Mississippi were indefensible in the event of conflict with Spain, Fort Bute at Manchac, just north of where the Iberville enters the Mississippi, was dismantled and the fort at Natchez that had been partially repaired after 1763 was converted to a trading post.[21]

Promoting West Florida: Natchez and a Natchez District

Montfort Browne arrived in Pensacola in January 1766 to serve as Johnstone's lieutenant governor and served as de facto governor from Johnstone's 1768 departure until Chester took over two years later. Browne extolled the virtues of West Florida and, like his predecessor, looked to promote his own interests as well as those of the colony, securing at least one land grant. Browne traveled extensively through the western part of the province to encourage the govern-

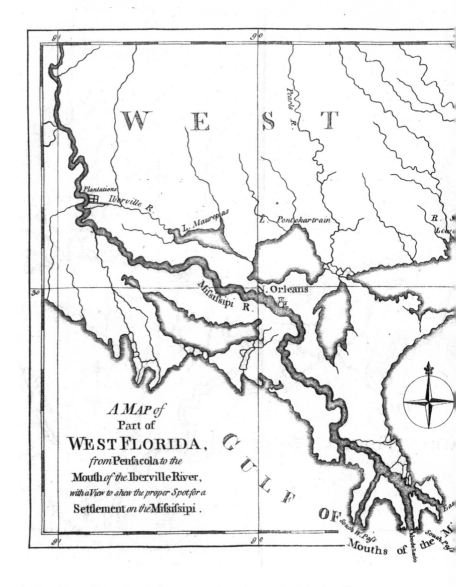

A Map of Part of West Florida from Pensacola to the Mouth of the Iberville River to show the Proper Spot for a Settlement on the Mississippi River, 1772. The map depicts many of the Gulf islands between the Chandeleur Islands in the west and Dauphin Island at the mouth of Mobile Bay as well as the water route bypassing New Orleans provided by the Iberville River and Lakes Maurepas and Pontchartrain. The English often used this route to travel from Biloxi, Mobile, and Pensacola to the Mississippi River and points such as Natchez to the north after 1762–63, when Louisiana, including New Orleans, became Spanish and West Florida became English. From *Gentlemen's Magazine and Historical Chronicle*, February 1772. Courtesy of the Archives and Research Services Divisions, Mississippi Department of Archives and History, Jackson.

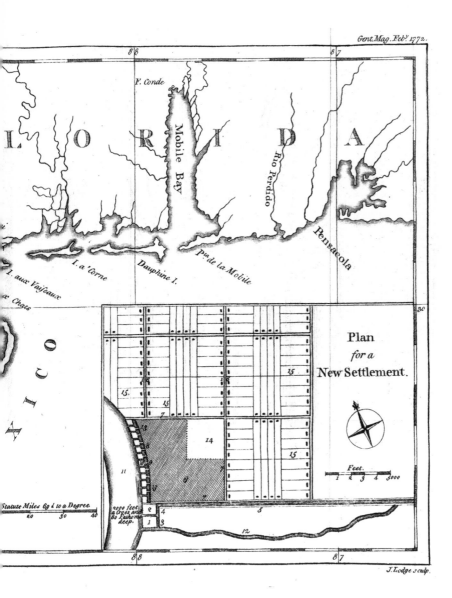

Plan
for a
New Settlement.

ment to do more to attract settlers from other parts of America. His journey took him from Pensacola along the Gulf Coast to the Rigolets, through Lakes Pontchartrain and Maurepas and the Bayou Manchac to the Mississippi River, and then upriver through the Natchez District to the smaller "Natchez Country" centered on the homeland of the Natchez Indians and the French fort. Along the way, Browne administered oaths of allegiance to French people who had left Spanish Louisiana and smoked the calumet with some Indian groups.[22]

Using language much like that of Rémonville's 1697 memorandum, Browne lauded the attractions of the area stretching "from Fort Bute to the Natchez": the land "increases in goodness as we approach the latter and is undoubtedly . . . one of the finest in the British American Dominions. The soil is exceedingly fertile, consisting of black mould, three feet deep on the hills and much deeper in the bottoms, & with little trouble will produce Wine, Oyls, Wheat, Barley, Rice, Indigo, Tobacco, Cotton and many other items." He rhapsodized that the view from the fort at Natchez offered "the most charming prospects in the world, extensive plains intermixed with beautiful hills, and small rivers" and "fruit trees of most excellent kinds . . . as good in their kind as any in the world and in as great abundance."[23] Botanist and cartographer Bernard Romans, whom Chester and Stuart hired to survey West Florida and make maps of the region in 1771, echoed Browne, describing the region as a "noble country" blessed with "a perfect climate."[24]

Such accounts and maps helped promote West Florida, especially the Natchez district.[25] Among those who applied for land grants in the province was George Washington, who unsuccessfully sought fifty thousand acres.[26] Washington had already joined others to form a new Mississippi Company with the ambitious goal of acquiring as much as 2.5 million acres. Seizure of the British fort at Michilimackinac by some Ojibwa warriors on the same day the company was created led to the end of that venture.[27] Land grants were made further to the south beginning in the late 1760s. A 1770 or 1771 map of the Mississippi River from the Yazoo River south to the Iberville River in West Florida identifies as many as forty-two lots granted to settlers, including 152,000 acres reserved for Anthony Hutchins and families from Virginia and the Carolinas. One Virginian, Jacob Winfree, came to the Natchez Country with his extended family and dozens of enslaved Africans to begin a one-thousand-acre plantation.[28]

Along with other officials, Browne obtained grants of land, including one of almost twenty thousand acres north of the Iberville River and at least one in the Natchez Country. And among the settlers that Browne helped bring people to the province was a small group of French Protestants (Huguenots) who with generous help from the British government were settled at the new Campbell Town at the mouth of the Escambia River east of Pensacola in

1766, though by January 1770, Campbell Town was almost deserted. A much larger contingent of Irish immigrants accompanied Browne to Pensacola in 1766. Some remained there, but others ended up in Mobile as part of a private initiative financed by him for his own profit, leading to the characterization of Browne as an "unscrupulous profiteer who showed no regard for the poor Irish colonists who ventured with him to West Florida."[29]

Another attempt at settlement was headed by Phineas Lyman of Connecticut, who was responsible for "the most promising of immigration schemes that brought newcomers to West Florida." After organizing the "Company of Military Adventurers," a group of veterans of the French and Indian War and farmers, Lyman initially focused on the acquisition of lands adjoining the Loosa Chitto, known today as the Big Black River, envisioning the creation of a new colony with him as governor. Its capital would be on the Big Black and would have a college where French and English would be offered and agriculture would be taught to children of Native Americans. Having newly taken up the West Florida governorship and eager to support immigration, Chester said he would allow each Adventurer family 2,000 acres, and in early February 1770, Lyman asked for 150,000 acres in and around Natchez. Though Lyman's request was rejected, he did secure approval for a personal grant of 20,000 acres along the Bayou Pierre below the Loosa Chitto. At the time of his death in 1774, however, that land remained empty.[30]

By the end of the decade, settlement along the Big Black remained sparse, with households of five or six people that essentially did no more than produce what they needed for themselves. A few of the households had one or more enslaved workers. In Grand Gulf, where the Big Black empties into the Mississippi River, a free woman of color, Eleanor Price, operated a store. Price had perhaps been enslaved in one of the English colonies along the Atlantic but either escaped or was freed. Like others in the area, such as Indian trader John Turnbull, much of Price's business centered on the trade in furs and skins with Choctaws and other Native groups. However, she sold and traded goods for local farmers. She had established a partnership with John Fitzgerald, a prosperous Manchac merchant who had come to America from Ireland during the Seven Years' War. He served as a colonial ranger, experienced Indian captivity in the last year of the war, and eventually made his way to New Orleans and then Manchac. Financial losses during the American Revolution contributed to major falling out between Fitzgerald and Price, but she established another business partnership with Miguel López.[31]

Though many land grants exceeded one thousand acres, most were much smaller.[32] The first Natchez-area land grant by the governor and his council occurred in May 1766, when Captain Francis Vignolles received 2,000 acres near the site of the fort. A London merchant, Samuel Hannay, secured a 5,000-acre grant the following December, when the largest grant, 20,000 acres, went to Archibald Montgomerie, the Earl of Eglinton, a "drinking companion of George Johnstone," who remained an absentee landlord in London. A year later, Browne presided over a meeting of the council at which ten people won approval for grants, and in 1768, one hundred grants were awarded. The pace quickened further in early 1769, when twenty-nine grants were made in January and February alone.[33]

The population of the Natchez country began to grow. According to Fabel, West Florida experienced its first wave of immigration in the mid-1760s after the "flurry of publicity" about the region. After a pause in the late 1760s, a second wave began in 1772–73 and continued into the second half of the decade as Anglo-Americans heard about good land along the Mississippi River. Elias Durnford, the surveyor-general of West Florida who created numerous maps of the region, received a modest 1767 grant of five hundred acres near Fort Panmure at Natchez. In his glowing 1774 "Description of West Florida," he estimated that 2,500 Euro-Americans and 600 Atlantic Africans lived in the area bordering the Mississippi River and that 1,200 whites and 600 enslaved Africans resided in the remainder of the province, for a total of 4,900 residents on the eve of the American Revolution. The population may have reached six thousand by 1779, when Spain entered the revolution on the side of the Americans and British rule in West Florida ended, before reaching as high as seven to eight thousand two years later.[34]

Native American Relations

Despite the influx of newcomers, the most numerous and diverse population in British West Florida remained Indian, and the different Native groups responded in different ways to the Euro-American settlers. In the late summer of 1764, an expedition led by Arthur Loftus set out from New Orleans to travel up the Mississippi to replace the French force at Fort Chartres in the Illinois Country. Loftus had difficulty getting started—he needed two weeks to travel from Mobile to New Orleans and another month to get his men prepared for the journey—and got only as far as the vicinity of present-day Fort Adams Landing, about forty miles south of Natchez, before the Tunicas and other Native groups attacked and forced his expedition to turn back.[35]

Robert Farmar assumed command of the next attempt, which occurred in 1765. Farmar's effort benefited from more careful planning and a military escort led by Franchimastabé from West Yazoo, a village that was part of the western division of the Choctaws that served as a center for negotiations with foreign diplomats. A British military officer, Thomas Ford, who earlier had recognized the village's importance, had persuaded Franchimastabé to assist the British, launching a long career during which the chief gained maximum advantage for himself and his people by cultivating good relationships with first British and later Spanish officials and traders. Franchimastabé and his party cleared a trail from Mobile to the Mississippi River and dissuaded other Indian groups from attacking the British. Those actions impressed Ford, who recommended that the British provide Franchimastabé with a British commission and special gifts and provisions that he could distribute to his followers.[36] Farmar and his band reached Fort Chartres in December 1765, but only after another British force led by Thomas Stirling had successfully occupied it.[37]

Not all Choctaws were as cooperative as Franchimastabé. On January 31, 1770, a band of roughly eighteen Choctaws entered a British trading post in Natchez and plundered the store of John Bradley, who in December 1767 had been granted a thousand acres of land. Bradley and some friends pursued the Choctaws and killed two and wounded another. Bradley's group then headed down the Mississippi River to New Orleans to warn other traders that the Choctaws were about to take the warpath. The Choctaw chiefs ultimately expressed a desire for peace and arranged to have the stolen goods returned to Bradley. Durnford, briefly serving as acting governor, attempted to deal with the problem and others related to the Indian trade.[38]

Security for newcomers preoccupied British officials as the movement of people into the region accelerated in the 1770s. In July 1770, a group migrated from western Pennsylvania to the Natchez region, bringing with them equipment to build a sawmill and a gristmill. According to the pilot who brought the group, other settlers were interested in coming if adequate security were provided. The newly arrived Governor Chester relayed these concerns to his superiors.[39]

In addition, Chester and his council sought to reassure prospective settlers. Affidavits were provided so that those with claims could come without making a special trip to Pensacola to register, and newcomers were promised enough corn and salt to get by until they could support themselves. In response, petitions for land increased and more people came, including some from Lyman's Company of Military Adventurers, whom the council permitted to select suitable tracts of land. Before late 1773, when the British government temporarily barred governors from freely granting land, among those who received grants and settled in West Florida were Thomas Hutchins; his older brother, Anthony; Garrett Rapalje of New York; and members of a Congregational church in New Jersey and their minister, Samuel Swayze.[40] By 1774, the Natchez area and points along the Big Black River had enough settlers that they asked the governor's council for a court to deal with conflicts and debt collection.[41]

The American Revolution

The beginning of the American Revolution prompted an easing of restrictions on migration and settlement to help those who preferred to remain loyal or simply neutral but were unable or unwilling to resist the violence of their neighbors. West Florida served in effect as "an asylum for those who refused to participate in the rebellion," and the governor was instructed to make liberal land grants and suspend quitrents for ten years.[42] That action not only contributed to the resumption of the flow of migrants but also led to the 1778 creation of two new electoral districts, Manchac and Natchez, with each allotted four delegates for a new assembly to meet that year. By then, Chester and his council had ordered the creation and surveying of three towns: Dartmouth (November 1775), at the junction of the Iberville and Amite Rivers; Natchez (February 1776); and Harwich (August 1776), just to the north of Manchac. Dartmouth apparently never came into existence, but between 1777 and 1779, almost sixty lots were sold in Harwich, and by 1776, Natchez had ten log houses, two frame houses, and a deserted fort.[43]

In May 1777, another major congress attended by some 2,800 Choctaws and about 40 Chickasaws met in Mobile with John Stuart along and various British commissioners. British officials secured from the Choctaw chiefs attending— particularly those from the Six Villages—a cession of a large portion of land along the Mississippi River that included Natchez. The agreement defined the grant as all land east of the Mississippi River as far as a line that ran south from the mouth of the Yazoo River across the Houma Chitto River where it intersected a road leading from the fort at Natchez to a boundary line determined in an earlier treaty. In exchange, the British agreed to give the Natives eight hundred guns and "other valuable presents." Among the chiefs who placed their marks on the agreement was Franchimastabé, listed as a small-medal chief from "Yassou."[44] By 1779, Joseph Purcell had surveyed the line, and at an early January meeting, some chiefs from the West Party of the Choctaws signed a formal agreement renouncing any Choctaw claims to that land.[45]

Stuart told attendees that the rebellion by colonists to the east posed a threat to both the Chickasaws and the Choctaws and that they consequently needed to work closely with the British. He pointed to recent actions of the Cherokees "to take up the Hatchet" and resist attempts by the rebels to seize their lands. He urged his listeners to disregard the advice of "rebel agents and worthless traders" to "remain inactive spectators of the present Rebellion." More specifically, he alleged that preparations had long been underway for rebel forces to sail from the "back parts" of North Carolina and Virginia down the Tennessee River to get a foothold on Chickasaw land and then move down the Tombigbee all the way to Mobile. And, he added, they should take seriously the rumors that the French were using the American rebellion as an excuse to seize Native lands.[46]

By this time, Stuart had many years of experience as superintendent of Indian affairs, and his thoughts regarding the meeting are noteworthy. Chickasaw chief Taska Oppaye had responded very positively to the speech, confirming that boats were prepared to transport people down the Cherokee River and that the rebels sought to take Chickasaw land. According to Stuart, the principal chief of the Choctaws had then agreed. Stuart also noted Natives' complaints regarding "the unlimited importation of rum to their nations and the miseries" caused by it. One of the principal chiefs of the Choctaws reported that he had lost more than a thousand of his people to excessive drinking in little more than eighteen months and that he feared a total "extirpation of their nation" if the traffic did not stop.[47]

Stuart further reported that a conspiracy of rebel commissioners, traders, and "packhorsemen" was striving to counteract the work of people in his department. The governor would again instruct officials to make sure traders and other people had appropriate licenses. The British commissioner to the Choctaws, Farquhar Bethune, (another Frenchman who had decided to stay) had toured Choctaw villages and reported that 4,400 men were available to bear arms. Some of them had already been stationed on the Mississippi River to watch and report on the movement of "any number of Batteaus coming down the River." According to Bethune, the Choctaws had agreed to keep a group ready to help the Chickasaws or Creeks in the event of an attack. Though the Mobile meeting had required a larger number of presents, especially guns and ammunition, than usual, a clearer definition of boundaries had begun to be established.[48]

Despite the promised monitoring, the Choctaws failed to notice the passing USS *Rattletrap* from Fort Pitt on the Ohio River down the Mississippi in early 1778. James Willing, an unpopular resident of Natchez, had left the town in early 1777 and gone south to New Orleans, where he met some rebel sympathizers—most notably patriot merchant Oliver Pollock—before heading north to Pennsylvania, arriving there in December. He secured a commission as a captain in the US Navy and organized a group of volunteers for an expedition, and these were the men aboard the *Rattletrap*. British officials knew of the possibility of an attack on West Florida, but Willing's force eluded them and the Choctaws. They reached Natchez and raised the American flag at Fort Panmure on February 19, 1778. They then proceeded to plunder the property of well-known Loyalists, especially Anthony Hutchins and Alexander McIntosh, and forced the remaining settlers to sign pledges of neutrality. Willing's expedition continued down the river, inflicting havoc at Pointe Coupée, Manchac, and just north of Baton Rouge. Like Natchez, none of these places had been warned.[49]

The British quickly launched a counteroffensive.[50] One involved the Choctaws in a more active way, in a sense affording them an opportunity to atone for their mistake in overlooking Willing's party. In April, shortly after Willing and his band departed Natchez, a group of more than 150 Choctaw warriors led by Franchimastabé arrived in town and set up camp at the old fort and repaired its defenses. According to Bethune, "their conduct during their stay was such that gave universal satisfaction." No American invasion occurred during the Choctaws' stay, which lasted until late May, by which time British reinforcements had arrived. Franchimastabé had clearly defined himself and his warriors as anti-American, in part as a warning to any sympathizers in Natchez. "We are behind you," he told the British, making the point the people in Natchez, too, needed to remain loyal. Franchimastabé thus enhanced his stature as a war leader, a position that again came into play, albeit with less success, after the Spanish entered the war in 1779 on the side of the American rebels.[51]

Spain and the Revolution: Campaigns of Bernardo de Gálvez

Although Spanish officials had little or no sympathy for the American rebels, Spain was bound to France by the third Family Compact, dating from 1761. That agreement led to the 1778 Treaty of Aranuez, in which France promised to help Spain recover Gibraltar, Minorca, and Florida and Spain joined France against Britain. In August 1779, Spain's principal minister of the Indies, José de Gálvez, who had previously spent six years as an inspector general in the viceroyalty of New Spain, declared that his country's principal objective in America was the expulsion of the British from the Gulf of Mexico and the shores of the Mississippi. Gálvez appointed his young nephew, Bernardo, as governor of Louisiana in late 1776.[52]

The young governor and other local Spanish officials viewed both the Americans and the British as threats to Spanish control over Louisiana. After Willing's expedition, the British strengthened their positions along the Mississippi River, prompting the Spanish to do the same. Although Gálvez had an official policy of neutrality, with encouragement from Oliver Pollock, who had assumed the role of de facto American consul, the governor had already made preparations for a first strike. During the summer of 1779, those plans ostensibly focused on an attack on New Orleans. Covertly, however, they consisted of assembling supplies, ammunition, and boats for an offensive action against the British. In August, Gálvez received news from Cuba that Spain had declared war on Britain, and in September, after being delayed by a major hurricane, he launched an expedition against Manchac, Baton Rouge, and Natchez. Later, aided by help from Cuba, he attacked the major British positions in Mobile and Pensacola.[53]

The expedition up the Mississippi benefited from the help of many groups, some of whom joined along the way and helped overcome a substantial attrition of the original force caused by sickness and fatigue. The additions included some six hundred Germans and Acadians, almost two hundred Indians, enslaved Africans, and free people of color who were members of the militia in New Orleans. The Acadians had been among those whom the British expelled from Canada during the Seven Years' War, and according to historian John Caughey, "they had not forgotten the persecutions they had suffered at the hands of the English."[54] Gálvez also saw both the Indians and free people of color as valuable in any conflict with the British, maintaining a cunning and flexible policy toward them that worked to his and Spanish Louisiana's benefit. The force that took both Manchac and Baton Rouge included militia units consisting of free people of color with their own officers as well as white ones. Indians and free people of color served as scouts, while enslaved Africans rowed boats carrying equipment up the river to British posts, a role that the Spanish intendant, Martín Navarro, later deemed essential to the effort.[55] The Spanish success against both Manchac and Baton Rouge also secured the surrender of Natchez's Fort Panmure. When a justice of the peace in Natchez learned of the surrender of both Baton Rouge and Panmure, he characterized the Baton Rouge commander as something of a coward who preferred drinking tea.[56] Gálvez sent Juan de la Villebeuvre, previously the commander of the Spanish fort across the river from the British Fort Bute at Manchac, with about fifty men to replace the British forces in Natchez. Pollock aided the transfer of Natchez to Spanish rule by sending a letter to the people of Natchez telling them that Spain now supported US independence and had entered the war on the side of the Americans. He urged Natchez residents to support the Spanish, telling them that Gálvez not only would purchase the current crop of tobacco but also had sufficient force both to take Pensacola and to protect Natchez from Indian hostilities. Spanish officials also began a campaign to convince inhabitants that the Spanish had no intention of treating them harshly. Residents would be allowed full use the river and access to the port of New Orleans. Suspicion of the Spanish nevertheless remained substantial. Villebeuvre secured oaths of allegiance from just over thirty settlers and offered to allow the rest to leave, though most chose to stay, and additional settlers continued to arrive from areas suffering from the war. On the whole, Gálvez's "Mississippi campaign was little short of brilliant."[57]

The campaigns against Mobile and Pensacola were complex but ultimately successful. Even before Spain had entered the war, Spanish officials in Havana and New Orleans were gathering information about the struggle between Britain and its Atlantic coast colonies and the implications for Spain on the Gulf Coast. Of the secret agents engaged in this effort, the most useful of these was Jacinto Panis, who was sent to Mobile and Pensacola to ensure Spain's rights as a neutral and who provided detailed information about both cities.[58]

In March 1780, after a two-month campaign aided by reinforcements from Cuba, Gálvez secured the surrender of Mobile's Fort Charlotte, which then became Fort Carlota. He left José de Ezpeleta to serve as governor of the district of Mobile and defend the post against a British counterattack and then turned to Pensacola, the commercial and administrative center of British West Florida. After another hurricane-related delay in the autumn of 1780, Gálvez brought about seven thousand men from Cuba, New Orleans, and Mobile and secured the surrender of Fort George and Pensacola in May 1781. Several hundred Choctaws led by Franchimastabé initially resisted, but when the British commander refused to provide gifts, the Choctaws angrily withdrew, leaving only some Creeks to provide Indian help. On May 8, a Spanish shot hit the magazine of the Queen's Redoubt, reduced it to rubble, and killed forty-eight Loyalists from Pennsylvania, twenty-seven British sailors, and an enslaved person. The next day, the British agreed to terms of surrender and gave up their last major position on the Gulf Coast.[59]

A Revolt in Natchez

In the meantime, a local rebellion had begun in Natchez. A few days before Pensacola's surrender, the Spanish commander at Fort Panmure, Villebeuvre, agreed to surrender that fort to a group of British Loyalists who had laid siege to the garrison with the endorsement of local leaders John Blommart and Jacob Winfree. British officials in Mobile and Pensacola also encouraged the Loyalists, who believed that British influence remained strong among the Chickasaws, or at least among those associated with Scottish-born trader James Colbert, who had lived among them for four decades and had a large Chickasaw family that included many sons, some of whom had become chiefs.[60] Though the insurrectionists secured the surrender of the fort, dissension among the rebels and the fall of Pensacola led rather quickly to the collapse of the revolt. The British surrendered Natchez on condition that a general amnesty be granted.[61]

Many of the Natchez Loyalists subsequently fled to Chickasaw Country, while some escaped to the Choctaws. A small group, Anthony Hutchins and his family, set out to reach Georgia and the Carolinas. A Spanish emissary caught up with them, bringing a letter of apology from Spanish officials that persuaded the group to return. Some who went to the Chickasaws joined Colbert's ongoing efforts on behalf of the British, which included taking hostages from Spanish vessels heading up the Mississippi River, among them Nicanora Ramos, the wife of the Spanish commandant in St. Louis, Francisco Cruzat, and members of her family. In 1783, Chickasaws attacked the Spanish post on the Arkansas River. Many Chickasaws, however, especially Payamataha, who had metamorphosed from a war chief to a leading advocate of peace, and young Natives questioned the wisdom of supporting what they recognized was a lost cause. By 1783, even Colbert realized that he could not go on being an enemy of the Americans.[62]

An Ambiguous Peace Settlement

The treaties of 1783 that concluded the American Revolution were not conclusive, especially with respect to boundaries. The preliminary agreement between Britain and the new United States identified the new republic's southern boundary as Thirty-First Parallel from the Mississippi River to where the Chattahoochee and Flint Rivers unite to form the Apalachicola River and then continuing east to the source of the St. Marys River to follow that stream to the Atlantic Ocean. Other treaties between Britain and Spain and the United States ceded East and West Florida to Spain but said nothing about a southern boundary for the United States.[63] According to historian David Narrett, the agreements and treaties helped thwart "Spanish and French efforts to keep an independent United States east of the Appalachians and as far above the Gulf as possible."[64] For the Spanish, the northern border of West Florida remained as it had been defined since 1763: from the mouth of the Yazoo River east.

Other boundary-related questions, including use of the Mississippi River, also remained unresolved, and this ambiguous peace settlement defined much of the politics of the subsequent period, which now involved the Spanish, the Americans, and Native Americans, who were still the region's most numerous peoples. Loyalists in Natchez and in other parts of West Florida weighed the advantages of shifting their allegiance to Spain, thereby encouraging local Spanish officials to treat leniently those connected to resistance or even rebellion.[65]

CHAPTER FOUR

Resurgence of Empire?

A "Spanish" Mississippi, 1779–1798

For the British, the loss of both East and West Florida to Spain and the loss of the Atlantic coast colonies to the new United States marked a significant contraction of empire in North America. Britain did, however, retain Canada and a number of colonies in the Caribbean. Some observers saw the successful conclusion of the Pensacola campaign as augmenting the Spanish claim of an empire stretching from the southern tip of South America to Alaska, including both sides of the Mississippi River as far north at least as the Ohio and Tennessee Rivers and even as far east as the Appalachian Mountains. Spain certainly laid claim to the east bank of the Mississippi River up to the Yazoo River.[1] According to one assessment, the independence of the thirteen colonies "strengthened Europe's oldest and largest empire"—that of Spain.[2]

Yet this view remained exclusively European. Native Americans had no say in the negotiations to end the war and thus no say in what happened to their lands, even though they were still the most populous and dominant presence in the trans-Appalachian region.[3] The treaty between the United States and Britain established the Thirty-First Parallel as the new republic's southern border, but Britain's treaty with Spain said nothing about borders, and the Spanish insisted that the northern border of West Florida remained unchanged from the British definition—well to the north of the Thirty-First Parallel. In addition, the new American state of Georgia took the position that its western boundary was the Mississippi River.[4] As a consequence, Natchez found itself a focal point of continuing postwar border disputes between Spain and the United States.[5]

The Spanish proceeded to treat the East and West Florida as securely theirs, incorporating them into a captaincy-general of Cuba that was part of the Viceroyalty of New Spain.[6] During the American Revolution, British Loyalists had seen East Florida as a haven for them and their enslaved chattel, expecting that East Florida would remain British and creating a special challenge for officials there after Spain took over. In the end, some Loyalist immigrants became Spanish subjects, while others departed or disappeared into the backcountry.[7]

A formidable challenge to the enlarged vision of the Spanish empire came from the United States, with its rapidly growing population.[8] Over the quarter century beginning in 1790, the population of about 3.7 million more than doubled, with many moving to the west beyond the Appalachians. The region that became the US state of Kentucky in 1792 had a population of about 12,000 in 1783, 73,000 in 1790, more than 220,000 a decade later.[9] In contrast, an estimate based on censuses ordered in 1785 and 1788 by the Spanish governor-general in New Orleans, Estevan Miró, put Louisiana and West Florida's population at 42,611, including 19,445 "whites," 1,701 "free blacks," and 21,465 enslaved. Comparing the data from the two counts, Miró optimistically concluded that Louisiana's population had increased by well over ten thousand in three years.[10] The first Spanish census of Natchez, taken in 1784, recorded a total population of 1,619: 616 white men, 505 white women, 275 male "Negro slaves," and 223 female "Negro slaves."[11] A 1792 census recorded an increase to more than 4,500 people, half of them "negro slaves."[12]

These crude numbers perhaps hide more than they reveal. Spanish officials both in the Americas and in Europe instituted a variety of policies designed to entice Americans to immigrate. During the American Revolution, the Mississippi River was opened to American trade, only to be closed in 1784 and then reopened in 1788–89 but subject to a 15 percent duty charge for use of the port of New Orleans. The 1795 Treaty of San Lorenzo between Spain and the United States sustained use of the river for American citizens "for its whole breadth." Beginning in 1782, Spanish subjects in Spain or Louisiana benefited from a more liberal policy that allowed them to trade directly with some ports in France and the West Indies.[13]

Religious tolerance existed to the extent that non–Roman Catholics could settle in West Florida but could not practice their faith publicly. English-speaking Irish priests were secured to take charge of parishes in the Natchez district and to encourage non–Roman Catholics to convert. Most immigrants were Anglo-American Protestants, attracted by a generous land policy that commonly provided four- or five-hundred-acre land grants free of all costs except secretarial and surveyor fees and offered quick processing of those grants. Few immigrants converted to Roman Catholicism, however. The British period had seen the arrival of some Protestant clergy, such as Samuel Swayze, a Congregational minister and planter from New Jersey who settled in what came to be known as the Jersey settlement near Natchez in 1773. Despite assurances that Baptists were harmless, Spanish governor Manuel Gayoso de Lemos attempted to check their activity, though he also allowed a Baptist clergyman to preach at Anthony Hopkins's house on one Sunday in 1789–90.[14]

Under the Articles of Confederation, the United States had a weak government that Alexander Hamilton described as "destitute of energy" with representatives who were "mere pageants of mimic sovereignty." For Spain, that weakness posed problems as well as opportunities. Individual state governments could and were easily manipulated by a population that included many "audacious and independent men" who were moving or eager to move in ever-increasing numbers to four American frontier areas north of the Floridas and Louisiana: Georgia, Holston, Cumberland, and Kentucky.[15] Some of those who settled in Kentucky considered initiating a separatist movement as early as 1782, and settlers in what became eastern Tennessee formed a state, Franklin, that existed marginally from 1784 until 1789.[16]

And in 1798, the population of "Spanish Mississippi," especially Natchez, remained primarily Anglo-American, numbering roughly 7,000, about one-third of them enslaved Africans.[17] Although Natchez was a district within a Spanish province, it was not Spanish.[18] Not only the settlers but political and administrative officials were a diverse lot: Jean de la Villebeuvre and Charles de Grand-Pré were of French or French-Canadian heritage, Francisco Bouligny was of French-Italian heritage, François Louis Héctor de Carondelet was of Flemish birth, and Stephen Minor was from Pennsylvania.[19] What became a "city" of Natchez in the 1780s was described as a "heterogeneous society and cosmopolitan culture" that was becoming part of a larger "Creole world" in the Mississippi Valley.[20] Not all immigrants were Anglo-Americans. The superintendent of the Royal Hospital in Natchez in 1782–83, Manuel García de Tejada, chose to become a permanent resident, purchasing a house and becoming a planter and prominent businessperson. And not all Spanish were Roman Catholics. Two brothers, Benjamin and Manuel Jacob, were Jewish, as was Benjamin's wife, Doña Clara. The Jacobs' parents had been born in the Netherlands but were of Spanish extraction, and Clara's family came from the Dutch island of Curaçao.[21]

Until 1789, the Natchez district was governed by commandants, military officers who served as police captains, justices of the peace, consular officers, notaries, sheriffs, judges, and military leaders. Subsequently, however, the district was headed by a governor who exercised both military and civil functions. The shift to an emphasis on civil functions elevated the town of Natchez to a city as part of an effort by the Spanish to attract people through liberal inducements and a more effective social and political order. For those who identified themselves as Spanish and who had some awareness of the Iberian Peninsula's history as part of the Roman empire and of the more recent but lengthy Reconquista, the city—a word deriving from the Latin *civitas*, a union of citizens—served as a key element in creating an effective empire or nation-state. In some matters, Natchez's new governor could communicate directly with Madrid, but he generally worked with and through the governor-general of the province of Louisiana in New Orleans, who in turn was responsible to the captain general located in Havana.[22]

The district's first commandants were Jean (Juan) de la Villebeuvre (1780–81), Charles (Carlos) de Grand-Pré (1781), Estevan Miró (1781), each of whom served for only a short time, followed by Pedro Piernas (1782–83), Francisco Collell (1783), and Felipe Treviño (1783–85).[23] Treviño's successor, Francisco Bouligny (1785–86), described the district for his superiors in New Orleans, depicting most of the white population as natives of North America and the rest as English royalists, a few French, and a handful of Spaniards. Most of the colonists were engaged in agriculture, and residents were concentrated in three locations: along the banks of St. Catherine's Creek, about a league from the fort; at Second Creek, about five leagues from the fort; and Coles Creek, which emptied into the Mississippi River twelve leagues away. Agricultural activities centered on production of tobacco, cotton, corn, vegetables, lumber, and livestock. "The small growing town of Natchez" had a nascent merchant community. Confirming the assessments of earlier commandants, Bouligny reported that "vagabonds" entered and left easily and often went to nearby Choctaw and Chickasaw villages.[24]

These officials and their successors worked within a legal system that had begun in Louisiana in 1769 when Alejandro O'Reilly replaced French laws with what came to be known as the Code O'Reilly, which drew from and conformed to such basic Spanish laws as the Laws of the Indies and the Siete Partidas but also included some influences from the French Code Noir (Black Code) of 1724. He also created a *cabildo* (town council), which Gayoso later attempted to establish in Natchez during his tenure as governor there.[25] Continuation of the Code Noir proved temporary, for it conflicted with basic Spanish laws that held that slavery was against reason and that slaves were human beings with rights as well as obligations. Spanish law supported enslaved people who sought their freedom and hence opposed enslavers who tried to prevent it. The law also supported freedom by purchase. Spanish law essentially prevailed in the Natchez district until Spain began to withdraw from the region in the late 1790s.[26]

Spanish legal documents provide glimpses into life in Spanish Natchez. In 1784 George Rapalje was unable to pay for some enslaved Africans purchased from François Farrel and had to provide a mortgage, and Rapalje eventually went bankrupt. A 1788 will lists possessions left by Gabriel Fuselier, a native of Lyon, France. Another document records a land transaction involving James Kirk and William Ferguson, both probably of Scottish descent.[27] Eleanor Price, a free person of color, took full advantage of her rights under Spanish law and operated a store at the mouth of the Big Black River. In 1781, a former slave, James, obtained an order from Grand-Pré requiring two white men, Clement Dyson and John Staybraker, to pay the debt they owed James.[28] Two years later, Jeannette, a free woman of color, registered the purchase of her mulatto son from Grand-Pré and the child's manumission in the commandant's court in Natchez. In November 1783, "La Negresse Betty," a creditor of James Willing, submitted a letter written in French to the commandant in Natchez, Treviño, asking that she be paid the sum of ten piastres and four escalines "for washing his clothes and also for having mended the same," apparently while Willing was in Natchez during his raid. She went on to plead with Treviño's "great humanity to think of her" after learning that Willing had left the district. The sum was paid.[29]

The sacramental records of the Roman Catholic Church also provide evidence of the status accorded people of color and demonstrate that enslaved Africans of Protestant owners embraced Roman Catholicism and the opportunities it offered to establish legitimacy and status for their offspring and connect with the community. In 1791, Isog, the son of a white man, Doshy, and an enslaved woman, Nenny, was baptized. Isog's parents took care to enhance his status through the institution of *compadrazgo* (godparenthood), naming as his godparents a soldier, José García, and a Black woman, Rachel.[30] On May 24, 1795, Francisco Lennan, a priest in Natchez, baptized "a boy of Black color, son of unknown parents, slave of Diego Kerk," with the boy's birth date, August 21, 1791, provided by his godparents.[31]

Secular and ecclesiastical law in Spanish Louisiana may have recognized the enslaved people as people and may not have seen blackness and liberty as diametrically opposed, but in practice, those who were enslaved took advantage of opportunities to become runaways. Bouligny's lengthy attention to the phenomenon of "vagabonds" that "stole" enslaved people, among other things, may have been influenced by his earlier experience with runaways when serving as acting governor in Louisiana. The phenomena of *cimarrones* that established whole communities in the swamps of Louisiana and vagabonds for him and other officials underscored the artificiality not only of law but also of borders and boundaries in a world characterized more by fluidity and mobility than by stability.[32]

Tensions with the American Republic

In August 1785, Bouligny sent the governor of Louisiana, Miró, a general description of the district modeled after the much lengthier 1776 *memoria* on all of Louisiana. Spanish officials had faced a significant challenge six months earlier, just after Bouligny replaced Treviño, when the Georgia legislature authorized the creation of Bourbon County, with Natchez as its focal point for settlement. Spanish officials interpreted the act as imperialist aggrandizement.[33]

The man behind the creation of Bourbon County was Thomas Green, who had been born in Virginia about sixty years earlier. In 1782, he led twelve families—some if not all of them related to him—and about two hundred enslaved Africans to Natchez. The next year, he angered the Spanish by distributing medals to Indians to gain their friendship as well as by developing a friendship with an English fugitive living among the Chickasaws. The Spanish commandant in Natchez drafted charges against Green, but he fled to Georgia and persuaded the state legislature to create the county and appoint him and three others as justices of the peace. In June 1785, he informed Spanish officials that the district was now part of Georgia and spread word that military forces of more than a thousand men were approaching by both land and sea. Although no armies were approaching, Spanish officials became alarmed.[34]

Green's scheme had its opponents, however, among them some members of his own family. In June 1785, Tacitus Gaillard, Richard Ellis, and Sutton Banks issued a statement "to the Citizens of Natchez" in which they urged local residents to meet and formulate a plan to prevent "the ruin and destruction of this country if it should fall under the government of Georgia." William Brocus and the fort's storekeeper, Juan Rodríguez, proposed that Spain should make the Natchez District independent.[35]

Neither idea generated much support, but they did cause much concern among Spanish officials. American settlers in Natchez generally seemed content under Spanish rule. They had received support for their tobacco crop and consequently netted economic gains. In August, Bouligny reported the district calm. Green and his supporters either had fled or languished in jail.[36]

The May 1785 arrival of Diego de Gardoqui as Spain's chargé d'affaires to the new United States provided added means to deal with issues of boundaries and the movement and behavior of people, even though the Spanish minister who appointed Gardoqui, the Conde de Floridablanca, instructed the diplomat to treat navigation of the Mississippi River as a nonnegotiable item. That position moderated after "intrigue between American frontiersmen and Spain" led by Pierre Wouves d'Argès, a "middle-aged French gentleman of misfortune" who had lived "in the backwoods of Kentucky" for three years, and North Carolina congressman James White.[37] The "intrigue" centered on Wouves d'Argès's 1787 proposal to remedy Spanish weakness in Louisiana by attracting American frontiersmen through liberal land grants concentrated in Natchez and by opening the Mississippi. In October 1785, the US Congress reaffirmed its commitment to the Treaty of 1783 between the United States and Britain but criticized the conduct of Americans like Green, who undermined harmonious relations with Spain. Learning of Congress's action in February 1786, Bouligny proclaimed it to the residents of Natchez, who accepted it quietly.[38] Although Georgia's attempt to create Bourbon County had failed, it did continue to claim the land and sell pieces of what it called the Yazoo Strip to speculators.[39]

Native American Diplomacy

Spanish officials were also dealing with other matters. Like their French and British predecessors, the Spaniards prioritized enlisting and sustaining the support of Native Americans, who still outnumbered the other people living in the region, which the Natives still regarded as theirs. The Indians, and especially their chiefs, needed to be convinced that a Spanish presence would be to their advantage by sustaining the economy of exchange and dependence that provided Native Americans with at least some degree of autonomy.[40]

Alexander McGillivray, the son of Scottish trader, Lachlan McGillivray, and Sehoy Marchand of the Wind Clan of the Creeks, emerged as the most notable of these chiefs. Toward the end of the American Revolution, he supported the Americans, believing that close ties with them would strengthen his position as a leader.[41] McGillivray became a shrewd diplomat and a master at playing off both the Americans and the Spanish to advance his own as well as Creek interests. He became a Creek "Beloved Man," a title bestowed on individuals for their wisdom and experience.[42] Franchimastabé of the western division of the Choctaws benefited from a similar position. Even though many Choctaws saw him as "the English chief," he, like McGillivray, became quite skillful at exploiting competing foreign interests for his own and the Choctaws' benefit.[43]

One trader who established kinship with Native groups and served as an important intermediary in these matters was Simon Favre, who also served as an interpreter.[44] Favre proved valuable to the Spanish in the context of the challenge posed by Georgia. In November 1783, he reported that Franchimastabé and another important Choctaw leader, Taboca, as well as others had traveled to Savannah, Georgia, seeking gifts and trade. According to Favre, the two chiefs had refused to go to Louisiana to receive gifts and had refused to see him as well as prohibited their warriors from receiving Favre's message. Favre immediately went with four great medal chiefs to Bay St. Louis to see a veteran Louisiana trader, Gilbert Antoine de St. Maxent, who had just returned from Spain after completing a mission begun in 1781 on behalf of his son-in-law, Bernardo de Gálvez. While in Spain, St. Maxent had made a recommendation for postwar Indian policy and been appointed lieutenant governor to supervise trade with the Indians.[45] Georgia apparently failed to satisfy the Choctaws during their visit to Savannah, thereby helping Favre and other Spanish traders.[46]

In early 1784, Spanish officials on both sides of the Atlantic began to respond to some of these challenges and opportunities. The lower Mississippi River was closed to all non-Spanish ships, and the Ohio River was identified as the northern border of the Spanish territory, moves designed to control the flow of Americans and goods of American origin into the Mississippi Valley.[47] At about the same time, McGillivray requested and received Spanish protection for the Creeks. To formalize that relationship, the governor-general in New Orleans, Miró, and the intendant, Martín Navarro, invited McGillivray and the Creeks to attend a May 1784 congress in Pensacola and Chickasaws and Choctaws to a gathering in Mobile a month later.[48]

Those meetings continued and expanded the complex diplomacy involving Native groups, Spanish officials, and representatives of a weak central government in the new United States. Native groups hoped to sustain the flow of goods on which they had become dependent. In so doing, however, they risked their land and their autonomy. Ultimately, many determined that closer cooperation among themselves and with the Spanish was the best way to deter American encroachment.[49]

Miró recognized the importance of formal meetings in establishing and sustaining friendship and trade with the various Native groups and their leaders, and he wanted Navarro in attendance to provide assurances of the Spanish commitment. Navarro accompanied Miró to both conferences despite the press of other duties and the state of his health.[50] West Florida's governor, Arturo O'Neill, also attended. The Pensacola congress approved thirteen articles of a treaty regarding peace and trade that recognized the complex reality of the Creeks by listing not only McGillivray as the principal representative of the upper, middle, and lower villages of the "Talapuches" but also the individual chiefs of different towns or groups. Gifts were then distributed, and eight chiefs received large medals, while six chiefs received smaller ones. The Indians departed with enough *aguardiente* (whiskey) and powder for ten days of travel as well as full of thanks and affection for the Spanish.[51]

Following the Pensacola meetings, Miró appointed McGillivray as Spain's commissioner to the Creeks and charged him with maintaining the subordination of his villages to the king of Spain and with monitoring traders to make sure that they adhered to the prices established at Pensacola. That action further enhanced McGillivray status and power among the Creeks by assuring him access to goods to distribute. In keeping with McGillivray's preference for Pensacola as the locus of Creek trade and the availability of English goods there, Miró also enlisted the services of a veteran Scottish trader and Loyalist, William Panton. McGillivray became a silent partner in the trading firm formed by Panton and two other Loyalist exiles in Florida, John Leslie and William Alexander. Panton's firm became the preeminent trading company in Creek Country and in the late 1780s assumed responsibility for trade with the Chickasaws and Choctaws.[52]

The Mobile meeting attracted about two thousand Choctaws from fifty-eight villages, more than four hundred Chickasaws from all their villages, about the same number of Alabama Indians from nine villages, and some Talapuche Indians from one village. Chouckafalaya, the village from which the Chickasaw chief Piomingo (Piominko) came, apparently sent enough people to consume almost a thousand pounds of bread and about fifteen hundred pounds of rice. Enough gifts were available to satisfy those who attended. Agreements similar to those of Pensacola were reached. The Spanish decided to work with traders in the area, awarding the privilege of supplying the Choctaws and Chickasaws to New Orleans merchants James Mather and Arthur Strother, who agreed to use Mobile as an entrepôt. The arrangement with Mather and Strother ended in 1789 after Indians complained that they had failed to supply goods at the agreed prices. Panton's firm stepped into the breach, assuring Miró and Navarro that the integrity of the trade would be maintained to deter the United States from gaining Indian friendship and trade.[53]

Groups of Choctaws, Chickasaws, and Cherokees engaged representatives of the American government at three meetings in Hopewell, South Carolina, beginning in late 1785 and continuing into 1786. Other meetings with some Creek chiefs and Cherokees had already taken place in October and November. In late December, the Choctaws arrived at Hopewell and began meetings that continued into early January. Franchimastabé and Taboca had organized the delegation. The meeting produced a treaty that included provisions designed to satisfy the Choctaw desire for trade goods. More important, the meetings provided the Choctaws an opportunity to educate the American commissioners regarding expectations for talk and exchange. Chickasaw representatives led by Piomingo then met with the American commissioners and secured some definition of a land boundary. In addition, the Chickasaws agreed to allow Americans to establish a trading post at the mouth of Ocochappo Creek—later known as Bear Creek—on the Tennessee River.[54]

Many other such meetings large and small brought together Spanish and various Native leaders and peoples, furthering a culture of diplomacy as a means to resolve issues into the 1790s. Helped by a variety of reforms undertaken after the succession of Charles III in 1759, the Spanish took advantage of their earlier diplomatic successes, and their American empire enjoyed something of an apex. Controversy between Spain and Britain over control of the Nootka Sound on the western coast of North America almost led to war in 1790, but the Spanish gave up their claim, an action that signaled the beginning of the empire's contraction.[55]

Settler Transitions: Opportunities and Opportunists

The Spanish encouraged Americans to come and settle in the region, essentially requiring that immigrants only take an oath of allegiance to Spain.[56] Spanish officials also had some success in attracting new arrivals from the Canary Islands.[57] Imports of enslaved Atlantic Africans led people of African origin to become the largest segment of the area's population by 1790, when estimates put the number of Indians at just under 19,500, the number of Europeans at almost 20,000, and the number of those of African descent at 23,500. In just thirty years, Indians had declined from nearly two-thirds of the region's people to less than one-third.[58]

Americans and enslaved Africans continued to pour into the Natchez Country and other parts of Louisiana and West Florida. Like earlier arrivals, they focused on agriculture, with indigo, tobacco, and to a lesser extent rice the principal money crops prior to 1790.[59] A major shift to cotton production subsequently occurred, however. Louisiana tobacco had proved to be of an inferior quality and simply did not sell, so Spain withdrew subsidies for the crop and opened its markets to American tobacco. The advent of Eli Whitney's modified cotton gin, which could process the short-staple cotton grown in the Natchez Country, and the growing demand for the staple in textile mills in England and the northeastern United States meant that cotton provided a suitable substitute over the next decades. But enslaved labor was essential for growing cotton, meaning that slavery became very much a central institution and defining feature of what became Mississippi. By the end of the decade, Spanish officials opened commercial use of the Mississippi River to Americans and allowed them the right of deposit in New Orleans for three years.[60] Enterprising and adventurous individuals such as James Wilkinson exploited this Spanish openness to advance their interests. "A frontier power broker, U.S. general, paid Spanish agent, and schemer extraordinaire" as well as "an adventurer by choice," Wilkinson traveled to New Orleans to ingratiate himself with Miró and Navarro.[61] Similarly, in 1788, James Robertson and other leaders of American settlements along the Cumberland River offered to name their district after Miró if he would help them deal with Indians and secure access to the Mississippi River.[62]

And in July 1789, another adventurous and ambitious young person interested in pursuing business opportunities and acquiring property in Natchez, Andrew Jackson, took an oath of loyalty to the king of Spain and began offering legal services to residents of the town. Jackson had studied law in North Carolina before traveling west in 1788 and settling in Nashville, which had become part of the newly created "Mero district" in western North Carolina. With decidedly negative views of Native Americans and diplomacy, Jackson went on to distinguish himself as an Indian fighter and eventually to become president of the United States.[63]

Manuel Gayoso de Lemos and the Beginnings of a City

The change to a military and civil administration, the creation of the city of Natchez, and the 1787 appointment of Manuel Gayoso de Lemos as both commandant and governor helped the district serve as an effective check to American expansion, at least briefly. Born in Portugal, the son of the Spanish consul and a Portuguese mother, Gayoso attained a high degree of education, much of it in England, and a fluency in many languages, including English. For example, in 1796, the well-educated son of a Virginia settler encountered the governor during a walk. Gayoso addressed the young man in Spanish, and although he did not understand, he recognized the words as similar to Latin and replied in that tongue. To his surprise, Gayoso answered "in perfect Latin and introduced himself as the governor." Gayoso was also skilled in military matters, having served as a cadet in the Spanish army beginning in 1771. His talent, conduct, and facility in languages impressed Miró when the two served together in the Lisbon regiment, and Gayoso went on to hold the post of assistant to Alejandro O'Reilly in Cádiz in the 1780s, attaining the rank of lieutenant colonel in 1786. In the fall of 1787, on the recommendation of the minister of the Indies, who sought someone "skilled in prudence and diplomacy and who spoke fluent English" to command the fort at Natchez, Gayoso was appointed to the dual position of commandant of the post and fort and civil governor for the Natchez District.[64]

Gayoso gained support from François Louis Héctor de Carondelet, who succeeded Miró as governor-general of Louisiana and West Florida in 1791 despite having "a dismal knowledge of affairs" in Spanish territories abutting the United States.[65] Both Gayoso and Miró worked to inform Carondelet about

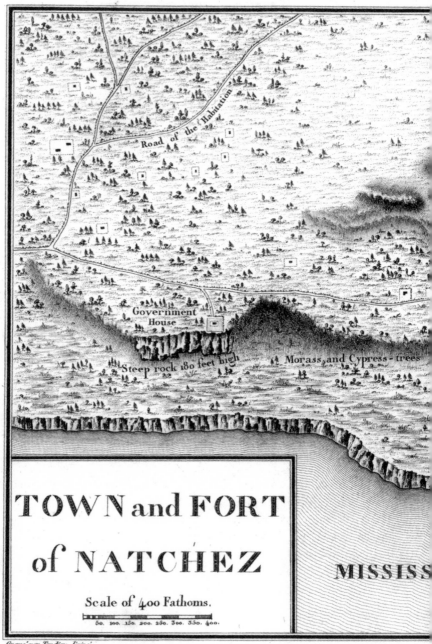

Georges-Henri-Victor Collot, *The Town and Fort of Natchez*, 1796. On behalf of the French ambassador to the new United States, Collot traveled down the Mississippi River in 1796 to assess separatist and pro-French sentiment among area residents. He created drawings of towns and military installations such this one. They were not always accurate, but they were detailed and artistic. Courtesy of the Archives and Research Services Divisions, Mississippi Department of Archives and History, Jackson.

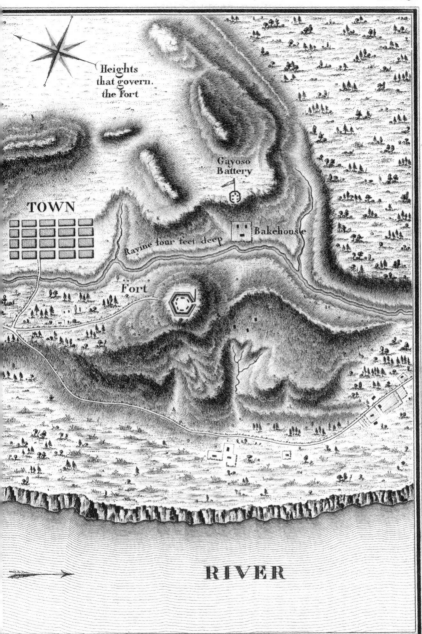

PL. 34.

Heights
that govern.
the Fort

Gayoso
Battery

TOWN

Bakehouse

Ravine four feet deep

Fort

RIVER

his new jurisdiction, and he ultimately agreed with Gayoso that good relations with Native American groups would make the province a more effective barrier against the United States. Carondelet appointed commissioners to serve as representatives of the Spanish government among the Creeks, Chickasaws, Choctaws, and Cherokees and became a strong supporter of a Spanish-affiliated confederation of these groups. Seeing the Mississippi River as a possible invasion route for American adventurers, the British from Canada or by French supporters of the republican or Jacobin cause, he expanded the Mississippi River fleet. After a group of Cherokees led by Bloody Fellow visited New Orleans in late 1792, Carondelet backed the establishment of additional posts, including one at Muscle Shoals and another on the site of the former French fort Tombecbé on the Tombigbee River.[66]

During the 1790s, Natchez continued its modest urbanization, making what had been just a fort surrounded by a village into a city that would both secure and express empire and perhaps even civilization. According to Jack D. Elliott Jr., "Urban planning in the Spanish empire was part of centralized and coherent vision of the world and society." In 1785, Bouligny had urged Miró to authorize measures to strengthen the whole district and its population, and the governor had drafted plans for parishes at Natchez and at Cole's Creek. English-speaking Irish priests from the Irish College in Salamanca came to serve the parishes and convert some of the predominantly Protestant population to Roman Catholicism, though that endeavor failed. Officials also developed a basic plan for the city, with a central plaza and streets laid out in a grid pattern, and constructed buildings on the common, including a royal hospital, a barracks, a market house, and a bakery. Gayoso continued the effort, attempting to establish a *cabildo* (town council) to hear and resolve legal disputes.[67]

In the late 1780s, Ezekiel Forman of Philadelphia emigrated with his family and some sixty "colored people" to Natchez, where he intended to acquire land and cultivate tobacco. Forman's nephew, Samuel, was among the group, and he recalled Natchez as "a small place"—no more than "a village"—"with houses of mean structure built mostly on the lower bank of the river and the hillside." The fort occupied a "handsome commanding spot, on the elevated ground," with a view "up the river and over the surrounding country." He found Gayoso "very affable and pleasant."[68]

Another account of Natchez during this era comes Georges-Henri-Victor Collot, a Frenchman who visited in 1796 while traveling down the Ohio and Mississippi Rivers to gather information about the possibility of establishing a "Francophile republic" in the region.[69] Collot described Natchez as a town of about one hundred houses "built of wood and painted different colors" and surrounded by "a number of fine farms and orchards," which he deemed "a high standard of industry and prosperity." He estimated the district's population at about ten thousand and divided them into three classes of immigrants: those who came when the colony belonged to Britain, those who were Loyalists during the American Revolution, and those who had come after American independence.[70] When Collot reached New Orleans, Carondelet ordered the Frenchman's arrest as a suspected "secret agitator and spy," but the governor quickly relented and came to respect Collot, granting him permission to go to Philadelphia.[71]

The following year, Francis Baily, a "cultured Englishman" who "had difficulties with the Spanish government," visited Natchez. Baily noted that the streets had been laid out in a grid pattern but that so much space existed between the eighty or ninety houses he counted that it appeared that "each dwelling was furnished with a plantation." Because the place had been settled for so long, he found little "attention to neatness, cleanliness, and the comforts attending thereon." He estimated the population of the district to be about five thousand.[72]

American Greed and Spanish Diplomacy

Gayoso's 1789 arrival in Louisiana coincided with a number of significant events on both sides of the Atlantic. The outbreak of the French Revolution had repercussions in America that eventually included such activities as those of Collot. More immediately, the Georgia legislature, undeterred by the failure to create Bourbon County, granted three enterprises collectively known as the Yazoo Companies, twenty-five million acres of land that had been expropriated illegally from Indians. Most of the land belonged to the Chickasaws, Choctaws, and Cherokees and stretched north from just above Natchez to the Thirty-Fifth Parallel and east from the Mississippi River to the Tombigbee River. All of the land north of the mouth of the Yazoo River and east of the Tombigbee River and extending to the Thirty-Third Parallel went to the Virginia and South Carolina Yazoo companies, while the land east of the Tombigbee went to the Tennessee Company.[73]

Of the three grants, the one to the South Carolina Yazoo Company received most of the attention from Gayoso, Miró, Carondelet, and other Spanish officials through 1792. The grant in effect allowed the company to establish itself as a kind of "autonomous buffer state." The company had its genesis in John Wood's 1786 acquisition from some Choctaws of two to three million acres of land that included an area at the mouth of the Yazoo River that the English called Walnut Hills and the Spanish labeled Nogales. Wood turned his land over to others, and they acquired a quantity of goods, some of which were used to satisfy the

Choctaws while the rest helped settle people at Walnut Hills.[74] In July 1790, the general agent for the South Carolina Company, James O'Fallon, wrote to Miró, identified himself as a friend of James Wilkinson and "an avowed friend of Spain," and attempted to persuade the governor of the company's value to Spain's interests. According to O'Fallon, the Yazoo Companies would offer the province "a Barrier of impregnable defence."[75]

After consulting maps of the Virginia and South Carolina Yazoo Companies' land claims, Miró and his superiors concluded that the Yazoo projects should be scuttled. The Spanish decided to construct a fort and settlement there, and while traveling to make a preliminary visit to the site in March 1791, Gayoso learned that a number of Choctaws had expressed opposition to the project. Gayoso returned to the site thirteen months later, after a plan had been drafted and Elias Beauregard had been appointed commandant. On this trip, the governor examined the site again with surveyor John Girault and met with a group of Choctaws, some of whom danced the calumet, a gesture Gayoso interpreted as an expression of peace and goodwill. Gayoso returned to Natchez confident that the project had gained Choctaw approval.[76]

Gayoso soon discovered that he had been overly optimistic. He received a letter from Franchimastabé and Taboca, probably written by trader Turner Brashears. A native of Maryland, Brashears had established himself among the Choctaws and married a daughter of Taboca who may also have been a niece of Franchimastabé. The letter expressed displeasure at the prospect of the Spanish taking and occupying Choctaw land and set in motion almost a year of additional negotiation that included two missions to the Choctaws by Stephen Minor and a congress in Natchez that lasted for over a week and was attended by more than three hundred Choctaws and Chickasaws. It concluded successfully for the Spanish, according to Gayoso, with a treaty, the distribution of gifts, and a ball game, "one of the most splendid that has been seen."[77]

Helped by such traders as Favre and Brashears who had kinship ties to Native leaders and peoples, and the commissioners to the various Indian groups appointed after 1791 by Carondelet, Gayoso continued to play a key role in sustaining good relations with the Choctaws and Chickasaws in particular. The Spanish policy of encouraging immigration of Americans and others required efforts to reassure Native groups that these newcomers did not threaten their interests. In 1789, Miró established a new Spanish post, San Estevan (St. Stephen), about sixty miles upstream from Mobile on the Tombigbee River to provide such reassurance.[78]

Establishment of yet another Spanish post on the Tombigbee River on the site of the former French Fort Tombecbé resulted from a diplomatic endeavor supported strongly by Carondelet and led by Villebeuvre, whom Carondelet

had appointed resident Spanish commissioner to the Choctaws and Chickasaws. At Boukfouka, on the Pearl River, Villebeuvre, assisted by interpreters
Favre and Thomas Price, obtained a May 1793 land grant from the Choctaws
that included the site of the former French fort. The construction of the new
Spanish fort, along with a commitment to establish a store to supply Choctaws
with trade goods, served as a tangible expression of the Spanish commitment
to the Native peoples.[79]

Spanish success continued with a major October 1793 congress at Nogales.
The congress had initially been planned for the preceding spring but, like the
building of the fort on the Tombigbee, was delayed. The gathering achieved a
major objective of both Native American groups and the Spanish: the creation,
at least on paper, of a confederation of major Native groups and the Spanish.
More than two thousand Indians attended, a good fifteen hundred more than
Gayoso had wanted. It produced a treaty of "friendship and guaranty" among
the Choctaws, Chickasaws, and Creeks; added the Cherokees to Spanish
protection; and defined the relationship among all the groups as an "offensive
and defensive alliance." The Spanish named the new post on the Tombigbee
Confederación (Confederation) to lend some additional substance to the
achievement at Nogales.[80]

Spanish officials hoped that the confederation would check the ongoing
American threats, which received another dimension in the spring of 1793
when Edmond Charles Genet, who represented France's new republican government in the United States, appealed to Americans, especially those west of
the Appalachians, to embrace an expansionist ideology that would expel the
Spanish under the guise of creating "an empire for liberty." Genet and his projects
had little appeal for those living in the Natchez Country, and the American
government under the new US Constitution eventually required the French
government to withdraw Genet.[81] The Nogales meeting did not achieve all
Spanish officials or many of the Indian participants wanted but at least provided
another opportunity for extended interaction, talk, and ceremony, to which the
Natives especially attached great importance. The Choctaws honored Gayoso
with an elaborate ceremony in which Taboca, wearing a special collar placed
around his neck by Franchimastabé, awarded Gayoso the title Chactimataha,
"King of the Choctaws." Gayoso then made a speech that he described as having
"a comic tone, with allusions to the nature of the Chacta, which made them
all laugh a lot." Some ninety chiefs "of all the nations" then dined with him.[82]

Chickasaw chief Ugulayacabé chose to use that title in many of his letters to
Gayoso as part of the final Spanish effort to prevent Americans from acquiring
land and strengthening their position along the Mississippi River. In 1795, the
Georgia Mississippi Company, chartered by a bribed Georgia legislature, tried

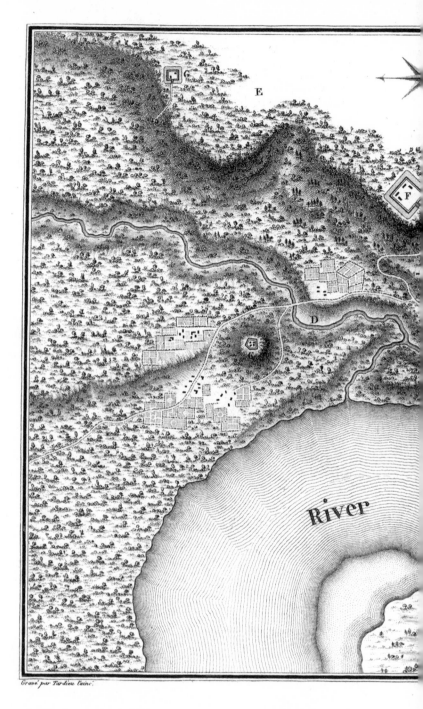

Georges-Henri-Victor Collot, *Plan of Nogales*, 1796. Collot spent time in
Nogales, where Vicksburg is now located, during his 1796 trip down the
Mississippi. Both this detailed drawing and his representation of Natchez
appeared in his published narrative of that trip. Courtesy of the Archives
and Research Services Divisions, Mississippi Department of Archives and
History, Jackson.

A Fort of the great Battery
B Block-House
C Fort Sugar-loaf
D Ravin 12 feet deep
E Elevated Plain
F Fort Mount Vigie
G Fort Gayoso
H Fort St Ignace   E

PLAN

OF

NOGALES

Scale of 300 Fathoms.

10. 20. 30. 40. 50.   100.   150.   200.   250.   300.

MISSISSIPI

to secure about thirty-five million acres of Choctaw and Chickasaw lands. This "Yazoo Land Fraud" failed, in part because of action by the American president and Congress to condemn the grants as fraudulent.[83] During the American Revolution, Spanish officials had focused on what the French called Écors à Margot and the Spanish translated as Barrancas de Margot, another high point on the eastern shore of the Mississippi at the mouth of the Margot River. The English name, Chickasaw Bluffs, acknowledged that site as part of Chickasaw Country, and with Carondelet's approval and the help of Ugulayacabé and the Chickasaw sons of James Colbert, Gayoso attempted to secure from the Chickasaws a grant of land there to establish a post and build a fort. He received the grant in late May 1795 and work began on the post to be called San Fernando de Las Barrancas, in honor of the prince and future king of Spain.[84] George Washington told some Chickasaws visiting Philadelphia later in the summer that he regarded that enterprise as an aggression against both the Chickasaws and the United States and that he would work through diplomatic channels to persuade the Spanish to remove the new post.[85]

Spanish Departure

In the fall of 1795, on the other side of the Atlantic, other officials undid, at least on paper, all that Gayoso and his assistants thought they had accomplished at Chickasaw Bluffs in the spring. In the royal palace of San Lorenzo, a short distance northwest of Madrid, Thomas Pinckney, representing the United States, and Spain's Manuel Godoy signed a treaty in which Spain accepted US demands that the Mississippi River be opened to American commerce and that the Thirty-First Parallel be the southern boundary between the two countries. Spain thereby agreed to evacuate such posts as San Fernando, Nogales, and Natchez on the Mississippi River and Confederación and San Estevan on the Tombigbee. That treaty came about as the result of political changes and conflicts caused mainly by the French Revolution and of Jay's Treaty between the United States and Britain, under the terms of which the British agreed to evacuate their posts in the American West and to ease restrictions on American trade with Britain and the British West Indies. In the summer of 1795, the French and Spanish mended relations and became allies by means of the Treaty of Basel, which nullified the alliance between Spain and England and ensured Pinckney's success that fall.[86]

The Treaty of San Lorenzo was not ratified by both nations until the spring of 1796, and by the fall, Godoy had changed his mind and concluded that implementation should be delayed to prevent the possibility of a joint American and

British plan to invade Louisiana. By the time Carondelet received instructions from Godoy, however, both San Fernando de las Barrancas and Confederación had been evacuated. In August 1797, shortly after the appointment of members of a commission to survey the new Spanish-American border, Carondelet departed for Quito, Ecuador, to become president of the royal *audiencia* there. In turn, Gayoso became governor of Louisiana. Not until March 1798 was the Spanish flag in Natchez replaced by the American flag.[87]

When news of the treaty reached Indian country, Native leaders expressed distress and even anger. They sensed that the balance of power had been altered significantly and that the play-off system that had worked in their favor might have come to an end. Chiefs such as Franchimastabé feared that they could no longer count on generous gifts, and indeed, when he returned to northern Alabama to trade in 1797, he received no gifts and instead had to "beg for a coat and a horse 'to carry him back to his Nation.'" Others doubters had already expressed in a forceful way their unhappiness with what they saw as Spanish penury. Another Choctaw leader, Pooscoos II, told his warriors in June 1795 to kill the cattle herds of both Villebeuvre and Favre.[88]

In late 1796, Chickasaw chief Ugulayacabé, accompanied by Payehuma and a large group of others, came to San Fernando de las Barrancas to express their discontent about being abandoned by those they had come to regard as their friends. Ugulayacabé eloquently explained how his people had accepted the Spanish promise of friendship and protection and now felt abandoned to the Americans, whose speeches and behavior reminded them "of the rattlesnake who caresses the squirrel in order to devour it." He accused the Spanish of abandoning the Chickasaws like "small animals to the claws of tigers and the jaws of wolves."[89]

The Spanish appreciated those words. Both Villebeuvre and Gayoso warned of the danger of hostilities. When Andrew Ellicott, one of the Americans appointed to serve on the boundary commission, raised an American flag on a Natchez hill a short distance from the Spanish fort in 1797, Gayoso told him to take it down. Ellicott refused, resulting in what Ellicott described as much "insolence on the part of the Indians." They "insulted a number of our men, walked about the camp with drawn knives, and one night we were informed that they intended attacking us." Other Indians sought to move south of the new boundary line. A group of four hundred Alabama Indians secured permission from the Spanish to settle in the District of Opelusas rather than stay in their villages, which they said would be cut by the new line.[90] Spanish authorities viewed such movement and settlement as supportive of their ongoing endeavors to create a buffer against American expansion and to check stronger and sometimes hostile Native groups such as the Osages. By the time France sold Louisiana to the United States in 1803, about five hundred Native families—Chickasaws, Cherokees, Delawares, Shawnees, Miamis, and Peorias—were living along the St. Francis River near New Madrid and Cape Girardeau.[91]

Before leaving Natchez in July 1797 to replace Carondelet in New Orleans, Gayoso had to deal with what became known as the Revolt of 1797. Barton Hannon, a Baptist preacher who had raised livestock prior to his arrival in Natchez in 1795, took advantage of Gayoso's tolerant policy regarding non–Roman Catholics. Hannon, who had a penchant for anti-Catholic and in effect anti-Spanish sermons, went too far, and one of his orations caused a revolt by those who wanted to hasten Spanish withdrawal and led to his arrest and imprisonment. The incident ended peacefully after an official inquiry ordered by Gayoso. The governor asked everyone to maintain neutrality in the transition period and promised no retaliation against those who involved in the commotion.[92]

Stephen Minor, who served as an interpreter for Hannon during the official inquiry and as a liaison between the governor and rebels, assumed the role of interim governor when Gayoso left for New Orleans. Minor, a Pennsylvanian who had been a loyal adjutant to Gayoso, agreed with his predecessor that implementation of the Treaty of San Lorenzo needed to be slowed and earlier in 1797 had attempted unsuccessfully to persuade Ellicott to remain at Nogales. Panton, too, felt betrayed by the treaty, which he believed had left him and his company "entirely abandoned to the mercy of the Americans." Despite such views, Spanish officials in Madrid reversed the earlier decision to delay evacuation of posts. In March 1798, the Spanish finally evacuated Natchez. In the fall, the border commission began surveying the new border.[93]

A friend of both Minor and Gayoso, José Vidal, who served as the latter's secretary in Natchez, asked the governor for a grant of land on the Mississippi River across from Natchez because he preferred to continue living in Spanish territory. Vidal became civil and military commandant of what became for a short time another Spanish post, Concordia, which he named in honor of what he hoped would be continued friendly relations between Americans and Spaniards. Minor briefly served as commandant in 1803, three years after completion of the border survey, mainly to transfer that post to the Americans after the Louisiana Purchase. However, the name *Vidal* lived on: in 1811, the town he had helped establish renamed itself Vidalia.[94]

CHAPTER FIVE

A Gulf Coast, 1779–1821

By the time José Vidal had his name attached to a town across the river from Natchez, Spanish Louisiana no longer existed. Spain had retroceded Louisiana to France in 1800, and the United States had purchased the still very vaguely defined territory from France three years later. The successful slave revolt that began in French Saint-Domingue on the island of Hispaniola in 1791 resulted in the creation of an independent Haiti and prompted Napoleon Bonaparte to abandon any aspirations of empire in America. Loss of Saint-Domingue diminished significantly whatever value Mississippi had for France. Spain objected to the sale of Louisiana to the United States, because the treaty of retrocession stipulated that the territory that had been returned to France could not be transferred to a third power.[1] Nevertheless, Spain tacitly accepted the purchase and evacuated New Orleans in late 1803 but continued to object to the American view that the purchase included Texas all the way to the Rio Bravo (today the Rio Grande) and West Florida.[2] The Spanish intended to keep West Florida, albeit without the Natchez District. From their perspective, West Florida extended east from the Mississippi River to at least the Perdido River between Mobile Bay and Pensacola. Final resolution of those issues did not occur until representatives of Spain and the United States agreed to the 1819 Adams-Onís Treaty. It transferred both East and West Florida to the United States and extended American territorial claims to the Pacific. The treaty was ratified by the US Senate in 1821.[3]

Spanish West Florida consisted of essentially three regions. The western began at the Mississippi River and extended east to the Pearl River and lay north of the Bayou Manchac, Amite River, and Lakes Maurepas-Pontchartrain and Borgne and south of the Thirty-First Parallel. Today the area includes the so-called Florida parishes of the state of Louisiana. The eastern region centered on Mobile Bay and Pensacola, with the Apalachicola and Chattahoochee Rivers as the boundary between what the Spanish established after 1783 as their provinces of West and East Florida. After holding a number of offices in the region beginning in 1787, Vicente Folch y Juan, nephew of Louisiana governor Estevan Miró, served as governor of the province of West Florida from 1803 until 1811.[4] The third region lay between the Pearl and Pascagoula Rivers and eventually became the state of Mississippi's Gulf Coast.[5]

Villebeuvre: From New Orleans to Grand Yazoo, 1787

On behalf of Miró, Jean de la Villebeuvre traveled some of the Gulf Coast water route in 1787 from New Orleans to reach the Choctaw village of Grand Yazoo. There he heard complaints from Choctaws about trade practices and attempted to persuade both them and the Chickasaws not to turn elsewhere for better prices for deerskins. He left New Orleans in September and traveled along the coast to somewhere near the mouth of the Pascagoula River before turning north toward Grand Yazoo. Villebeuvre reported traveling from New Orleans by what is now known as the Bayou St. John to reach a fort at its end on Lake Pontchartrain, whence he and his party continued by water to reach the Rigolets, or passes, that connect Lake Borgne with the Mississippi Sound.[6] Then the trip took him to Bay St. Louis, the Choctaw villages of Yellow Canes and Grand Yazoo, and the rivers leading to or close to them, the Pascagoula and the Chickasawhay.[7] He arrived in the village of Yellow Canes on October 7, staying for two days to talk with chiefs of the Six Villages and encourage them to attend the meetings in Grand Yazoo. They departed Yellow Canes on October 10 and arrived in Grand Yazoo three days later.[8]

Villebeuvre's trip took him through the middle portion of Spanish West Florida. The Spanish definition initially followed pretty closely that of the British at the end of the Seven Years' War: the Apalachicola River on the east, the Gulf of Mexico on the south, the Mississippi River on the west, and on the north a line running from the mouth of the Yazoo River east to the Apalachicola. Beginning with the 1795 Treaty of San Lorenzo, revisions began, with the border first moved to the Thirty-First Parallel and subsequently to the Perdido River.[9] Villebeuvre became a Gulf Coast inhabitant when he established a residence in Mobile, where he died in 1797 and was buried in the cemetery of the parish of Nuestra Señora de la Concepción.[10]

A Multilingual/Multiethnic Gulf Coast

The names of many Gulf Coast places and families sustain the memory of the French presence in the area. Villebeuvre is not among them, but Iberville, who led the way in establishing the French colonial presence there, is. In 1988, the community of d'Iberville, north of Biloxi on Biloxi Bay, incorporated itself as a city. Other place-names easily reveal a French origin: Pass Christian, Bay St. Louis, Bienville Forest (named after Iberville's brother), and the Rivière aux Perles (Pearl River). Perhaps more important for aficionados of sailing are the many islands along the Mississippi Gulf Coast. In addition to the Isle Dauphine (Dauphin Island), to the west are Isle aux Chats (Cat Island), Isle aux Vaisseaux (Ship Island), Isle a la Corne (Corn Island), and the Isles de Chandeleur (Chandeleur Islands).[11]

The French compiled lists of people coming to the Gulf Coast, and Spanish censuses in 1786, 1787, and 1788 provide names beginning the year before Villebeuvre's trip, thus providing some insight into the nature of the people Villebeuvre would have encountered.[12] In addition, the record of an ecclesiastical visitation in 1791, a listing of wartime donations, and remnants of the final colonial census, conducted in 1805, offer further documentation.[13] These records and others indicate that by the time the area became part of the British empire in 1763, a number of families with such names as Carriere, Ladner, Morin, Favre, Carco, Dubuisson, Labat, Fayard, Saucier, Bousage, and Krebs—some two or three generations removed from their forbears—had already become well established. Although the British had made land grants to nonresidents, few immigrants came during the time of British rule.[14]

The 1786 census enumerated Bay St. Louis, Pass Christian, Biloxi, Pascagoula, Bayou la Batre, Dauphin Island, Fish River, Deer River, Dog River, and Mobile, all of which authorities designated French, as well as Tombigbee River and Tensaw River, which were identified as American. Although the official language of the colonial administration and documents was Spanish, officials and the people whose names were recorded often were not. The documents record a mix of languages, spellings, and classifications of people. The existence of *libres* (free people of color) provided an added challenge, with Native Americans occasionally assigned incorrectly to that category, as in the case of Mongula.[15]

The censuses reveal the decline or stagnation of population along the coast, where the sandy soil and humidity were not conducive to agriculture. In contrast, rather dramatic population increases occurred in what came to be categorized as the American region centering along the Tombigbee and Tensaw Rivers. The Spanish evacuation of San Estevan in the late 1790s may have prompted some of these settlers to move south, where the Spanish continued to offer generous land concessions for modest investments.[16]

Documents from the Spanish period also reveal that the Gulf Coast had a more sedentary population, with families the norm and few single men. For the Tombigbee-Tensaw area, in contrast, single males, often listed as transients, were common and indeed may have been the norm. The French and American areas also differed significantly with regard to free people of color. No free persons of color appear in the three censuses for the Tombigbee-Tensaw area, whereas between thirty-two and thirty-five appear for the Gulf Coast. In both areas, most landholdings were located along or very close to navigable waterways or the coast itself, which seemed to have no Indian trails. Rivers such as the Pearl to the west and the Tombigbee to the east constituted important areas of settlement. The fact that thirty-nine of the fifty-five horses recorded along the Gulf Coast in 1787 grazed near the Pascagoula River also demonstrates the importance of waterways.[17]

Nature affected where and how people lived, and inhabitants of the Gulf Coast seemed to have a more relaxed and less possessive attitude toward space.[18] They accepted what has been described as a vernacular landscape, one that lacked elements of political organization.[19] Boundaries tended to be imprecise, with economic potential rather than proximity to neighbors or similarity to European landscapes governing choice of land. Throughout the colonial period and regardless of French, British, or Spanish dominion, land came to be treated in an inexact manner. For the British period in particular, surveyors often were not available, and the numerous petitions for land concessions were not processed. The result was a settlement pattern that was dispersed and that often offered little possibility of social contact, although it was eagerly sought.[20]

For example, in late May 1806, Andres Brey of Bay St. Louis completed a warehouse for bricks and invited two of his neighbors to celebrate with him and two hired workers. The party expanded when Brey sent Ayche, a Choctaw, across the bay to invite Felix Antonio Judiss, known as "the Jew," to attend. He came in a piragua with two Black men, who remained with the vessel. The party turned into a drunken brawl that eventually involved thirteen men—five Frenchmen, four Anglo-Americans, two African Americans, one Native American, and one Jew. A local official in Bay St. Louis, Philip Saucier, subsequently recorded depositions by various participants in French, although the two Anglo-Americans could not communicate in that language. An additional interview took place with Lieutenant Juan Bautista Pellerín, apparently in Spanish. The testimonies reveal that the people of French extraction knew both French and Spanish, while the Anglo-Americans could communicate only in English.[21]

These legal proceedings provide evidence of an attempt to establish more order and formality in a region characterized by a mixture of many ethnicities, languages, and inexactness of both land and social boundaries that many regarded as an advantage—a settlement pattern that generally was socially, culturally, politically, and economically diverse and dispersed. Another attempt to strengthen the administrative and military presence on the Gulf Coast occurred in 1805. Previously, Saucier and his counterpart at Pascagoula, James White, sent letters, reports, and juridical proceedings to officials in Mobile and Pensacola. The arrival of Francisco Bellestre in Pascagoula and Juan Bautista Pellerín in Bay St. Louis/Pass Christian prompted an effort to organize communities more effectively, but both experienced much frustration, deriving in large part from what was the most prevalent disregard of authority: contraband. Almost no cargo was more valuable than enslaved Africans, and the Spanish controlled and taxed the arrival and sale of enslaved workers in West Florida. Smuggling, therefore, was rampant. In 1807, for example, an American schooner landed a cargo of enslaved from Jamaica.[22]

By 1807, the social and ethnic mix of people on the Gulf Coast had changed significantly from what Villebeuvre encountered twenty years earlier. Those sometimes identified in Spanish documents as *anglo-americanos* constituted a rising portion of the single males in the total population, suggesting the beginning of the Americanization of a region that had only small enclaves of Spanish or French settlement. Americans had also settled farther inland, especially just north of Mobile. Creeks, Choctaws, Chickasaws and smaller groups of Native Americans such as the Alabamas, Tuskegees, and Yuchis remained the largest segment of the population in inland coastal areas and extending beyond the Thirty-First Parallel. Despite the growing presence of Americans, the region remained very mobile, fluid, and diverse.[23]

Observations of Andrew Ellicott, 1803

During the 1798–1800 survey of the boundary agreed upon in the 1795 Treaty of San Lorenzo, Andrew Ellicott, commissioner for the United States, recorded his observations and thoughts, which were published in 1803. Ellicott was joined on the commission by the Spanish representative, Stephen Minor; surveyor Thomas Power; and planter-scientist William Dunbar. A young trilingual man, Juan Pedro Walker, born in New Orleans in 1781 to an English father and a French mother, also served on the Spanish side. Walker's father had moved to the Natchez District and become closely associated with the Spanish governor, Manuel Gayoso de Lemos. Ellicott was also assisted by his son, Andrew, and

David Gillespie, who had studied mathematics in the University of North Carolina. President Washington had also appointed Thomas Freeman to serve as the other American commissioner and official surveyor, but Ellicott dismissed Freeman after alleged "improper" conduct and appointed Gillespie as "surveyor pro tem."[24]

Much of Ellicott's journal centers on physical features, but it also provides insight into such populated places as Mobile and Pensacola. In general, he concluded that the "upland" of West Florida as defined by the boundary contained land of very little value for plantations or farming and that the river bottoms, although fertile, were too small to be of any value to the province. Although West Florida seemed to be largely insignificant considered alone, when connected to "all the avenues of commerce to, and from [the] large productive country" to the north, it could become of "immense consequence." Those avenues consisted of the Pearl River as well as the Pascagoula, Tombigbee, Alabama, Escambia, Chattahoochee, and Flint, which stretched "at least 300 miles from east to west." Ellicott described the coast as abounding in live oak and red cedar trees "fit for ship building."[25]

Ellicott identified "a commanding eminence" along the Pearl River as an appropriate site for a fort that could deter travel up the river by boats and "periaguas" (piraguas). Although he admitted having little knowledge of the Pascagoula, he suggested that given its distance from both the Pearl and Mobile Rivers and its "magnitude," it might merit more attention than the Pearl. In light of their navigability for square-rigged vessels from the Gulf of Mexico and the fact that lands along their shores had already been "partially settled," the Mobile, Tombigbee, and Alabama Rivers had much greater value and importance to the United States than the area's other rivers.[26]

The Beginning of the End for the Spanish Empire

Ellicott's journal was published in 1803, the same year that the United States acquired Louisiana, much to the dismay of Spanish officials. By that time, events in Europe as well as America had set in motion the effective end to Spanish political hegemony in both East and West Florida, and that authority "completely disintegrated" when Napoleon invaded Spain and Spain's colonies began their independence movements.[27] Andrew Jackson's 1818 seizure of San Marcos de Apalachee and Pensacola made West Florida a de facto part of the United States. Ten years earlier, a movement had begun in the Viceroyalty of New Spain that led to an independent Mexico in 1821, the same year that the United States assumed de jure possession of all of Florida. The Spanish empire in North America had come to an end, while in the Caribbean, only Cuba and Puerto Rico remained.[28]

In December 1804, the former first consul of France's authoritarian republic, Napoleon Bonaparte, was crowned the country's emperor in a ceremony at the Cathedral of Notre-Dame de Paris. The new emperor was positioned to pursue his goal of becoming, in the words of historian Ernest Knapton, "a new Charlemagne" and creating a "Napoleonic Europe."[29] Napoleon suffered a temporary setback when the British navy scored a victory at Trafalgar in 1805 but rebounded with important victories over combined Austrian and Russian forces at Austerlitz in December of that year and over the Prussian army at Jena the following summer. He then set out to wage economic warfare against Britain by means of the so-called continental system, an embargo in the form of seizure of all goods coming from or going to Britain. He also secured permission from Spain to send an army to seize Portugal, a task that proved easy and allowed the movement of the French army across Spain to become something of a parade.[30]

Napoleon continued to send troops across the border on the grounds that they were protecting Spain from a possible British invasion. A French army arrived in Madrid in March 1808. Charles IV abdicated in favor of his son, Fernando, and Napoleon summoned both men to Bayonne, France, to negotiate. Ultimately, however, the emperor imprisoned both men and forced them to accept his brother, Joseph, as the new Spanish king. Joseph reigned for the next two years, although most Spaniards remained loyal to Fernando and supported a temporary alternative government in the form of the Central Junta based in Seville and local juntas.[31]

The events of 1807–8 merely continued what historian John Lynch characterizes as a "crisis of Bourbon Spain" associated with Charles IV, the worst "among inept Bourbon monarchs."[32] That monarchical ineptness was evidenced by the 1795 Treaty of San Lorenzo; the 1800 Treaty of San Ildefonso; the 1802 transfer of Louisiana to France and its subsequent sale to the United States in violation of the terms of that treaty; and Spain's 1821 acceptance of the American claim that the acquisition of Louisiana included West Florida.[33]

West Florida remained a marginal part of Spain's empire at least until 1818. A politics of play-off persisted given both the complexity of the international situation and the continued presence of a heterogeneous population of Native Americans and peoples of European and African origin. In general, that local population remained loyal to and supportive of Spain—when the right kind of leadership was provided. Charles (Carlos) de Grand-Pré, who was part of the Baton Rouge community after 1783 and served as governor beginning in 1799, and Vicente Folch y Juan, who held various positions between 1787 and

1811 and served as governor of West Florida for the last eight years of that period, merit some credit for maintaining at least the fiction of a Spanish West Florida. Despite the Napoleonic invasion and the conflicts that followed, Spain attempted to sustain the old order and provide some help to officials in Cuba and in East and West Florida.[34]

An 1803–1806 Spanish Map

Spanish cartographers and their maps endeavored to help the cause. Beginning in the fifteenth and sixteenth centuries in Europe, maps—visual representations of how people imagine, record, and define space—assumed particular significance as symbols of possession and authority. As Ricardo Padrón argues, the "invention of America" depended much on the "invention of the map."[35] For Spain, the beginnings of at least dynastic unity with the marriage of Fernando of Aragón and Isabella of Castilla and the activities of Columbus, Cortéz, Pizarro, Soto and many other explorers and conquistadores who followed required such documents to help define and claim parts of America. Spain consequently became an important center of cartography. One map of parts of what the Spanish regarded as the province of Louisiana and West Florida provides a very good visual expression of the debate that ensued after the sale of Louisiana to the United States in 1803.[36]

The sparse detail and the focus and rich coloring of the map, which probably dates from 1803–6, highlight two borders to help illustrate and argue the Spanish view of the country's territory and its divisions after what they saw as the illegal 1803 sale of Louisiana to the United States. The right-hand side of the map emphasizes the straight line of the Thirty-First Parallel beginning at the Mississippi River and running due east to the edge of the map above Lake Pontchartrain and New Orleans. The second highlighted border takes the form of a ninety-degree corner to follow what writers and other maps identified as Arroyo Hondo (not shown), which separated Los Adaes (spelled Adais) in the province of Texas from Natchitoches in the province of Louisiana. The line then runs south and connects with the Sabine River. A less highlighted border continues along the eastern bank of the Mississippi River south from the Thirty-First Parallel to the mouth of the Bayou Manchac (Iberville River) and then to Lake Maurepas along the lake's north shore to its connection with Lake Pontchartrain, and finally along its north shore to the right-hand side of the map. That less highlighted line emerged from the complex negotiations ending the French and Indian War, providing assurances—perhaps disingenuous—that the British would have access to the mouth of the Mississippi River.[37]

Other details provide visual reinforcement of verbal representations. In general, the map expresses the basic Spanish position that both Texas and West Florida remained Spanish. It labels territory north of the Thirty-First Parallel and east of the Mississippi River "American" and locates a "Fuerte Americano" (American fort, Fort Adams) at Loftus Heights. The territory to the south is clearly identified as a portion of "the dominion of His Majesty [the Spanish king] belonging to Florida." The more central focus of the map, however, is Texas, clearly offering a visual refutation of the position taken by Thomas Jefferson and other Americans that Louisiana extended all the way south to the Rio Bravo. The map does not, however, include that area of south Texas but rather highlights the northeast corner of Texas centering on Adaes and Natchitoches, which had become a place of potential conflict between Spain and France in the early eighteenth century when the French established a post at Natchitoches on the Red River.[38]

The map's depiction of the area of the map above Lake Pontchartrain and south of the new American territory of Mississippi also merits some attention. It is carefully marked as belonging to "His Christian Majesty, the King of Spain." From an agricultural point of view, this territory it seemed far more attractive than the coastal areas. Before moving north to the Natchez Country in the 1790s, William Dunbar found this region attractive for the cultivation of indigo, tobacco, rice, corn, and sugar. Historian F. Andrew McMichael concludes that at least until 1805 the international situation, Spanish policies, and a sensible, restrained style of governance under Grand-Pré generally worked to keep the area happy under Spanish rule.[39]

But the border issue and the question of whether West Florida had been included in the Louisiana Purchase remained open. In the words of Thomas D. Clark and John D. W. Guice, the Gulf Coast became "a perimeter of conflict" within a larger "land of speculation." The five major rivers, especially the Mississippi and the Tombigbee-Alabama systems, added to the conflict. The need to keeping these waterways open made the border issue central and played into the hands of the adventurers, opportunists, filibusters, army deserters, and criminals who seemed to thrive in such an environment.[40]

A Golden Age for Adventurers and Adventurism: Toward a Lone Star Republic of West Florida

Between 1799 and his death a decade later, Grand-Pré served as governor of the Baton Rouge District, which included an area known as Feliciana. With the involvement of Ohio senator John Smith and influential New Orleans

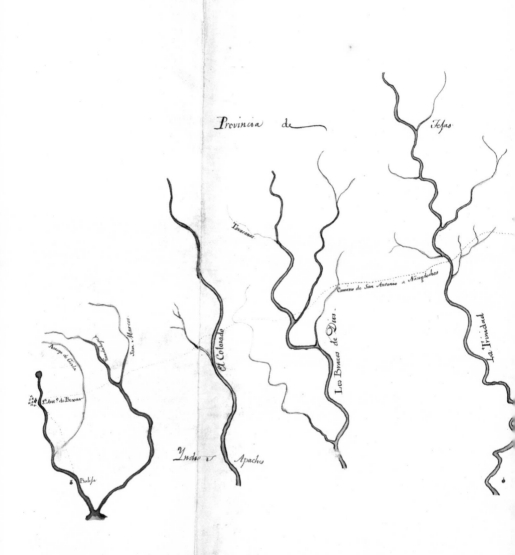

Spanish map from ca. 1803–1806, *Plano de una parte de la Provincia de la Luisiana y de otra de la Florida Occidental y de la Provincia de Texas*. See also book jacket. Reproduced with kind permission of Graham Arader, Arader Galleries, New York.

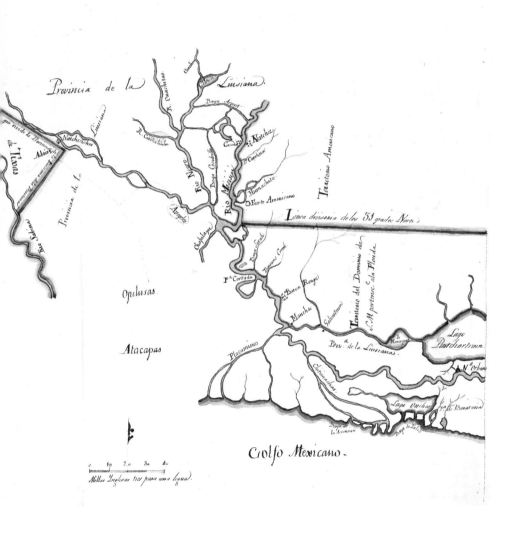

Provincia de la ... Lusiana.

que riba de la Provincia de Texas

Adaes

Natchitoches

Provincia de la

Rio Sabino

R. Ouachitas

R. Cocilachitas

Catahoula

Bayou Apgent

Rio Nero

Natchez

Catahoula

Bayou Crocodillo

Fuerte de Catahoula

Rio Mary

Humachito

O Fuerte Americano

Angola

Chatalagua

Territorio Americano

Linea divisoria de los 33 grados Norte

Bayou Sarah

Tunicas Creek

Pto Cortada

Baton Rouge

Mancha

Galvestown

Placaminos

Chitimacchas

Bayou de la Ascension

Opelusas

Atacapas

Territorio del Dominio de
S.M. pertenec. e a la Florida

Manapac

Brazo de la Lusiana.

Lago Pontchartrain

A No Orleans

Lago Onchas

Pto de Banataria

Bayou de Lafit

Golfo Mexicano.

0   10   20   30   40

Millas Inglesas tres para una legua.

merchant Daniel Clark Jr., Feliciana became a central area of attention and conflict. As early as 1802—before the Louisiana Purchase—Smith and Clark sent agents into Feliciana to acquire land. Brothers Reuben, Samuel, and James Kemper settled just north of the border in Pinckneyville, where they sustained something of an offensive against the Spanish and helped lend support to an American position on the border and its importance for a republican "empire for liberty." In September 1805, Grand-Pré reported that the Kemper brothers had been captured by "persons unknown" who were apparently working on behalf of specially created patrols to secure the border and interior settlements of Feliciana from "the inroads committed by that turbulent Banditti headed by the Kempers." These "turbulent Banditti" ultimately failed to secure much support from Feliciana residents, who saw them as no more than "leaders of a group of land pirates" interested only "in stealing slaves and cattle."[41] The Kempers and their ilk remained a problem and proved a significant factor in the collapse of Spanish authority. In 1805, Reuben Kemper and others went to the Bahamas to secure British help for an invasion of the Baton Rouge area.

Well before Kemper's arrival, however, a much more formidable fellow, William Augustus Bowles, a native of Maryland and a sublieutenant in the British army, had arrived in Nassau and begun a career as an adventurer par excellence.[42] Bowles had served in a Loyalist infantry during the Revolution, was either dismissed or deserted, and joined a group of Creek Indians in Pensacola. He then went to Nassau and spent four years reading literature and history and honing his theatrical and artistic skills. He took a job with a British merchant and returned to mainland North America in 1783, appealing to the imagination of and garnering support from the Creeks by promising that his employer and others in Nassau could provide goods. He married a Creek woman and set out to challenge the Spanish by posing as director-general of an autonomous Muscogee nation. In so doing, he also challenged Alexander McGillivray's position as leader of the Creek confederation and the monopoly on the Creek trade that the Spanish had granted to William Panton's company. In addition to the Bahamas and Creek Country, Bowles's career took him to such far-flung places as Jamaica, Canada, and Britain, and he was imprisoned in Spain and the Philippines. With support from the American commissioner to the Creeks and Creeks themselves, the Spanish finally apprehended him, and he was again imprisoned, this time in the El Morro castle in Santiago de Cuba, where he died in August 1803, about a hundred days before the end of Spanish rule in Louisiana.[43]

Bowles and other adventurers, conspirators, and filibusters, posed challenges not only for the Spanish but also for the American government. Another member of that group was former US vice president Aaron Burr, who arrived in New Orleans in 1805. With initial support from James Wilkinson, a friend from the era of the American Revolution, Burr had undertaken the journey with a large group of men intending to make contact with the Spanish, though his objectives were and remain hazy. He did meet some members of "a shadowy organization of swashbucklers" dedicated to "liberating" or revolutionizing Mexico and then annexing it to the United States. He may also have sought to bring about the secession of the western part of the United States.[44]

Spanish officials in Texas took a more aggressive stance toward deterring the United States than did their counterparts in West Florida as a consequence of the high priority Spain accorded to retaining Mexico. Burr apparently saw an opportunity to take advantage of what seemed to be growing sentiment in favor of American annexation of the Floridas and told people he met along the journey west whatever they seemed to want to hear, including the assertion that he intended to seize West Florida for the United States. In 1804, Congress had sought to mollify that sentiment by passing the Mobile Act, which techni-cally annexed Mobile and defined it as a customs district. The legislation had no practical effect, but it did demonstrate some support for the view that the purchase of Louisiana had included West Florida.[45]

Whatever his goals, Burr did not achieve them. In 1807, he found himself on his third and final visit to the Mississippi Territory, having lost Wilkinson's backing.[46] Sent to New Orleans to command an enlarged American force to help defeat any expedition put together by Burr, Wilkinson provided enough evidence to authorities to have Burr arrested on charges of treason. A territo-rial grand jury failed to indict him and he fled. He was reapprehended, held prisoner at Fort Stoddert, above Mobile, and eventually sent to Richmond, Virginia, to face trial on the same charge of treason. After a federal district court found him not guilty, he faced yet another charge, this one a misdemeanor for initiating an expedition to invade the "dominions of the King of Spain," but again was absolved.[47]

Proponents of a break with Spain in Baton Rouge and Feliciana achieved their objective, helped in part by Burr and his supporters but more significantly by international developments. The alliance and then break between Spain and France brought about by Napoleon's invasion of the Iberian Peninsula, the abdication of Charles IV, and Joseph Bonaparte's installation as Spanish king initiated movements that led ultimately to the demise of the Spanish empire. Local juntas enabled towns to assert at least temporary autonomy in Spain and in its American colonies. In 1807, the year before Charles's abdication, the United States proclaimed an embargo directed mainly against Britain, but its prohibition on American ships entering foreign ports and on foreign ships entering American ports translated into an economic disaster for West Florida.[48]

Growing hostility leading to a kind of francophobia on the part of Spanish Creoles throughout the entire Caribbean, including Louisiana and the Mississippi Territory, caused some to flee to Orleans Territory. Grand-Pré became a victim of this hostility in 1808 when he received Octaviano Davilmar, supposedly a distinguished visitor from a friendly nation. In reality, Napoleon had sent Davilmar and other agents to Spanish colonies by Napoleon before revealing his intentions regarding Spain. Both Wilkinson and the American governor of the Orleans Territory, W. C. C. Claiborne, advised the Spanish vice consul in New Orleans, José Vidal, of Davilmar's presence, and Vidal, in turn, informed the Mexican viceroy. Vidal believed that Davilmar was a man of talent and "high enterprise" who nevertheless had "no morality." Grand-Pré received Davilmar with hospitality and provided him with a boat to travel up the Red River toward Texas, where he was subsequently arrested. After learning that Grand-Pré had received the emissary, West Florida governor Vicente Folch questioned Grand-Pré's loyalty, resulting in his recall to Havana and his replacement by Carlos De Hault de Lassus, whom many West Floridians came to despise.[49]

Lassus proved unable to check the more radical elements in the population who favored an end to what they characterized as corrupt Spanish rule. More moderate parties pursued a conciliatory policy that they hoped would establish a more effective government. A convention sanctioned by Lassus met fourteen times beginning in July 1810 to this end but never succeeded. The interception of letters sent by Lassus to Folch asking for military reinforcements did not help. Folch had already attempted to suppress unrest in Bayou Sara via military action, but the force he sent never arrived. Lassus's letters further strengthened radicals' determination to depose him, and they succeeded in late September when a small group attacked and took what remained of a fort in Baton Rouge, in the process killing Grand-Pré's son. After Lassus's resignation, the insurgents issued a declaration of independence, adopted a flag, and chose a president for the Republic of West Florida, known colloquially as the Lone Star Republic, but it lasted only a few days.[50]

The End of Spanish West and East Florida

Florida's final status had to await other developments in what the Spanish still regarded as the provinces of West and East Florida. US president James Madison expressed his approval of the insurgent actions with an October 27, 1810, proclamation authorizing the seizure of all of Florida from the Mississippi to the Perdido River. Congress provided qualified approval to take possession in the event that West Florida seemed likely to fall into other foreign hands. American forces immediately occupied Pass Christian, Pascagoula, and Dauphin Island. By 1812, the year war between the United States and Great Britain began, all of West Florida with the exception of Mobile and Pensacola was effectively in American hands. East Florida then became the principal focus of American expansionists.[51]

On August 6, 1812, the Spanish secretary of state in Cádiz linked the taking of the fort at Baton Rouge with Madison's proclamation. From the Spanish perspective, a union of adventurers of various nations along the Mississippi, equipped, armed, and maintained by the American government, had seized the fort at Baton Rouge. The Spanish minister to the United States, Luís de Onís, protested these actions, though to limited effect because of the ambivalent political situation in Spain, he had not yet been recognized as the country's official representative. Madison defended the actions by reasserting that West Florida had been part of the Louisiana Purchase and adding that Spanish authority in West Florida had disintegrated to an extent that endangered the United States.[52]

W. C. C. Claiborne played an important role in securing West Florida for the Americans, helped by others including Mississippi's territorial governor, David Holmes. Claiborne reinforced what had already been accomplished, reporting in early December 1810 that all of West Florida had been effectively occupied with the exception of the Mobile District associated with the fort there. He also announced that a county of Feliciana had been created to include the parishes of Feliciana, East Baton Rouge, St. Helena, St. Tammany, Biloxi, and Pascagoula and that various officials had been named for all these parishes.[53] Though Spain had not yet conceded, Congress admitted Louisiana, including the region west of the Pearl River, as a new state in April 1812. The outbreak of war with Britain two months later and some negotiation by Folch helped modify what Claiborne and Congress did. Through diplomacy Folch obtained at least occasional alliances with some Native Americans, thereby checking US officials willing if not eager to use military action to take what remained in Spanish hands. The war ultimately undermined his efforts, however, leading Madison to authorize former Georgia governor George Matthews and Choctaw agent John McKee to arrange the secret surrender of East Florida with the help of former Georgians living there. The fact that East Florida served as a haven for enslaved runaways helped Matthews garner support on both sides of the border. Wilkinson launched two military assaults, successfully seizing Amelia Island off the northeast coast of Florida but failing in his bid to take St. Augustine, where the Spanish had concentrated their limited military force. In December 1812, the Spanish parliament decided to pardon those who had helped the Americans, and the following March, the American government, seeking to avoid an additional war with Spain, decided that military action in East Florida should be terminated and US forces withdrawn.[54]

During the evacuation of East Florida, American troops finally took possession of Mobile. In the spring of 1813, Wilkinson led a military expedition to compel the Spanish to evacuate Mobile. His expedition began in New Orleans and continued to Pass Christian, where he intended to join Commodore John Shaw. Though Shaw was not there, Wilkinson moved on and requested help from Fort Stoddert to the north of Mobile. The fort at Mobile was in a dilapidated condition and the sixty troops there were "dispirited and starving." On April 15, 1813, the Spanish commander gave up, and he and his troops boarded American vessels and went to Pensacola.[55]

Still not recognized by the US government, Onís protested in June. The Spanish Council of State met in August and concluded that war was not appropriate and that negotiations should continue, beginning with US recognition of the General and Extraordinary Cortes and of Fernando VII as king. The council recommended that negotiations should seek the return of all US-occupied land, acceptance of the boundaries of Louisiana as they had been when the territory was retroceded to France, abstention by the United States from cooperation with insurgents in Spanish America, and the recall by the United States of commercial agents sent to areas in revolt.[56]

The following year, 1814, saw more military action on the part of American forces, this time led by Andrew Jackson. In May, a detail of American troops arrived along the Escambia River a short distance from Pensacola. They were pursuing some "Red Stick" Creeks as part of a larger war led by Jackson against Natives who were opposing American encroachments to the north. In November, Jackson and about fifty-five hundred men occupied Pensacola for three days. The fort there, San Miguel, surrendered on condition that it would remain Spanish while Spain sent sufficient forces to sustain its neutrality in the context of the ongoing war between the United States and Britain. The Spanish flag continued flying, and Americans agreed to protect the property of inhabitants.[57]

The United States chose not to remain in Pensacola because the British had completely destroyed the posts of Barrancas and Santa Rosa guarding the harbor of the city and because Jackson had received word that the British were planning to attack Louisiana in December and that needed to focus on its defense. The British began to land troops at the mouth of the Mississippi River to block traffic from the north, but Jackson defeated them in early January 1815 at the Battle of New Orleans, which won him national fame, after the war had officially ended. The peace agreement between the United States and Britain negotiated at Ghent in Belgium on December 24, 1814, provided for the restoration of the prewar status quo, with both countries agreeing on paper to evacuate what they had occupied in the Floridas. However, all of Florida west of the Perdido River had already been annexed by the United States, and only five years later the United States finally took possession of East Florida under the Adams-Onís Treaty.[58]

Additional American military action had occurred when Jackson ordered a land and water expedition to destroy a British-built fort on Prospect Bluff near the mouth of the Apalachicola River. The British had abandoned the fort, leaving behind a large quantity of weapons and ammunition, and it became a refuge for enslaved Africans who had escaped from Pensacola as well as from Georgia. It also attracted belligerent Creeks and Seminoles. Despite the fact that Jackson's raid violated Florida territory still accepted as Spanish, local Spanish officials welcomed the removal of what they, like the Americans, viewed as a menace.[59]

By the beginning of 1818, the only places of importance in East and West Florida still not occupied by Americans were Pensacola; San Marcos de Apalache, just to the east of Pensacola; and St. Augustine. Within four months, all were in American hands. The occupation of Pensacola provided a short-term setback to the ongoing negotiations between the United States and Spain. As in 1814, the restoration of the Spanish flag blunted "the clamor raised by the invasion" among the Spanish, and on February 22, 1819, John Quincy Adams and Luís de Onís placed seals on the treaty that bore their name, and after ratification by both governments, it went into effect two years later.[60]

CHAPTER SIX

From Borrowed Land to Possessed Land, 1798 and Beyond

Whatever political or imperial role Spanish Florida had played came to an official end with the Adams-Onís Treaty. The United States secured what it wanted and more, including the Gulf Coast of what had become the new state of Mississippi in 1817. After the retrocession of Louisiana by Spain to France, US president Thomas Jefferson had the modest goal of acquiring New Orleans and the Floridas. In 1803, he instructed his representatives in Paris, Robert Livingstone and James Monroe, to try to achieve that end. When Napoleon decided to abandon the French empire in America, he offered Louisiana to the Americans at a low price. Perhaps exceeding their instructions, the American representatives accepted, and those so inclined in the United States could begin to talk about an "empire for liberty" and a "manifest destiny" to achieve it. Spain objected to the American purchase but after nearly two decades had to accept that all of Louisiana and the Floridas had come under US control.[1]

But European imperial and colonial interests in America did not end with Spain's loss of most of its American empire by the 1820s. Canada remained part of a British empire, as did islands in the Caribbean and a portion of Guyana on the coast of northern South America. The Portuguese sustained an imperial presence in Brazil, encouraged, somewhat ironically, by Napoleon's 1807 invasion of the Iberian Peninsula. With British help, the Portuguese royal family escaped to Rio de Janeiro, where they received an enthusiastic reception in January 1808, and Brazil remained an empire for another eighty years.[2] For a short time in 1820, Mexican conservatives sought without success to create an imperial form of government for that newly independent country. In the 1860s, however, their successors, with help from the French now led by Napoleon's nephew, Louis Napoleon Bonaparte, persuaded Maximilian, the younger brother of Austria's Franz Joseph, to become emperor of a revived Mexican empire. That episode ended when he and two of his Mexican generals were executed near Querétaro, just north of Mexico City, in 1867.[3]

A New Empire?

With the Northwest Ordinance of 1787, the United States seemed to reject empire as a model for its political evolution. The legislation may have done no more than ensure that pursuit of empire would continue in the form of an "imperial republic" initiated by the American Revolution and the emergence of "imperial revolutionaries." The ordinance provided a plan for the political evolution of parts of the United States not yet organized in a way that would admit new states on an equal political basis with the old, laying out a procedure whereby territory north of the Ohio River relinquished by the new American states could evolve into between three and five new states. Preceded by two land ordinances in 1784 and 1785, the 1787 ordinance also recognized that land held by Native Americans could be acquired only by peaceful purchase by the United States and banned slavery in that area, which became the Northwest Territory.[4]

Though the Northwest Ordinance seemed to outline a commitment to political equality, subsequent US actions and rhetoric undermined that commitment. Slavery spread across the South, becoming even more rigid and harsh, and public policy removed Native Americans from their homelands, especially in the American Southwest. The US House of Representatives tried and failed to extend the ban on slavery to the new Mississippi Territory when it was organized after 1798. Little or no support for such a ban existed in an area that had long depended on slavery and that had thrived when cotton became the preferred cash crop in the 1790s.[5] Between 1830 and 1836, the state's slave population grew by about 250 percent, from just over 65,000 to more than 164,000.[6]

The phrase *empire for liberty* came to mean liberty for propertied white men, but not for enslaved African Americans. Land surveyor Andrew Ellicott played an important but controversial role in the initial phase of territorial organization. Ellicott argued that the Northwest Ordinance should be the model for the new territory, a position that garnered opposition from some prominent Mississippians because it would have eliminated slavery. Ellicott recorded in his journal that although slavery was "extremely disagreeable" to "people in the eastern states," it would be "expedient to tolerate it in the district of Natchez, where that species of property is very common." He also recorded observations on disposing of vacant lands in ways that would avoid creating a "monopoly the most dangerous of any other to the liberties of the people." He believed that the ideal form of land tenure would involve relatively small parcels of land owned by many rather than large parcels owned by a few. According to Ellicott, Anthony Hutchins had taken the lead in championing the latter view. Nevertheless, Ellicott expressed optimism that a good 90 percent of the inhabitants of Mississippi were "warmly attached to the interests of the United States." In August 1798, Winthrop Sargent, the first territorial governor, arrived in Natchez.[7]

Four years later, in the published version of his journal, Ellicott noted the acquisition of Louisiana and offered some comments on what it might mean for the US political situation. He saw positives in greater security for the navigation of the Mississippi River but worried about what sales of land west of the river and the dispersal of people over an even broader territory might have on "the advantages of society, civilization, the arts, sciences, and good government."[8] In his discussion of rivers, Ellicott noted other potential problems with transportation and communication.

Roads, People, and King Cotton

On December 10, 1798, Secretary of State Timothy Pickering sent some letters from Philadelphia to Governor Sargent in Natchez. After traveling by flatboat and trail, the letters finally reached Sargent on April 20, 1799—more than four months later. As Pickering observed, "the passage of letters from Natchez is as tedious as from Europe."[9] The Spanish had already attempted to improve communication and transportation to secure their presence in the Southwest. The 1803–6 map (see chapter 5) shows a road leading from San Antonio northeast to Los Adaes and then east to Natchitoches—a portion of a *camino real* (royal road) that connected the viceregal capital, Mexico City, with Natchez.[10]

Another important project began as a post road linking Natchez with Tennessee. Building it required August–October 1801 meetings with the Cherokees, Chickasaws, and Choctaws through whose lands it would pass. The Cherokees rejected the portion of the road between Nashville and Knoxville, but the Chickasaws and Choctaws proved more amenable. The three American commissioners—General James Wilkinson; North Carolina's Benjamin Hawkins, who served from 1796 until 1816 as the US government's principal agent for Indian affairs south of the Ohio River, and Andrew Pickens of South Carolina—met with Chinubbee, who had succeeded his brother, Taskietoka, as leader of the Chickasaws, and other Natives, with George Colbert speaking for Chinubbee. The Chickasaws agreed to the use of their land for the road but stipulated they should own and operate ferries and places of accommodation. The Choctaws not only agreed to allow the road to cross their territory but also ceded to the Americans some 2.6 million acres of land—essentially all that the British had defined as the Natchez District within the province of West Florida.[11]

The Choctaw land cession and the opening of the Natchez Trace in 1801 initiated more Choctaw and Chickasaw land cessions to Americans in Mississippi. For the Choctaws, it continued what had begun at Hopewell, South Carolina, in 1786, when they ceded almost seventy thousand acres in exchange for the establishment of trading posts and guarantees of protection by the United States. Seven more treaties followed in which the Choctaws gave up more than twenty-five million acres, including ten million in the final agreement, 1830's Treaty of Dancing Rabbit Creek. Securing land, historian Martin Abbott argues, came to be one of the four objectives of American "Indian management" in the Mississippi Territory, along with removal west of the Mississippi River, fostering trade, and encouraging manufacturing and agriculture.[12]

Other roads, sometimes at first no more than paths, became especially important in facilitating movement of people, free and enslaved, into the Mississippi Territory. That influx of free and enslaved Americans from Virginia, the Carolinas, and Georgia effectively Americanized the territory and strengthened the American South's "peculiar institution," African American slavery. The ten thousand newcomers who arrived in the Natchez region between 1810 and the beginning of the Red Stick War in 1813 "quickly swamped the small creole population of native-born whites, blacks, and *metís.*" The eastern part of the territory near the Tombigbee and Tensaw Rivers received even more people.[13]

The so-called Federal Road began in 1806 as a post and military road connecting Fort Wilkinson, at Milledgeville, Georgia, and Fort Stoddert, north of Mobile. In 1811 improvements enabled wagons to traverse the road, thereby expediting the movement of settlers. A branch of it went to Fort St. Stephen (the former Spanish San Estevan), on the Tombigbee River, where it connected with St. Stephen's Road and Fort Stoddert Road, both of which went to Natchez. The Gaines Trace followed a former Indian path south from the Tennessee River to the Tombigbee, crossing it at Cotton Gin Port, where a cotton gin was constructed in 1801. That road first served as an important conduit for supplies going south to Fort Stoddert before becoming an important immigration route into the Tombigbee River Valley. These and other roads facilitated the Mississippi Territory's "steady if unspectacular" population growth from 1798 to 1812 and the post-1815 "great migration" to what became the Cotton Kingdom and its associated "flush times." The population more than doubled between 1810 and 1820 in what became the state of Mississippi in 1817 and increased sixteenfold in the part of the territory that became Alabama two years later.[14]

Andrew Jackson found these roads and others useful in the many operations he sustained against Indians through his presidency in the 1830s.[15]

Among these newcomers during this period of growing American nationalism and westward expansion were Christian evangelicals and missionaries. They were part of the Second Great Awakening, a movement of growing religious awareness and enthusiasm that manifested itself in a variety of ways, including camp meetings lasting for as long as a week and attracting crowds as large as six thousand people to hear rousing sermons. Missionaries saw opportunities among Indians and in time established schools and churches among them. Many of these early Protestant evangelicals saw themselves as critics of social evils including slavery but went on to become plantation and slave owners and ultimately "the most ardent defenders of a hierarchical social system grounded in slaveholding." James Smylie, for example, was a Presbyterian minister who migrated from North Carolina to Mississippi with his father and other family members. Smylie also received encouragement to move from the organizer of the first Presbyterian church in Mississippi, Joseph Bullen, who in 1799 had "a good long talk" with the Chickasaw chief Ugulayacabé "to tell him all sorts of good things about the faith."[16]

Both George Washington's secretary of war, Henry Knox, and Thomas Jefferson criticized the people who made their way west of the Appalachians, declaring them "uncivilized," "fractious," or "ungovernable frontier whites" who included "Indian fighters" and "haters." Such views led to efforts to purchase land from Native Americans for later resale to settlers in an orderly way that would respect Native interests, maintain peace, and make the frontier more governable by giving white settlers a stake in society through ownership and cultivation of land. In 1803, Jefferson suggested that the United States incur debt to get Indian lands and embraced a policy of "civilization" espoused by George Washington, Knox, and others that sought to convert Indians to "white-style" agriculture and encourage them to sell unneeded hunting lands to secure needed capital goods. This "peace and civilization policy" would, Jefferson believed, protect Native Americans and even enable them to become US citizens. In the end, however, most Natives chose removal under the terms of the Indian Removal Act of 1830 rather than, in the words of Robert Remini, "become subject to state law and jurisdiction—in other words, white law and jurisdiction."[17]

"Civilization" or Survival?

For the most part, Native Americans offered little initial resistance to these newcomers, who included missionaries and Benjamin Hawkins, the new federal agent south of the Ohio River who arrived in 1786 to promote "civilization" and whom Washington appointed in 1796 as his principal agent to the four southern "nations" (Chickasaws, Creeks, Choctaws, and Cherokees). To these officials, *civilization* meant adopting white ways of living and working. Their task was made somewhat easier by what French, English, and Scottish traders had already done by living among Native Americans and establishing mixed families. Many of these traders' children assumed positions of leadership—the Colberts among the Chickasaws and Alexander McGillivray among the Creeks. By the late eighteenth century, Native Americans had begun using plows and wagons and raising some cotton, though they still hunted and therefore required control of substantial tracts of land.[18]

Creek men and women "vacillated between extremes in their opinions of Americans," with sentiments tending to become more extreme after 1800.[19] With encouragement from Native leaders such as Tecumseh and his brother Tenskwatawa, who promoted the creation of a pan-Indian confederacy to preserve Native ways and resist American demands for land, the Red Stick faction emerged among the Creeks. Members of this group embraced the option of using violence to resist Americans. A civil war that broke out among the Creeks in 1813 ended the following year when a force led by Andrew Jackson defeated the Red Sticks.[20] Tecumseh also visited the Choctaws to appeal to "traditionalists" and their dismay with mixed-blood "modernizers." No "civil war" resulted, and Chiefs Pushmataha and Mushulatubbee persuaded their people not to support a pan-Indian confederation.[21]

Perhaps "the most important agents of cultural change" among Native peoples were the enslaved African Americans who had become part of their societies.[22] The enslaved workers toiled on plantations established by individual Native slaveholders, and captive Atlantic Africans were seen and treated as valuable personal property. For example, in April 1806, the governor of the Mississippi Territory, Robert Williams, wrote a letter seeking the arrest of the men "who stole Negroes from the widow of Wolf's Friend [Ugulayacabé] in the Chickasaw Nation."[23]

In 1830, the same year that the US government and the Choctaws signed the Treaty of Dancing Rabbit Creek, Congress passed the Indian Removal Act. Although the treaty allowed Choctaws to remain in Mississippi under certain conditions, well over half chose to move west across the Mississippi River, continuing an out-migration that had begun as early as the 1790s.[24] What some of them had previously considered "borrowed" or "lent" lands were becoming "owned," first by the American government, then by the "squatters, whiskey traders, and peddlers" who had begun arriving with a vengeance after 1800, and finally by land speculators who sold it to migrating slaveholders. By 1820, most Native chiefs saw removal as the only option, and Jackson's election to the presidency eight years later "signaled to Choctaws and Americans alike that the Choctaws' tenure in Mississippi would no longer be tolerated."[25]

Removal

In February 1829, Mississippi's governor signed a law that extended the authority of the state over Choctaw lands, and with the Indian Removal Act, Native chiefs and others faced a choice: "Remove and be Happy" or "disappear and be forgotten."[26] There was no question about which was preferable. As Daniel K. Richter puts it, Jackson and William Henry Harrison, "two of the most successful political leaders of the United States" in the 1820s and 1830s, completed the process of "ethnic cleansing that had begun in 1763."[27]

Choctaw chief Greenwood LeFlore, previously a leader of the "modernizers," had begun to revise his views and to predict that "white men" would soon settle on vacant Choctaw land and cheat Natives out of their property. He urged Choctaws to accept removal, others agreed, and on March 16, 1830, chiefs of the eastern and southern towns resigned in favor of centralizing decision-making in one person. LeFlore became chief of the entire nation, affirming his commitment to refuse to submit to Mississippi law and promising to oppose further land cessions. In addition, he pledged to negotiate a treaty that would provide the best possible terms for removal.[28]

More than six thousand Choctaws joined LeFlore at a September 1830 meeting to discuss a treaty. On the other side of the table were "a large portion of white people" made up mainly of "rowdies, gamblers, and saloonkeepers—in short, the bad element of the American frontier." They gathered between two prongs of Dancing Rabbit Creek in Noxubee County, Mississippi. The Choctaws had chosen not to attend an earlier meeting in Franklin, Tennessee, with Jackson and representatives of other Indian groups including the Chickasaws. That meeting had failed to secure an agreement from the Chickasaws to move west, angering Jackson. Nevertheless, the Chickasaws later indicated an interest in removal after they, too, concluded they could not "endure the laws of Mississippi." At Dancing Rabbit Creek, Jackson was represented by secretary of war John Eaton and the commissioner for Indian affairs in the southern region. The three major Choctaw factions were represented by LeFlore, "dressed in a suit of citizen clothes"; Mushulatubbee, who wore "a new blue military uniform," a present to him by General Jackson; and Nittakechi, "wearing full Indian garb." Many other chiefs also attended.[29]

In his lengthy account of the meeting, nineteenth-century historian Henry Halbert (1837–1916) noted that a range of activities kept most of the people occupied. Much "dissipation and revelry" characterized life night and day, but no "licentiousness" occurred thanks to the "chaste" nature of the Choctaws. A major "Indian dance" occurred every night. In contrast, the "Christian Indians" attended religious services directed by David Folsom, "preaching, praying, and singing every night into a late hour."[30]

On September 18, the US commissioners presented to the various chiefs, captains, and warriors in attendance the basic terms of the proposed treaty. The Choctaws should consent to "remove" to the other side of the Mississippi River and settle on a "large and fertile" area "double the size" of their current landholdings that could support a population two or three times as large as their current numbers. There they would be "contented and happy," free from "white man's laws interrupting and disturbing you."[31] The tone of the meeting quickly turned negative, however, when, much to the commissioners' surprise, the Choctaws announced that they had already voted to reject the proposal. Only after Eaton told them that an army would be sent to expel them did they accept the treaty and agree to move to the area west of the Arkansas Territory that had been set aside for them. In addition to that stick, the US officials offered carrots in the form of sections of land reserved for chiefs, along with small stipends, a general annuity for the nation, and other gifts. The final treaty was signed on September 27.[32] Halbert concludes that the treaty was accomplished via "intimidation and moral coercion," while according to modern historian James F. Barnett Jr., the Choctaws were both confused and angry when they learned the terms of the treaty their leaders had signed.[33]

More than twelve thousand of the approximately eighteen thousand Mississippi Choctaws moved across the Mississippi River to the new "Indian Territory." For those who remained, article 14 of the treaty provided grants of land to adult males who agreed to occupy it for five years and live according the laws of Mississippi.[34] James Culberson, the son of Tushpa, related the journey undertaken by a hundred "full-blood Choctaw" led by his father in the early spring of 1834. The group crossed the Mississippi somewhere in "Desha County," in southeastern Arkansas, before trekking west to "the Post" (Little Rock); "Dardanelle," on the Arkansas River; and "Fort Smith" or "Skullyville." The "four-hundred mile walk" to the promised land of Oklahoma's Indian Territory finally ended on July 1. Many of the Choctaws had died along the way.[35]

Three years earlier, a talented young French aristocrat, Alexis de Tocqueville, touring the United States, found himself on the Chickasaw Bluffs, which had become part of Memphis. In the book that resulted from that trip, *Democracy in America*, Tocqueville noted that a large group of Choctaws had tried to cross the river to "an asylum that had been promised them by the American government." The winter had been unusually cold, and blocks of ice drifted in the river. Many of the Choctaws were wounded or sick people; the elderly were on the verge of death. According to Tocqueville, "They possessed neither tents nor wagons, but only their arms and some provisions. I saw them embark on the mighty river, and never will that solemn spectacle fade from my remembrance."[36]

Greenwood LeFlore was among the six thousand Choctaws who remained in Mississippi. He embraced "white civilization" and did well, expanding his treaty reserves into a fifteen-thousand-acre plantation, came to own about four hundred enslaved Africans and served briefly in the Mississippi legislature. When he died in 1865, he was buried not with the traditional objects that had given chiefs power—"gorgets, copper ornaments, and sacred objects"—but rather "wrapped in an American flag," "a token of his sources of power—the practices of Anglo-America—and evidence of the possibilities of creolization."[37] The Choctaws, in the view of Clara Sue Kidwell, remained something of an anomaly in Mississippi, but over time they learned how to use that position to their advantage. Indeed, they effected a "Choctaw miracle" by maintaining their identity and manipulating the rhetoric of race to resist a second removal attempt in 1898. In 1945, with the help of more favorable laws for Native Americans, they achieved recognition as the Mississippi Band of Choctaw Indians, and they subsequently worked out a way to embrace and use much of modern life yet still preserve a distinctive ethnic identity.[38]

In contrast, few Chickasaws stayed. Even before the 1801 Treaty of Chickasaw Bluffs gave the United States the right to build the road connecting Natchez and Nashville across Chickasaw land, the group had made small land cessions. Indebtedness to such traders as John Forbes and his company added to the pressure the Chickasaws faced to give up land. In 1805, American commissioners James Robertson and Silas Dinsmoor met with Chickasaw leaders near the house of the late Ugulayacabé and secured the first major cession of land to the United States—a large tract south of the Tennessee River. The price was a very low twenty thousand dollars, half of which earmarked to cover the debt to the Forbes company. Other treaties followed over the next three decades, culminating in the 1832 Treaty of Pontotoc Creek, which set in motion the surrender of the remaining Chickasaw lands in the East and the beginning in earnest of their removal to the West. Thousands of Americans streamed in even before final questions regarding the 1832 agreement were resolved.[39] The Chickasaws survived and ultimately prospered in their new setting, but they continue to regard northern Mississippi as their homeland.[40]

CHAPTER SEVEN

Remembering, Recovering, and Representing a Mississippi Past, 1500–1800

Beginning in the fifteenth century, Europeans sailed the oceans of the world as they never had before, encountering new lands and peoples. In 1492, the Spanish queen of Castile, Isabella, decided to support Genoese adventurer and entrepreneur Christopher Columbus's attempt to reach Asia by sailing west. Columbus indeed found land, but of course it was not Asia but rather a continent that was new to most Europeans. A Florentine clerk and inveterate traveler, writer, and publicist, Amerigo Vespucci, claimed to have explored much of southern portions of this continent, including the mouths of the Amazon River and the coastline to the south, and concluded that it was not Asia but rather a *novus mundus*—a new world. Reflecting on what Vespucci had written and claimed to have accomplished, Waldseemüller published in 1507 a tract on cosmography that included maps that depicted what Vespucci described and supported those depictions with more precise calculations of longitude. Waldseemüller's map of the world showed a single continent separate from Asia that bore the name *America*.[1] Some other European expeditions and activities might be noted. In 1498, a Portuguese expedition found an all-water route to India by sailing down the coast of Africa, rounding what came to be called Cape Horn, and continuing on to India. Two years later, an expedition to India led by Pedro Alvares Cabral got blown off course and sighted land that turned out to be the coast of what is now Brazil. Because the Spanish-Portuguese Treaty of Tordesillas, signed in 1494, had identified this portion of America as Portuguese, this contact resulted in a Portuguese colony. The Dutch, the Swedes, the French, and the English soon followed the Iberians across the Atlantic, conducting their own reconnoitering and making contacts. By 1700, the Spanish, French, and English had explored and begun to settle and develop relations with Native peoples in the lower Mississippi River Valley and along the Gulf Coast. New worlds opened up for these Europeans, as they did for the people with whom they came in contact. The first colonial empires of the modern era had been established, defined, and sustained by a rich literature and cartography of travel, "discovery," and economies and polities of trade and bureaucracy.[2]

The degree to which the Spanish and the other Europeans succeeded in creating empires and colonies varied and hence has been and remains discussed and debated. For that part of America that became first the territory and then the state of Mississippi, empire remained elusive. Thus, we characterize colonial Mississippi as a "borrowed" land. Perhaps even more accurately, it was a storied land before the arrival of Europeans and Africans, and it has remained a storied land—only the nature of the stories has changed. When Europeans arrived, they created a different America than that known or understood by its longtime inhabitants. Using new kinds of maps and an abundance of written accounts, they, as Mexican historian Edmundo O'Gorman argues, "invented" an America that constituted an empire of paper—millions of documents recording what Europeans experienced, observed, recommended, and decreed. They thereby added another dimension to Natives' long-standing practices of "emplotting" the land by creating narratives that recorded and gave meaning to where they were, what they were doing, and what might follow.[3]

European newcomers to the Americas encountered much to remember and represent: a varied natural environment and people and all they created—place-names, physical structures such as mounds and buildings, pictorial art, maps, and writings.[4] In what is now Mexico, the newcomers and those who followed were impressed—in some cases even awed—by what they found and set about attempting to decipher and understand it, often to support rationalizations for actions in quest of what some have described in English—perhaps only for the alliterative aspect—as "Gold, Glory, and Gospel."[5] To a slightly lesser degree than those to the south, Native Americans in Mississippi did much to emplot the land, a practice that resulted in more than six hundred Native American place-names in the state of Mississippi.[6]

Some of the counties created from the Choctaw lands ceded in the Treaty of Dancing Rabbit Creek sustained a Choctaw presence via their names: Oktibbeha, Neshoba, LeFlore, Noxubee, and Attala, which derived from a fictitious Choctaw princess, Atala, created by a French romantic writer, François-René de Chateaubriand in an 1802 novella. Chateaubriand later incorporated the novella into his *Les Natchez*, an "epic on the Man of Nature" that shifted the

The Natchez, a painting begun by Eugène Delacroix in the 1820s but not completed until 1835. Delacroix took his inspiration from an episode in François-René de Chateaubriand's 1801 novella, *Atala*, about the Natchez Indians in the wake of 1729. This painting was included in a major exhibit of Delacroix's work by the Metropolitan Museum of Art in New York and the Musée du Louvre in Paris in 2018–19.

focus to the Natchez and "the massacre of the colony in Louisiana." "All the Indian tribes conspiring, after two centuries of oppression, to restore liberty to the New World," he wrote, "seemed to me to furnish a subject nearly as happy as the conquest of Mexico."[7] That work inspired French romantic painter Eugène Delacroix's 1835 work *Les Natchez*, which depicted a young man holding a baby just born to the young woman traveling with him up the Mississippi River.[8]

More than a century later, Mississippi author William Faulkner changed the name of his own county, Lafayette, and surrounding counties to the more Native-sounding Yoknapatawpha. He divided it into regions with river bottoms where the land was rich and dark with soil washed down from surrounding hills when streams flooded. Faulkner's fictional world included both a cotton aristocracy whose members bore such names as Compson, Sartoris, Sutpen, and McCaslin and "plain folk" with such names as Gowry, Quick, Workit, Bundren, and McCallum. Yoknapatawpha encompassed much of the state and the South—both "old" and "new"—with Black Belts where African Americans constituted a majority or near majority.[9] Faulkner also wrote four "Indian stories" set in this land before the Sutpens and their ilk transformed it into cotton fields and towns, among them Jefferson.[10]

Europeans in eighteenth-century Louisiana and Mississippi left behind journals, memoirs, letters, histories, reports, maps, pictures, and fictional accounts. The works of Le Page du Pratz, Dumont de Montigny, and Caillot essentially constitute eyewitness narratives—the authors experienced in one way or another the Natchez events of the late 1720s—but also have an autobiographical dimension that makes them a kind of intermediate form between history and autobiography.[11]

Presbyterian minister James Hall spent eight months in the Natchez Country in 1800–1801, when portions of the area were still nominally Spanish. Based on an account by an unidentified French writer, a report of a US attorney general, and conversations with local settlers, Hall published *A Brief History of the Mississippi Territory*. Hall's 1801 account exhibits many of the same characteristics of both memoir and history as the earlier writings but also anticipates the more detached tone and style associated with later historical writing. Noel Polk has characterized Hall's volume as "much less a complete history of the area than an intelligent and informed historical sketch coupled with a description of some of the many things that fell under Hall's observant eye during his time in the territory." Hall treats such topics as boundaries, the "massacre of the French," the soil and produce, climate, population, and a hurricane. He also noted that a number of Chickasaws were "men of considerable property" and had "a number of slaves," and he identified Wolf's Friend (Ugulayacabé), as "a man of considerable influence in the nation."[12]

In 1851, Albert James Pickett published a more substantial work, *History of Alabama and Incidentally of Georgia and Mississippi*. Born in 1810 in North Carolina, Pickett moved with his family to Alabama in 1818. His father established a trading house and later at least one plantation; Albert studied law but never practiced it. Instead he turned to journalism, writing articles in various publications. *History of Alabama* was his only book, and he spent the last few years of his life promoting it. Among the writers and sources he acknowledges are Jared Sparks, historian and president of Harvard College; Charles Gayarré, author of many books on Louisiana's past; William Gilmore Simms of South Carolina, whom Pickett describes as his "muse"; and two Mississippi historians, John Francis Hamtramck Claiborne (1809–1884) and John W. Monette (1803–1851). Pickett devotes considerable attention to the Soto expedition and credits his major sources as Alexander McGillivray, the otherwise unidentified "Gentleman of Elvas," Hernández de Biedma, and the "Inca Garcelasso de la Vega." In addition to discussing "the terrible massacre at Natchez," Pickett describes the early Mississippi Territory: a place where "the forests began to be extensively felled," "houses reared as if by magic," and "the preacher was zealous in the discharge of his divine mission." His discussion of the events associated with the short-lived Republic of Florida devotes considerable attention to the "daring Kempers," who were "sons of a Baptist preacher."[13]

In 1880, Claiborne, the nephew of W. C. C. Claiborne, who served as governor of the Mississippi Territory from 1801 to 1803, published the first volume of *Mississippi, as a Province, Territory and State, with Biographical Notices of Eminent Citizens.* He completed the second volume, but it and many other manuscripts and documents were destroyed when his house was consumed by fire in March 1884, and he died two months later. Claiborne, Pickett, and Monette were "typical of the numerous 'gentlemen amateurs' of the nineteenth century who composed nationalistic history" that provided readers with "exciting melodrama full of heroes and villains, conspiracies and exposures of plots, triumphs and failures, conquests and defeats."[14] Claiborne waxed particularly eloquent in characterizing the Spanish as "a race of heroes, bold, arrogant, and generous, who believed it their mission to carry the religion of Christ, by conquest, into the territory of the Infidel." He was especially generous in his assessment of Hernando de Soto but noted that Soto's Florida expedition "encountered a race of men as patient, subtle, remorseless and intrepid as themselves."[15] In the foreword to the Mississippi Historical Society's 1964 reprint of Claiborne's work, Mississippi State College historian John Bettersworth (1909–1991) described the author as the "Father of Mississippi History and the author of the best history of the state ever written."[16]

Henry Halbert, a contemporary of Claiborne's who lived among the Choctaws for many years and taught Choctaw children in at least two mission schools, acquired a degree of fluency in the language and served as an editor of Cyrus Byington's dictionary of the Choctaw language. Anticipating later criticisms, Halbert pointed out Claiborne's penchant for putting fine speeches in the mouths of such Indian heroes as Pushmataha that were "nothing more or less than pure unadulterated fiction."[17]

Bettersworth also compared Claiborne with Herodotus, commenting that for both men, "history was a story—sometimes more story than fact." Much of what Claiborne wrote focused on the provincial and early territorial period, and his sources consisted of materials he had collected and "memory." Reflecting what has been characterized as "partisan bias," Claiborne judged people. He concluded that Americans liked Gayoso and that westerners were open to Genet and his mission on behalf of French interests. Andrew Ellicott, however, emerges as a villain. Claiborne attributes the Spanish delay in evacuating posts north of the Thirty-First Parallel to Ellicott, compares him to "the treacherous moccasin, ever ready to strike," and declares that his legacy was "the poisoned shirt of Nessus."[18]

A son of two missionaries sent to Mississippi by the American Board of Commissioners for Foreign Missions in 1820, H. B. Cushman (1820–1904) regarded Halbert as a good friend and acknowledged him as a valuable source for Cushman's major work, *History of the Choctaw, Chickasaw, and Natchez Indians*.[19] Published in 1899, almost twenty years after Claiborne's history, the volume focused primarily on the Choctaws, but as Clara Sue Kidwell points out in her introduction to an 1962 version, Cushman came to be "passionate in his respect for the nobility of Indian people" generally "and deeply affected by their degradation in American society."[20] In Cushman's view, that degradation began as early as the sixteenth century with "that memorable adventurer Hernando De Soto" and continued through the French, English, Spanish, and American periods until removal. According to Cushman, "The Choctaw people, amid all their vicissitudes and misfortunes," managed to become not only "the most dreaded in war of all the North American Indians" but also "the most to be admired in peace for the purity of their friendship and fidelity to truth." The United States, with its sustained "greedy avarice," emerges as the major villain.[21]

Cushman wrote primarily about specific events and characteristics of the people among whom he had lived since a child and considered he knew best. He stresses the Choctaw belief that all land was regarded as common until it was occupied; occupancy determined ownership. If an occupant abandoned a piece of land, it reverted to its previous status as common, but the occupant could return and reclaim it. According to Cushman, the Choctaws and the Muscogees (Creeks) were traditional enemies but sometimes cooperated in a limited way. He also notes the importance of places—rivers, creeks, lakes, rocks, hills, the site of "some incident or adventure of the past"—and the attaching of names to such places or locations as a way to remember them. He also relates an encounter between himself and his brother and a wild boar, the "most dangerous of all wild animals." "For reasons best known to himself," the boar chose to sleep with the "tame hogs belonging to the missionary station, Hebron," over which the elder Cushman had jurisdiction. Cushman and his brother chased the boar on horseback, ultimately tracking and killing it.[22]

As with Claiborne's history, Halbert found much to criticize in Cushman's book.[23] Of Cushman's account of an 1811 meeting between the Choctaws, the Chickasaws, and Tecumseh and other Shawnees as part of the campaign for a pan-Indian movement to resist American threats to their land and traditional ways of life, Halbert concluded, the "nineteen pages of the Plymouth Council given by Mr. Cushman is fiction from beginning to end, and has just about as much historical verity as some other matters in the book." Some of those matters included the location of the meeting, the assertion that several companies of Choctaws had served in the American army during the American Revolution, the presence of Chickasaws, and the "invented" speeches of Pushmataha and Tecumseh.[24]

These authors relied heavily on their and others' experiences and reminiscences as well as on locally available documents. With the exception of Halbert, who lived until 1916, none of these men had easy access to archival material and particularly to the European colonial archives considered essential to the creation of a better-informed memory of the state's past.

Near the turn of the twentieth century, however, such material began to become available in Mississippi and elsewhere in the United States, and historians began to discuss and evaluate how these documents might be used. In 1858, Natchez planter and naturalist Benjamin L. D. Wailes (1797–1862), Claiborne, and others had attempted unsuccessfully to create the Mississippi Historical Society. The effort was revived in 1890, and the organization subsequently advocated the creation of the Mississippi Department of Archives and History (MDAH) to preserve state documents and make them and other materials available with the goal of creating and sustaining a better-informed and more complete historical and public memory.[25]

Simpson County native Franklin L. Riley (1868–1927) played an especially important role in the revived historical society as well as in suggesting changes in the way people might think about, research, and represent the state's past. Riley graduated from Mississippi College and went on to earn a doctorate in history at Johns Hopkins University, at the time "the academic mecca for southern scholars." Riley studied under Herbert Baxter Adams, a leader of the movement to introduce into the United States the "scientific" German method that stressed the importance of writing history based on a systematic and dispassionate analysis of original documentary sources to provide a reasonably accurate representation of the past. Riley's dissertation was not related to Mississippi, in part because he could find no documents to support such a work. He returned to the state and became president of the Baptist Hillman College for Young Women in Clinton and then the first professor of history at the University of Mississippi. In the aftermath of Reconstruction, many southern whites sought to reshape the narrative of the events of that period and of leading to and during the Civil War. These efforts led to the creation of the myth of the Lost Cause, which, as historian Charles Reagan Wilson has argued, became something of a religion. Riley, however, was not among its most fervent adherents.[26]

Riley insisted that history be understood and practiced in a way that put complex questions into perspective through careful analysis of written, material, and oral evidence. He began the *Publications of the Mississippi Historical Society* and included in the first volume an essay on Adams. In 1900, Riley persuaded the state legislature to follow Alabama's lead by creating the Mississippi Historical Commission, which was tasked with inventorying all resources relevant to Mississippi and its history and suggesting measures for their acquisition and preservation. Based on the commission's findings, the legislature created the MDAH in 1902 and tasked it with responsibility for the "care and custody of materials bearing on the history of the state and territory included therein."[27]

Though Riley probably should have been chosen as the new department's first director, the post went to Dunbar Rowland (1864–1937), an attorney from northern Mississippi. An ardent believer in the Lost Cause, Rowland saw an archival institution as important in creating and sustaining that myth.[28] He nevertheless accepted much of European archival theory and used its principles to guide the collection of material, writing, "One of the cherished plans that the Department has in view is the collection of Mississippi historical material, which is preserved in Europe in order that copies may be made and filed as part of the archives of the state." The state archives were organized into three categories—provincial (pre-1798), territorial (1798–1817), and state (1817–)—and became an ample and open institution that in many ways served as a model for other state archives. In addition, Rowland suggested a focus on collecting historical material related to places such as Biloxi, Natchez and Fort Rosalie, Fort Maurepas, Pass Christian, Mobile, Fort Tombecbé, Manchac, Baton Rouge, and Yazoo; Indian tribes; explorations by water; land grants; and descriptions by traders, hunters, and explorers.[29]

Rowland secured one thousand dollars from the legislature for transcripts of documents housed in Europe. He traveled to England and France in 1906, visiting the Public Record Office in London and various archives in Paris to begin identifying documents that would be valuable for understanding early Mississippi history. Transcriptions of these materials were then prepared and sent to Jackson. Though he had used up all his funds, J. F. Jameson of the Carnegie Institution and W. R. Shepherd of Columbia University helped Rowland locate and obtain transcriptions of Spanish documents related to provincial Mississippi.[30]

Rowland's efforts resulted in a trove of valuable materials, including more than thirty volumes of transcriptions from France alone, that eventually grew to vast amounts of microfilmed documents as well. The MDAH's Record Group 24: French Provincial Archives is the most extensive of the three record groups in the provincial series. According to Rowland, the documents came from the Ministry of the Marine's Archives du Ministères des Colonies, Série C-13, Correspondence Général Louisiane (Archives of the Colonial Ministries, Series C-13, General Correspondence of Louisiana).[31]

No complete English translation of all the documents was done, but many were translated, edited, and published in *Mississippi Provincial Archives: French Dominion*, five volumes of which appeared between 1927 and 1984. Under the auspices of the Library of Congress, the Louisiana Consortium was formed in 1970 to obtain on microfilm all of the documents in the C-13 series in the French archives as well as numerous maps, drawings, journals, narratives of sea voyages, and other materials. The microfilms are now available at the MDAH and other institutions in the region.[32]

In England, Rowland focused on the papers of the secretary of state and particularly the records of the British Province of West Florida. He found records of grants of land in Mobile and grants, mortgages, and leases for Pensacola, Natchez, and the Amite and Iberville Rivers. He also found and identified maps, reports of exploration, descriptions of flora and fauna, and material related to Indians, including treaties, boundaries, and disputes. One volume of this material was edited and published.[33] The MDAH has subsequently added more microfilmed documents, mainly from the Public Record Office's Colonial Office 5 America and the West Indies section.[34]

Spanish colonial documents were primarily obtained from archives in Simancas, Madrid, and Seville. The repository at Simancas was established in the fifteenth century and evolved into the main archive of the Spanish Hapsburgs and early Bourbons. When it proved inadequate to house the abundance of material that began arriving in the eighteenth century, the Archivo General de las Indias (Archive of the Indies) was created in Seville. And in 1850, the Archivo Histórico Nacional (National Historical Archive) was established in Madrid. It provided the MDAH with thirty-three rolls of microfilmed documents, the Relaciones Diplomáticas entre España y los Estados Unidos, 1737–1820 (Diplomatic Relations between Spain and the United States, 1737–1820). Later additions to the Spanish Provincial Archives have included microfilm rolls of papers of the Panton, Leslie and Forbes trading companies.[35]

Many other institutions have also collected material relating to the region's colonial history. In addition to universities, such institutions include the Historic New Orleans Collection, the Center for Louisiana Studies in Lafayette, and the Adams County Court House in Natchez as well as Chicago's Newberry Library; the Library of Congress; the research division of the New York Public Library; the Huntington Library in San Marino, California; and the Bancroft Library at the University of California, Berkeley.[36]

In 1927, the MDAH initiated a project to identify and catalog the state's archaeological sites, locating about five hundred village and mound sites before World War II disrupted the effort. A research consortium that included the Harvard University's Peabody Museum, the University of Michigan, and the

American Museum of Natural History in New York revived the work after the war, and Congress's 1966 passage of the National Historic Preservation Act prompted the MDAH to resume active maintenance of the files and sites, and the department was given the power to comment on the potential impact of development projects on cultural resources identified as eligible for the National Register of Historic Places.[37] The act also led to the creation of the MDAH's historic preservation division, which focused primarily on the identification, recovery, and preservation of sites and structures. In 1989, the state's historical archaeologist, Jack D. Elliott Jr., completed a lengthy draft plan for historic preservation of cultural resources, including sites and buildings for the period of European colonization.[38]

In 1948, Mississippi's legislature had added to the activities of local communities and such organizations as the Daughters of the American Revolution by authorizing the establishment of a new Mississippi Historical Commission. Taking a cue from what Riley and others had set forth as a major objective of the first commission, the identification of "Points and Places of Historic Interest in Mississippi," the legislature tasked the commission with identifying and marking historic sites. The placement of such historical markers and even monuments and staging commemorative rituals related to them had become an important activity for such organizations as the Daughters of the American Revolution. Commission members therefore included the director of the MDAH, heads of history departments of the state's colleges and universities, and representatives from the Daughters of the American Revolution; representatives of the United Daughters of the Confederacy were later added. Despite the inclusion of professional historians, the places and events that the commission deemed important often merely reflected current views and opinions.[39]

In the late 1980s, the MDAH initiated a project in which Patricia K. Galloway, an ethnohistorian who had translated and edited the last two volumes of the *Mississippi Provincial Archives: French Dominion*, and archaeologist Samuel O. McGahey explored how the commission had determined the locations of sites to be commemorated. They concluded that much of the research had been hasty and careless. The attitude of members of the commission was indicated in a letter written by Mississippi State College's John Bettersworth regarding the location of a marker for a path: "Don't think I know where Three-Chopped Way really was. . . . I have discovered since my last letter that it will probably not do to put the Three-Chopped marker on Highway 13 W. Instead, it should probably go on Highway 27 south of Tylertown. I knew the reason why when I first made this decision, but now I have forgotten. But what does it matter?" Bettersworth's words may have reflected exasperation rather than indifference—the commission was pressed to act quickly and lacked the funding to do proper research.[40]

A similar example of the commission's penchant for "uncritical mythmaking of popular history" at the expense of academic historical research resulted in the misplacement of the marker for Ougoula Tchetoka, site of a battle during the first campaign of Bienville's 1736 war against the Chickasaws. In 1952, the Historical Commission had identified the location of the village using a 1931 book by journalist E. T. Winston, *The Story of Pontotoc*, celebrating the author's hometown. Although Rowland had published the first volume of *Mississippi Provincial Archives* four years earlier and Winston quoted from Rowland's introduction, he apparently overlooked or chose to ignore those documents.[41] Research into those documents as well as others that subsequently became available indicated not only that the marker for Ougoula Tchetoka and another Chickasaw village, Ackia, had been incorrectly placed but that accounts of what had happened during Bienville's campaign had to be revised.[42]

Recognition of inaccuracies in Mississippi history was not new. Thirty years earlier, National Park Service historian Dawson Phelps had looked into an expedition led by the Marquis de Vaudreuil-Cavagnal, the governor of Louisiana from 1743 to 1753, and found that it never happened. Fourteen authors had uncritically accepted and amplified an 1827 account by Louisiana jurist Francois-Xavier Martin that asserted, without citing sources, "The Marquis de Vaudreuil marched into their country at the head of a body of seven hundred men of the regular forces and militia, and a large number of Indians. He was not very successful: the enemy had been taught by the British to fortify their villages. Each had a strong block house, surrounded by a wide and deep ditch. The colony was badly supplied with field artillery and soldiers skilled in the management of the pieces. The Marquis lost little time in laying sieges, but wandered through the country, laying waste the plantations. He enlarged the fort of Tombecbé, left a strong garrison in it, and returned to New Orleans."[43]

The resources that became available through the MDAH played another vital role beginning in the 1950s when an effort was launched to preserve and restore the Old Capitol in Jackson and make it a modern state historical museum. A few rooms in the New Capitol had served as a sort of museum, but it largely conformed to a nineteenth-century view of museums as little more than "cabinets of curiosities." Among those who played key roles in the restoration plan were Bettersworth; William Winter, who served as governor of the state in the 1980s; and Richard McLemore, president of Mississippi College. MDAH director Charlotte Capers assumed responsibility for planning the new medium for educating the public in Mississippi history, and Bettersworth's high school Mississippi history textbook served as a guide for planning the exhibits.[44]

The museum opened on March 21, 1961, as part of a formal celebration of "Secession Day"—the centennial of Mississippi's secession from the United

States. The event focused on honoring the memory of those who had fought in what the 1959 edition of Bettersworth's text called the "War for Southern Independence," an event that began "like a glorious revolution." The day included a "three-hour-long parade of horse troops, artillerymen with very loud cannons, and infantrymen."[45] Capers rode in an automobile bearing a sign proclaiming the "Mississippi Commission for the War between the States," while students from Central High School carried "the largest Confederate flag in the world," which they had borrowed from the University of Mississippi.[46] The parade also featured three thousand members of the Mississippi Greys, "colonels" commissioned by the state's governor, Ross Barnett. The Centennial Pageant, written by Mississippi College professor Louis Dollarhide and directed by Lance Goss of Millsaps College, depicted the secession convention and was performed in front of the restored Old Capitol. The reenactment concluded with an appearance by "Jefferson Davis," who according to Capers "did very well from the balcony of the Old Capitol despite the fact he had been upset all morning for leaving his beard in the room that had been set aside in the Old Capitol for use of the cast after spending some two hours the night before making it" and subsequently finding "bits and pieces of it in a waste basket." "True to finest tradition of the stage," however, "Jefferson did the best he had to work with, and looked real bearded to an observer who did not know the background of the tensions."[47]

Secession Day coincided with a major protest against the arrest and detention of nine students from Tougaloo College who had attempted to integrate the main branch of the city's public library on State Street by staging a read-in.[48] As historian John Skates notes, "ghosts from Mississippi's racial past had arisen," and those celebrating Mississippi's Confederate past were juxtaposed with those working to change its present and future.[49]

At the museum's opening that afternoon, Capers related, five thousand men, women, and children "lunged through the building," and "madness reigned supreme." "Chains snapped, windows broke, doors rocked on their hinges," a "discouraging note" for those aware that between two and three million dollars had been spent on the restoration as well as those who had spent four years creating the exhibits.[50]

The museum's exhibits largely conformed to the values and expectations expressed on Secession Day. Those for the colonial period celebrated the white European story, although a pirogue provided a conspicuous Native American presence. One diorama depicted "De Soto's Discovery of the Mississippi River," an exhibit complemented by a painting commissioned by Rowland. Another diorama portrayed the 1820 Treaty of Doak's Stand, which had opened 5.5 million acres of Mississippi land to "white civilization." That phrase echoed the text on a small plaque installed on the site of Fort Tombecbé by the Colonial

Dames of Alabama in 1935: "Here Civilization met Savagery and the Wilderness beheld the glory of France."[51]

Beginning in the early 1980s, the museum undertook a major renovation of all of its permanent exhibits. The first exhibit to be updated was the one devoted to the twentieth century, and it was completed by 1984, when the Mississippi Historical Society devoted its annual meeting to the subject of the civil rights movement, with particular attention on Mississippi's 1964 Freedom Summer. The revisions to the exhibits relating to what had previously been represented as the "colonial" period focused on how, in the words of Galloway, who oversaw the effort, to "cast into sharp relief the new role of museums as forums for the discussion and contesting of community identities." She and the staff took the concept of the agora, the central meeting place and market in ancient Greek cities, as their "working assumption for the exhibits to be developed" and sought to enlist participation from "descendants of the communities whose history we were going to tell."[52]

This new attitude toward remembering, recovering, and representing the past was reflected in other historical commemorations starting in the 1980s. In 1982, the Mississippi Historical Society focused on the tricentennial of the La Salle expedition, requiring speakers to contribute written essays to a published anthology that would "move scholarly enterprises ahead."[53] The society's 1991 commemoration of the 450th anniversary of Hernando de Soto's *entrada* also resulted in the publication of an anthology of essays.[54]

The five hundredth anniversary of Columbus's "discovery" of America prompted international discussions of how—or even whether—to observe the event. The museum ultimately chose to do so in a way that stressed the mutuality of discovery and acculturation.[55] Work to revise the museum's "colonial" segment embraced that decision. The new exhibits would illustrate the interaction of Natives, Europeans, and Africans during a period identified simply as "1500–1800," and scholars' contributions to that effort were collected in another anthology.[56] To create an exhibit portraying this "shared history," the project solicited active involvement from members of three communities—Native Americans, western Europeans, and West Africans. As Galloway noted, "We wanted to come up with an exhibit which, while presenting facts correctly as they are understood by academic historians, also included new information and perspectives from within the communities we serve."[57]

The Mississippi Humanities Council made a significant contribution to these endeavors in the context of the 1992 Columbus Quincentenary with *Ethnic Heritage in Mississippi*, a book that added further scholarly support for the exhibit project. Editor Barbara Carpenter observed that the quincentenary afforded an opportunity to reevaluate not only Columbus's legacy but also previous commemorations of his voyages, most notably the 1893 Columbian Exposition, which had enormous influence on "American architecture, museums, entertainment, and the culture in general."[58]

Part 1 of *Ethnic Heritage* focuses on "the original Mississippians." It begins with an essay on "Prehistoric Mississippi" and continues with pieces on the emergence of Indian tribes, removal, and the Mississippi Choctaws in the nineteenth century. Using a word and concept foundational to activities related to the Columbus Quincentenary, part 2 turns to "Encounters: Native Americans, Europeans, Africans." These essays address the three major groups of people who comprised the region's population between 1500 and 1800, all of whom have contributed to the new stories narrated in the exhibits in the State Historical Museum.[59]

Complementing this initiative of the Mississippi Humanities Council, the Mississippi Department of Education and the Mississippi Institutions of Higher Learning obtained financial support from the National Endowment for the Humanities and the Phil Hardin Foundation to hold institutes at which specially created anthologies focusing on the state's Spanish and French heritages were used to help foreign-language teachers "integrate language, literature, history, and culture and thereby bring the humanities content into the classroom." These volumes also provided resources that the museum used to provide content for exhibits.[60]

The new 1500–1800 exhibit opened on April 12, 1997, with a calumet ceremony in the rotunda of the Old Capitol. A ceremonial pipe was lit and passed among representatives of the Choctaw, Chickasaw, Tunica-Biloxi, Spanish, French, British, and African communities. A two-day multicultural festival was also held on the Old Capitol grounds. Some highlights of the exhibit included a five-hundred-year-old canoe carved out of cypress; a video, *On the Edge of Encounter*, depicting the three major cultures around 1500; and a display about the *filles à la cassette* who were sent to New Orleans in 1728 to become brides.[61] An interactive video featured actors portraying eighteenth-century people who spoke in languages that included Choctaw and Arabic. Among those who appeared in the video were Choctaw chief Alibamon Mingo; trader and interpreter Simon Favre; planter and scientist William Dunbar; and Abdul Rahman Ibrahima, the son of the king of Futa Jalon in West Africa who was enslaved.[62] In the words of the project's director, rather than "just another enunciation from on high of another Euro-American presentation of the past," the exhibit told "a story in which all three communities could find themselves and recognize the stake that this past gives them in the present."[63]

Their stories, revisions, and new ones continue.

NOTES

Abbreviations

AGI	Archivo General de las Indias
CO	Colonial Office
LC	Library of Congress
MDAH	Mississippi Department of Archives and History
MPA-FD	*Mississippi Provincial Archives: French Dominion*, ed. Rowland et al.
PC	Papeles de Cuba
PRO	Public Record Office

Introduction

1. Tuskeatokamingo to Lavillebeuvre, April 2, 1793, AGI, PC, file 208, in Corbitt and Corbitt, "Papers from the Spanish Archives," 102. The letter was probably written in English for Taskietoka by someone among the Chickasaws, possibly a trader or another chief. For insight into issues related to the interpretation of such documents, see Galloway, *Practicing Ethnohistory*, 33–54. For context for the document, see James R. Atkinson, *Splendid Land, Splendid People*, 155; Charles A. Weeks, *Paths to a Middle Ground*, 87. Delavillebeuvre had come from France in 1764 as Jean de la Villebeuvre to serve in the French Company of Infantry and remained with it during a difficult period of transition from French to Spanish rule. As recorded on marriage banns published in 1764 in New Orleans, his full French name was Jean Louis François de la Villebeuvre. Villebeuvre was born in Brittany, and his first language was Breton. He acquired other languages, beginning with French and then some Spanish, some Choctaw, and English. As a military officer for the Spanish, he served as commandant of such posts as Manchac and Natchez. He undertook an important 1787 mission to the Choctaws on behalf of the Spanish governor-general of Louisiana (see chapter 6) and shortly thereafter became Spanish commissioner to both the Choctaws and Chickasaws. He lived in Mobile, where he died and was buried in 1797, about three years after Taskietoka's death. For more biographical data, see Holmes, "Juan de la Villebeuvre," esp. 98; Holmes, "Up the Tombigbee with the Spaniards." This volume uses *Delavillebeuvre* and *Villebeuvre* interchangeably. See also Charles A. Weeks, "Politics of Trade." On Taskietoka's death, see James R. Atkinson, *Splendid Land, Splendid People*, 167. On implications of a movement west

following the American Revolution, see Taylor, "Introduction." For further insight into how Indians viewed land, with particular emphasis on the Cherokees to the east and the subject of the nineteenth-century removal, see Garrison, *Legal Ideology of Removal*, 13–58. On Indian and Euro-American views of land and its importance to both, Shoemaker, *Strange Likeness*, 13–34.

2. R. R. Palmer and Joel Colton, *History of the Modern World*, 273–85, discuss the French and Indian War as part of the "Great War of the Mid-Eighteenth Century" beginning in 1748 and concluding with the "Peace of Paris, 1763." For more perspectives on this settlement and its limits, see Calloway, *Scratch of a Pen*, 68–69; Hämäläinen, *Comanche Empire*, 68–73; Mapp, *Elusive West*, 359–437.

3. John Stuart to the Earl of Egremont, Charles Town, June 1, 1763, PRO, CO 5, trans., LC, vol. 65, ms. 118. For more on Stuart and the context of this particular report, see Alden, *John Stuart*, 139, 156–91. Waselkov, *Conquering Spirit*, 18, notes that Creek leaders told the British that lands occupied above the Tensaw by colonists under the French had never been ceded to them but had only been settled on Creek "sufferance." For a discussion of "storied land" with focus on the Choctaws, see Galloway, *Practicing Ethnohistory*, 175–222. For Native American stories or legends of the Southeast, see Lankford, *Native American Legends*, esp. 137–38 for a Yuchi story, "Stealing the Land." For more theoretical discussion of "story" and "emplotment," see Hayden White, *Metahistory*, 5–11; Hayden White, *Content of the Form*, 20–57; Hayden White, *Probing the Limits of Representation*, 37–53. For a northern perspective on attitudes toward land, landownership, and boundaries involving Native Americans and the British, see Taylor, *Divided Ground*, 25–45. On stories as related to history museums, see MDAH, *Telling Our Stories*.

4. Galloway, *Native, European, and African Cultures*; Axtell, *Natives and Newcomers*, 9; Adelman and Aron, "From Borderlands to Borders," 814–16. For names of specific groups of Native Americans as well as a discussion of them, see Swanton, *Indians of the Southeastern United States*. For Mississippi, see Barnett, *Mississippi's American Indians*. Early America as Indian country is the subject of Richter, *Facing East*, 1–10. For an earlier exposition of this perspective, particularly for a French period in what became Mississippi, see Mary Ann Wells, *Native Land*. See also Ethridge, *Creek Country*; Galloway, *Practicing Ethnohistory*, 112. On the subject of land and European "hunger" for it, see Wallace, *Long and Bitter Trail*, 3–13. For perspectives on the word *creole* and the process of creolization, see Domínguez, *White by Definition*, 93–110; Gwendolyn Midlo Hall, *Africans in Colonial Louisiana*, 157–59; Klein, *Creole*, esp. the essay by Febintola Mosadani, "The Origin of Louisiana Creole," 223–39; Dawdy, *Building the Devil's Empire*, 5–6, 86, 163, 249, 288 n.50; Gitlin, *Bourgeois Frontier*, 1–12. On accounts of encounter, see Steigman, *Florida del Inca*. In the context of the five hundredth anniversary in 1992 of Columbus's first trip to what came to be called America, the word *encounter* came to be discussed and used as a way to remember that event and what followed from it.

5. On "landscape" and "dependency," see Richard White, *Roots of Dependency*, 1–96. A discussion of "perspectives on the land" found in what such early European visitors such as Ayllón and Soto recorded, for the South Atlantic region can be found in Timothy Silver, *New Face on the Countryside*, 7–34. See also Garrison, *Legal Ideology of Removal*, 35–36. For a discussion of various schools of interpretation of this region, see Paul E. Hoffman, "Nature and Sequence of the Borderlands," in *Native, European, and African Cultures*, ed. Galloway, 43–55.

6. Kirkpatrick, *Spanish Conquistadores*, 40–46. For more on this subject particularly for Mississippi, see Barnett, *Mississippi's American Indians*.

7. Hubert Herring, *History of Latin America*, 127; Quinn, *North America*, 139–40; Reséndez, *Land So Strange*, 71; Fuson, *Juan Ponce de León*; Turner, "Juan Ponce de León," 4.

8. Turner, "Juan Ponce de León," 4; Kirkpatrick, *Spanish Conquistadores*, 60–109. For an adulatory account of Cortés and the "conquest" of Mexico, see López de Gómara, *Cortés*. For a critical account by one who identified himself as a participant, see Díaz del Castillo, *Discovery and Conquest of Mexico*. For the "invention" of New Spain, see Padrón, *Spacious Word*, 92–136; Cortés, *Letters from Mexico*, 47–159. Cortés's name is now usually spelled *Hernán*, but *Fernando* and *Hernando* were commonly used during his lifetime. See Cortés, *Letters from Mexico*, 10 n.19; Altman, *Contesting Conquest*, 1. For a critical discussion of what is often described as a conquest of Mexico, see Restall, *Seven Myths*.

Chapter 1: La Florida and Mississippi: Early European Contacts and Native Responses

1. Ethridge, *From Chicaza to Chickasaw*, 42–44.

2. For more detailed accounts on precontact and initial contact periods in the lower Mississippi Valley, see for example Carson, *Searching for the Bright Path*; Ethridge, *Creek Country*; Ethridge, *From Chicaza to Chickasaw*; Ethridge and Shuck-Hall, *Mapping the Mississippian Shatter Zone*; Galloway, *Choctaw Genesis*; Charles M. Hudson, Pluckhahn, and Ethridge, *Light on the Path*; Charles M. Hudson, "The Historical Significance of the de Soto Route," in *Hernando de Soto Expedition*, ed. Galloway, 311–26; Charles M. Hudson, *Knights of Spain*; O'Brien, *Pre-Removal Choctaw History*; Ethridge and Hudson, *Transformation of the Southeastern Indians*. There is also an ongoing debate about how many Native Americans actually perished from the European diseases. Establishing numbers is hard but important, though it has little effect on our argument. Native Americans did survive in large numbers, and they remained significant power players in the Southeast at least until the War of 1812. However, because the population centers were hit by waves of disease, cultural changes occurred at catastrophic levels for the Mississippian culture. For estimated numbers of casualties and a rebuttal of these estimates, see Dobyns, *Their Number Become Thinned*; Henige, "If Pigs Could Fly"; Henige, *Numbers from Nowhere*; Henige, *Historical Evidence and Argument*. Soto's name is remembered today with De Soto County and its seat, Hernando. Pictorial and verbal representations also depict him as the "discoverer" of the Mississippi River.

3. The sole exception may be Cabeza de Vaca, who remained a captive of Native people to the west of the Mississippi River for several years. On Cabeza de Vaca, his journey, and related documents, see Adorno and Pautz, *Álvar Núñez Cabeza de Vaca*.

4. There are four known chronicles or narratives of the Soto expedition. Many archeologists, historians, and biographers of Soto and his expedition have critiqued the historical validity and truth of these four sources, and most agree that the account of Luys Hernández de Biedma is the most accurate and complete. We have consequently relied on Hernández de Biedma's account, although the other narratives do have value, in particular for the historical memory of the expedition. For discussion on the sources, see Ida Altman, "An Official Report: The Hernández de Biedma Account," in *Hernando de Soto Expedition*, ed. Galloway, 3–11; Martin Amalcolm Elbl and Ivana Elbl, "The Gentleman of Elvas and His Publisher," in *Hernando de Soto Expedition*, ed. Galloway, 45–97; Patricia Galloway, "The Incestuous de Soto Narratives," in *Hernando de Soto Expedition*, ed. Galloway, 11–44; Lee Dowling, "*La Florida del Inca*: Garcilaso's Literary Sources," in *Hernando de Soto Expedition*, ed. Galloway,

98–154. See also Galloway, *Choctaw Genesis*, 143–45. On the Luna expedition, see Charles M. Hudson, *Knights of Spain*, 422–23. See also the introduction to Priestley, *Luna Papers*.

5. Ethridge and Shuck-Hall, eds., *Mapping the Mississippian Shatter Zone*, 3–10; Wallace, *Long and Bitter Trail*, 18–20. Some scholars distinguish between simple chiefdoms consisting of one dominant village and perhaps six more with a total population of as many as 5,400 and paramount chiefdoms with one chief wielding power and influence over a larger area. Many places such as Coosa and Cofitachequi encountered by the Soto expedition in the middle of the sixteenth century have been identified as paramount chiefdoms. See Charles M. Hudson et al., "On Interpreting Cofitachequi," 468–69. See also Robbie Franklyn Ethridge, "The Native World before New Orleans," in *New Orleans*, ed. Greenwald, 13–29.

6. Ronald Wright, *Stolen Continents*, 90–91; Taylor, *American Colonies*, 15–16. F. Todd Smith, *Louisiana*, 7, has a more modest population size for Cahokia—about twenty thousand—as do Ethridge and Schuck-Hall, *Mapping the Mississippian Shatter Zone*, 5; Ekberg, *Colonial Ste. Genevieve*, 86; Pauketat and Emerson, *Cahokia*.

7. Reséndez, *Land So Strange*, 98–99; Mt. Pleasant, Wigginton, and Wisecap, "Forum," 227.

8. The Mississippi Mound Trail paralleling the Mississippi River includes more than thirty archaeological sites, many of which can be accessed from Highway 61. See the MDAH's Mississippi Mound Trail website, http://trails.mdah.ms.gov/mmt/. On the concept of chiefdom and in particular Moundville, see Paul D. Welch, *Moundville's Economy*. See also Ethridge, *From Chicaza to Chickasaw*, 3–20; Galloway, *Southeastern Ceremonial Complex*; Galloway, *Choctaw Genesis*, 27–74; Dye and Cox, *Towns and Temples*, especially Ian W. Brown, "Indians of the Lower Mississippi Valley"; Brain, *Winterville*. For the term *building blocks*, see Gallay, *Indian Slave Trade*, 23. Milne, *Natchez Country*. Reséndez, *Land So Strange*, 96–100, describes Apalachee as "the largest and most complex chiefdom of the entire Florida peninsula." The Spanish expeditions led by Narváez in 1528 and Soto more than ten years later encountered Apalachee. On the emergence of gathering and agriculture and the particular importance of corn, see Gayle Fritz, "The Development of Native Agricultural Economies in the Lower Mississippi Valley," in *Natchez District*, ed. Steponaitis, 23–47; F. Todd Smith, *Louisiana*, 6–15. On myths related to corn and other staples, see Lankford, *Looking for Lost Lore*, 24–69; for "storied land," see Galloway, *Practicing Ethnohistory*, 175–201.

9. For a general discussion of changes in Native polities for the colonial period, see Patricia Galloway, "Colonial Transformations in the Mississippi Valley: Disintegration, Alliance, Confederation, Playoff," in *Transformation of the Southeastern Indians*, ed. Ethridge and Hudson, 225–47. On the "shatter zone" concept, see Ethridge and Shuck-Hall, *Mapping the Mississippian Shatter Zone*, 1–3. See also Wallace, *Long and Bitter Trail*, 15–29; Galloway, *Choctaw Genesis*, 1–4, 338–60; Carson, *Searching for the Bright Path*, 9–26.

10. With regard to "beginning" or "discovery" or "rediscovery" as associated with Columbus, see Quinn, *North America*, 1–19; Kirkpatrick, *Spanish Conquistadores*, 3; Weber, *Spanish Frontier*, 30–31. See also James Axtell's interpretation that John Locke's characterization of America as the beginning of the world means that the state of nature into which Adam and Eve made their debut was like America. Axtell, *Indians' New South*, 4, modifies that idea as "All of America was Indian" and argues that for the so-called colonial period, the "Southeast remained unmistakably 'Indian' throughout." See also Axtell, *Natives and Newcomers*, 9. European fishermen were harvesting Newfoundland cod in the 1490s. Moogk, *Nouvelle France*, 1. In addition, there are stories of a "Prince Madog" (Madoc, Mdawag) from Wales who allegedly came west in 1170 and spent time in the Mobile Bay region. See Hoole and Moore, *Spanish Explorers*, 42–59.

11. Crosby, "Reassessing 1492"; Crosby, *Columbian Exchange*; Axtell, *Natives and Newcomers*, esp. 295–308. See also Barr, "There Is No Such Thing as 'Prehistory.'"

12. Samuel M. Wilson, *Hispaniola*, ix. See also Samuel M. Wilson, *Indigenous People*; Weber, *Spanish Frontier*, 30–31.

13. For a discussion of the milieu into which Columbus was born and lived, see Fernández-Armesto, *Columbus*, 1–44; William D. Phillips Jr. and Williams, *Worlds of Christopher Columbus*. For others from Italy important in this enterprise of discovery and rediscovery, see Quinn, *North America*, 48–50. See also Gilmore, *World of Humanism*, 28–29. For the quest for patronage, see Kirkpatrick, *Spanish Conquistadores*, 8–15; Fernández-Armesto, *Columbus*, 45–65. For a discussion of the meaning and significance of *capitulaciones* in the Spanish world, see Charles Gibson, "Conquest, *Capitulación*, and Indian Treaties." For an English translation of the *capitulación* granted by Charles I of Spain to Hernando de Soto for his 1539 foray into La Florida, see "Concession Made by the King of Spain." Fernandez-Armesto's *Columbus* provides more biographical detail, as does the earlier Kirkpatrick, *Spanish Conquistadores*, 3–39.

14. Stein and Stein, *Colonial Heritage of Latin America*, 14, question the view that the marriage can be seen as "the birth of the modern Spanish state." The marriage did not result "in the unification of the kingdoms of Castile and Aragon" but rather "in condominium in which the two parts of the 'Spanish Crown' coexisted as separate entities." Vicens Vives, *Approaches to the History of Spain*, 91, describes Fernando's view as the monarchy as "pluralistic."

15. Trouillot, *Silencing the Past*, 110–11; Lockhart and Schwartz, *Early Latin America*, 59–180. For various perspectives on the Reconquista, see William C. Atkinson, *History of Spain and Portugal*, 62–79, 106–17; Herr, *Historical Essay*, 37–41; Vicens Vives, *Approaches to the History of Spain*, 28–95. On the "conquest of America" as a continuation of the Reconquista, see Kirkpatrick, *Spanish Conquistadores*, 13–14.

16. For more on what motivated Spaniards, particularly Cortés, see J. H. Elliott, *Spain and Its World*; Cortés, *Letters from Mexico*, xi–lxxi. For contrasting accounts of the Cortés expedition, see López de Gómara, *Cortés*; Díaz del Castillo, *Discovery and Conquest of Mexico*. See also Hugh Thomas, *Conquest*, 156–57. For a critique of how the Cortés expedition has been interpreted, see Restall, *Seven Myths*. See also Padrón, *Spacious Word*, 98, which describes Cortés's second letter from Mexico addressed to Charles V as a "historical narrative with cartographic ambitions" that enabled Cortés to invent a New Spain for his monarch. Historian James J. Cooke, "France, The New World, and Colonial Expansion," in *La Salle and His Legacy*, ed. Galloway, 81–105, argues that French colonialists were motivated by glory more than by trade, commerce, or a desire for raw materials. Carole Shamas, "The Origins of Transatlantic Colonization," in *Companion to Colonial America*, ed. Vickers, 27–30, uses "Gold, Glory, and Gospel" to characterize much of the content of the promotional literature of the day that explains the motivations of "military adventurers" who dominated the migration of Europeans to America before 1550. Reséndez, *Land So Strange*, 46, offers another perspective on what motivated people to take part in such expeditions, especially the Narváez's ill-fated foray into Florida and points west that began in 1527: "None of the colonists were gold-crazed conquistadores madly brandishing their swords, but rather ordinary men and women with their own struggles and fears and dreams."

17. The treaty extended the line decreed in the papal bulls farther west, giving Portugal access to America. See Weber, *Bárbaros*, 205; Safier, "Confines of Colony," 139, 145.

18. Evan T. Jones and Condon, *Cabot and Bristol's Age of Discovery*, 1–2; Quinn, *North America*, 48–50, 115–22.

19. Magellan (Fernão de Magalhães) was Portuguese and had been influenced by Henry the Navigator and Vasco da Gama. Between 1497 and 1499, da Gama had rounded the southern tip of Africa, explored much of the coast, and reached India. Magellan served the Portuguese in India and Africa and proposed to the king of Portugal and his court a willingness to undertake a voyage to find a western route to Asia. The court was not interested, and Magellan went to Spain, where he found support. For more on Magellan and the Portuguese, see Hubert Herring, *History of Latin America*, 83–88, 134–35; Eccles, *France in America*, 2–3. Historian Paul Hoffman, *New Andalucia*, ix–xi, 3–21, 105–10, argues that Lucas Vázquez de Ayllón's report of finding a *chicora* (land of great wealth and promise) and Verrazano's account of an isthmus leading to the Orient became legends that motivated a generation of European explorers and colonizers to search the southeastern coast of North America for both.

20. See Richter, *Facing East*, 1–10; Taylor, *American Colonies*, x–xii. For more on the importance of revising the myth of westward expansion, see in particular Barr, "How Do You Get from Jamestown to Santa Fe?"; Saunt, "Go West."

21. On the precontact Native civilizations, see Barnett, *Mississippi's American Indians*, chapters 1–2. According to most recent research, the Mississippian cultures Soto encountered were in a down cycle, and Soto's *entrada* accelerated the cultural decline of the Native people inhabiting the area. See also Barnett, *Mississippi's American Indians*, 60–63; Carson, *Searching for the Bright Path*, 9–11; Ethridge, *From Chicaza to Chickasaw*, 60–88; Galloway, *Choctaw Genesis*, 128–49.

22. See Barnett, *Natchez Indians*; Barnett, *Mississippi's American Indians*, chapter 4.

23. De Soto served under Pizarro during the Peruvian episode: see Duncan, *Hernando de Soto*, 116–23. De Soto met with a survivor of the disastrous Narváez expedition, Cabeza de Vaca, while he was in Spain to receive his *capitulación* from Charles V. The knowledge gleaned from that meeting caused Soto to ask Cabeza de Vaca to join his expedition. See Charles M. Hudson, *Knights of Spain*, 44–45.

24. As Padrón, *Spacious Word*, 92–136, has argued, Cortés may have simply renamed the Aztec Empire "New Spain" and hence laid claim to the region for the Iberian monarch, thereby verbally "conquering" the region. He also aimed to enhance his status as well as the legitimacy of his undertaking—the governor of Cuba changed his mind and ordered Cortés to cut short his expedition. When he ignored the order, the governor sent Narváez to stop the effort. Charles I became king of Spain in 1516 and then became known as Charles V as the Holy Roman Emperor in 1519.

25. For a social history of Peru that shines light on Pizarro's expedition, which devolved from conquest into a civil war among the conquistadores and ultimately motivated Soto to abandon Peru, see Lockhart, *Men of Cajamarca*; Lockhart, *Spanish Peru*.

26. Charles M. Hudson, *Knights of Spain*, 32. See also Samuel M. Wilson, *Indigenous Peoples*.

27. Taylor, *American Colonies*, 51–66.

28. On hidalgos, see McKay, *Spain in the Middle Ages*, 47–50, 56–57. See also Charles M. Hudson, *Knights of Spain*, 1–38.

29. Charles M. Hudson, *Knights of Spain*, 32. For an in-depth look at Ponce de León's *entrada*, see Turner, "Juan Ponce de León"; for the influence of slavery expeditions across the Caribbean and the resulting maps that guided de León, see 4–5. A 1511 map identified an island, Bimini, for the purpose of slaving, but de León's 1513 mission was officially licensed for that purpose. See also Weddle, *Spanish Sea*, 185–233.

30. Turner, "Juan Ponce de León," 2.

31. F. Todd Smith, *Louisiana*, 17–18. For a more complete history of the Gulf Coast, see also Davis, *Gulf*, 1–51.

32. Steigman, *Florida del Inca*, 34.

33. F. Todd Smith, *Louisiana*, 18–19.

34. Reséndez, *Land So Strange*, 46; F. Todd Smith, *Louisiana*, 18–20. For the "legendary city," see Taylor, *American Colonies*, 70–72.

35. Charles M. Hudson, *Knights of Spain*, 39–40.

36. Cabeza de Vaca, *Cabeza de Vaca's Adventures*, 7–10; Reséndez, *Land So Strange*, 57–132. Weddle has called the Gulf of Mexico a Spanish sea, which is something of a misnomer (plenty of other Europeans, either in the service of Spain or as part of pirate expeditions, were also present), but Spanish conquistadores indeed dominated the gulf during the first decades of the sixteenth century. See Weddle, *Spanish Sea*.

37. Hoffman, *New Andalucia*, xvi, 87–91; De Soto was already extremely wealthy and well established in Spain through previous expeditions when he decided to explore La Florida. On Soto's thirst for power and glory, see Charles M. Hudson, *Knights of Spain*, 43–47; Taylor, *American Colonies*, 76.

38. "Concession Made by the King of Spain." *Adelantado* was a medieval title that "conferred extraordinary powers to a military leader [and] was used in the New World," a continuing of the tradition born in the Reconquista. Based on a *capitulación*, an *adelantado* was outfitted "with specific rights and interests affirmed and reserved by the crown." See Charles M. Hudson, *Knights of Spain*, 8.

39. Soto likely pursued his mission so doggedly precisely because his future titles were at stake. See Hoffman, *New Andalucia*, 88.

40. "Concession Made by the King of Spain," 183–84. See also Charles M. Hudson, *Knights of Spain*, 45–47.

41. Cabeza de Vaca, in contrast, used Christianity during his captivity to heal his Native captors of diseases he most likely introduced. He introduced Christian symbols like the cross to his captors but made no lasting missionary efforts among the Natives. See Reséndez, *Land So Strange*; Cabeza de Vaca, *Chronicle of the Narváez Expedition*. Soto at least once erected a cross on top of a mound for ceremonial purposes, but he never stayed in one place long enough to make a concerted effort to missionize the Amerindians. See Charles M. Hudson, *Knights of Spain*, 291–92.

42. Barnett, *Mississippi's American Indians*, 123–33.

43. Ethridge, *From Chicaza to Chickasaw*, 4–5.

44. There is considerable debate among historians, archeologists, and anthropologists about the exact route Soto took. Physical evidence is hard to come by, and sources can be unreliable. Charles Hudson has a map of the route that most people now cite, but it has been criticized because it occasionally relies on reports that have proven inaccurate in other areas. For the purpose of this book, Hudson's map is accurate enough. See Charles M. Hudson, "Historical Significance of the de Soto Route"; Charles M. Hudson, *Knights of Spain*. For deeper insight into the particular issues with locating the route and basic problems such as distance measurements, see the introduction to Charles M. Hudson, *Knights of Spain*, as well as an illuminating debate about the location of just one chiefdom, Coosa: C. Clifford Boyd and Schroedl, "In Search of Coosa"; Charles M. Hudson et al., "Reply to Boyd and Schroedl."

45. Weddle, *Spanish Sea*, 213, places 513 soldiers and 237 horses on Soto's ships, but Charles M. Hudson, *Knights of Spain*, 49, counts at least 657 men and 237 horses. Neither count includes

Soto himself or the entourages of the wealthier leaders of the expedition, including slaves. Duncan, *Hernando de Soto*, 243, counts 130 sailors and an entourage numbering 100. We will likely never know the exact number of people who accompanied Soto, but 700 seems plausible. Similarly, the number of survivors is difficult to determine, and all numbers provided here are approximations based on their testimonies, which rarely corroborate one another.

46. Charles M. Hudson, *Knights of Spain*, 48.

47. Ignacio Avellaneda, "Hernando de Soto and His Florida Fantasy," in *Hernando de Soto Expedition*, ed. Galloway, 212–15.

48. Cabeza de Vaca had been part of a previous Spanish expedition that failed miserably in the face of overwhelming Native resistance and natural disasters. Cabeza de Vaca survived in captivity of Natives in the Texas panhandle and was ultimately ransomed by the Spanish. His accounts prompted the last two Spanish missions to find more riches in North America, one of which was led by Soto. Cabeza de Vaca gave his testimony in 1537. See Reséndez, "Land So Strange," 219–20, 300n.4; Duncan, "Hernando de Soto," 215–19. On Cabeza de Vaca's uncertainty about joining Soto, see Hoffman, *New Andalucia*, 89–90.

49. Duncan, *Hernando de Soto*, xxxiv.

50. Duncan, *Hernando de Soto*, 1–200.

51. Charles M. Hudson, "Historical Significance of the de Soto Route," 318; Duncan, *Hernando de Soto*, 296.

52. Robert S. Weddle, "Soto's Problem of Orientation: Maps, Navigation, and Instruments in the Florida Expedition," in *Hernando de Soto Expedition*, ed. Galloway, 225–27.

53. Weddle, "Soto's Problem," 225–27.

54. Weddle, "Soto's Problem"; Duncan, *Hernando de Soto*, 370–84.

55. Weddle, "Soto's Problem," 228. See also Barnett, *Mississippi's American Indians*, 51–53.

56. Joseph M. Hall, *Zamumo's Gifts*, 1–5.

57. Joseph M. Hall, *Zamumo's Gifts*, 1–42; Ethridge, *From Chicaza to Chickasaw*, 11–42.

58. Charles M. Hudson, *Knights of Spain*, 13–15. See also Charles M. Hudson and Tesser, *Forgotten Centuries*.

59. Ethridge, *From Chicaza to Chickasaw*, 11–59; Barnett, *Mississippi's American Indians*, 46–66; Duncan, *Hernando de Soto*, 393–404. *Complex* here refers to the number of subordinated villages—that is, more complex chiefdoms had larger numbers of subchiefdoms under their control. The Chicaza town was likely located on what is commonly called the Black Prairie. "From southwest Tennessee, the Black Prairie forms a distinctive geological and vegetative arc that swings down through Mississippi and into central Alabama. In present-day Mississippi, it cuts from the Tupelo area southeast to the Columbus–Starkville–West Point area and then across the Tombigbee River into Alabama." Ethridge, *From Chicaza to Chickasaw*, 32.

60. Ethridge, *From Chicaza to Chickasaw*, 30.

61. Ethridge, *From Chicaza to Chickasaw*, 30–32.

62. Ethridge, *From Chicaza to Chickasaw*, 38–39.

63. Ethridge, *From Chicaza to Chickasaw*, 37–45; Joseph M. Hall, *Zamumo's Gifts*, 39–40.

64. Duncan, *Hernando de Soto*, 393–401.

65. Luis Hernández de Biedma, *Relation of the Island of Florida*, in *De Soto Chronicles*, ed. Clayton, Knight, and Moore, 1:236.

66. Duncan, *Hernando de Soto*, 398–99.

67. Luis Hernández de Biedma, *Chronicles*, in *De Soto Chronicles*, ed. Clayton, Knight, and Moore, 1:237; Duncan, *Hernando de Soto*, 399–400.

68. Duncan, *Hernando de Soto*, 399–400.

69. Hernández de Biedma, *Chronicles*, 1:237–38. Hernández de Biedma did not identify the group to which these Natives belonged.

70. Charles M. Hudson, *Knights of Spain*, 271–73.

71. Charles M. Hudson, *Knights of Spain*, 238.

72. Charles M. Hudson, *Knights of Spain*.

73. Duncan, *Hernando de Soto*, 402–4.

74. Duncan, *Hernando de Soto*, 419–25.

75. F. Todd Smith, *Louisiana*, 24–25. On the imperial goals of the Luna expedition, see Hoffman, *New Andalucia*, 144–68. Excavations have recently located the original site of Santa Maria de Ochuse in Pensacola. See Pruitt, "Early Spanish Colony."

76. F. Todd Smith, *Louisiana*, 24–25. One example of the difficulties faced by Luna and his expedition can be found in a letter he received from the viceroy of New Spain, Velasco: while looking for Mississippian settlement, Luna and his scouts had a hard time locating villages that corresponded to those described in the reports of the Soto expedition, and the Natives were much more cautious in their dealings with the Europeans. Velasco to Luna, May 6, 1560, in Priestley, *Luna Papers*, 93–94.

77. F. Todd Smith, *Louisiana*, 24–25.

78. Ethridge and Shuck-Hall, *Mapping the Mississippian Shatter Zone*, 1–2.

79. Ethridge, *From Chicaza to Chickasaw*, 68–88; Galloway, *Choctaw Genesis*, 134–60. Galloway is cautious about the influence of disease on the population and cultural changes that occurred, but recent evidence and scholarship seem to contradict her.

80. See Joseph M. Hall, *Zamumo's Gifts*.

81. The best example of continued cultural misunderstanding is the events that led to the 1729 Natchez uprising. The French never understood the Natchez people as a confederation but rather believed that their spiritual leader, the Great Sun, was as much as an absolutist leader as Louis XIV, the Sun King. See Barnett, *Natchez Indians*; George Edward Milne, "Picking up the Pieces: Natchez Coalescence in the Shatter Zone," in *Mapping the Mississippian Shatter Zone*, ed. Ethridge and Shuck-Hall, 388–417; Milne, *Natchez Country*. Despite some of these failures, which also include a misjudgment of the Choctaws and their intentions in the Natchez Wars, the French overall had a better track record with the Natives in the area than the English. But as Rushforth, *Bonds of Alliance*, and others have argued, the French may have done better only because the English Indian slave trade put enormous strains on the diplomatic systems employed by the French. See Gallay, *Indian Slave Trade*.

82. Richard White, *Roots of Dependency*, 34–96; Galloway, *Choctaw Genesis*, 67; Snyder, *Slavery in Indian Country*, 9, 14, 16, 20; Ethridge and Shuck Hall, *Mapping the Mississippian Shatter Zone*, 1–3, 10–42; Gallay, *Indian Slave Trade*, 1–10, 23–39; Rushforth, *Bonds of Alliance*; Carson, *Searching for the Bright Path*, 26. According to Stein and Stein, *Colonial Heritage of Latin America*, 117, "the pre-eminent social legacy of colonialism was the degradation of the labor force, Indian and Negro, everywhere in Latin America."

83. Snyder, *Slavery in Indian Country*, 4–5; Gallay, *Indian Slavery in Colonial America*, 2. See also Lauber, *Indian Slavery*. Milne, "Bondsmen, Servants, and Slaves," 115, argues that both Natives and the European newcomers in the heart of seventeenth-century North America were "enmeshed in unequal relationships" that for Natives included a variety of slaves, some of whom were sold like chattel, and for those who accompanied La Salle between 1669 and 1686 during his expeditions "ranged from contracted *voyageurs* to *donnés* who labored for Catholic missionaries."

84. Glenn R. Conrad, "Reluctant Imperialist: France in North America," in *La Salle and His Legacy*, ed. Galloway, 93–105; Guenin-Lelle, *Story of French New Orleans*, 12.

85. R. R. Palmer and Colton, *History of the Modern World*, 134–39; Knapton, *France*, 125–48.

86. Eccles, *France in America*, 22–59; Quinn, *North America*, 402, 404–6, 411–13, 447–48, 480–84. On France's weakness making it less than a nation and "scarcely a unified kingdom" and the implications for its colonial aspirations, see Moogk, *Nouvelle France*, 53–54.

87. Kupperman, *Indians and English*, 3; Calloway, *Indian World of George Washington*, 22. Some of the English colonies began as or reverted back to proprietorships and royal colonies.

88. Louisiana became what has been described as a colony of the Company of the Indies during the first years of the reign of Louis XV. For the argument that charter-based corporations, proprietary colonies, and merchant-based networks were a particular distinguishing aspect of English colonial efforts, see Roper, *Advancing Empire*.

89. Kenneth J. Banks, *Chasing Empire*, 14–19.

90. Kenneth J. Banks, *Chasing Empire*, xv, 22–27.

91. Eccles, *France in America*, 60–89; Moogk, *Nouvelle France*, 87–119; Gordon M. Sayre, introduction to Dumont de Montigny, *Memoir of Lieutenant Dumont*, 18.

92. On the *coureurs de bois*, see Havard, *Histoire des Coureurs de Bois*. For a biographical sketch of Frontenac, see Havard, *Great Peace of Montreal*, 196–97.

93. Conrad, "Reluctant Imperialist," 100.

94. F. Todd Smith, *Louisiana*, 47–50. For one account of this trip to the mouth or mouths of the Mississippi River, see Jean-Baptiste Minet, "Voyage Made from Canada Going Southward during the Year 1682, by Order of Monsieur Colbert Minister of State," trans. Ann Linda Bell, annot. Patricia Galloway, in *La Salle, the Mississippi, and the Gulf*, ed. Weddle, 29–68. On this account and other sources of La Salle's 1682 expedition, see Patricia Galloway, "The Minet Relation: Journey by River," in *La Salle, the Mississippi, and the Gulf*, ed. Weddle, 17–27; Patricia Galloway, "Sources for the La Salle Expedition of 1682," in *La Salle and His Legacy*, ed. Galloway, 11–40.

95. F. Todd Smith, *Louisiana*, 48; Minet, "Voyage Made from Canada," 56. "This land" came to be interpreted as lands drained by the Mississippi River and called, at least on French maps, La Louisiane. On such "ceremonies of possession," see Seed, *Ceremonies of Possession*.

96. "Memoir of Robert Cavelier, Sieur de la Salle, Addressed to Monseigneur de Seignelay on the Discovery Made by Him by Order of His Regent, Louis XIV, King of France," in *Historical Collections of Louisiana and Florida*, ed. French, pt. 7, 7; Villiers du Terrage, *Louisiane*, 1–10. Louis de Vorsey Jr., "The Impact of the La Salle Expedition of 1682 on European Cartography," in *La Salle and His Legacy*, ed. Galloway, 64–69; Conrad, "Reluctant Imperialist," 102–3; Guenin-Lelle, *Story of French New Orleans*, 12–15; O'Neill, *Church and State*, 11.

97. Falconer, *On the Discovery of the Mississippi*, 3. See also Jay Higginbotham, *Fort Maurepas*, 13–14.

98. Weddle, *La Salle, the Mississippi, and the Gulf*, 5–10. Jean Delanglez, *El Río del Espíritu Santo*, 145–46, concludes that the Río del Espíritu Santo was not the Mississippi River but rather most likely Galveston Bay. For more insight into vacillation on the part of the king and La Salle's flexibility in responding, see Jay Higginbotham, *Fort Maurepas*, 14–15.

99. For an eyewitness account of this expedition and its failure, see Joutel, *Joutel's Journal* (1906). See also Patricia Galloway, "Minet's Journal: The Cruise of the Joly," in *La Salle, the Mississippi, and the Gulf*, ed. Weddle, 71–81; Minet, "Journal of Our Voyage to the Gulf of Mexico," trans. Ann Linda Bell, annot. Robert S. Weddle, in *La Salle, the Mississippi, and the Gulf*, ed. Weddle, 71–126. Perhaps the best secondary account is Villiers du Terrage,

Expédition de Cavelier de La Salle. See also Weber, *Spanish Frontier*, 148–49; Boucher, *Nouvelles Francesbo*, 59–60. For the conclusion of the expedition and what followed, see Cavelier, *Journal of Jean Cavelier.* For the distance between the Mississippi River and Matagorda Bay, see Jack Jackson, Weddle, and De Ville, *Mapping the Texas and the Gulf Coast*, 3. According to Sayre, introduction, 18, La Salle's supporters in Paris, the abbés Claude Bernou and Eusèbe Renaudot, placed the mouth much farther west on the Gulf of Mexico, perhaps confusing it with the mouth of the Río Grande. On "pilot error," see Thomassy, *De La Salle et Ses Relations*, 12; F. Todd Smith, *Louisiana*, 48–50.

100. See Weddle, *Spanish Sea*, xi; Weddle, *Wilderness Manhunt*, ix–xi; Leonard, "Spanish Re-Exploration," 548; Weddle, *La Salle, the Mississippi, and the Gulf*, 4. See also Weddle, *French Thorn*; Weddle, *Changing Tides.* For more on the Spanish reaction, see Jack D. L. Holmes, "Andrés de Pez and Spanish Reaction to French Expansion into the Gulf of Mexico," in *La Salle and His Legacy*, ed. Galloway, 106–28. William Coker, "English Reaction to La Salle," 131, describes the reaction in Spain as "near panic."

101. Weddle, *Wilderness Manhunt*, 248; Wood, "La Salle," 294.

Chapter 2: L'Espérance de Mississippi: The French in Mississippi, 1699–1763

1. Information on Telemann comes from the program notes by Lynn Raley for the Mississippi Symphony Orchestra chamber orchestra program of March 6, 2015, and from notes by Adolf Hoffmann on the score *Corona/Werkreihe für Kammerorchester Nr. 100.* For Law and his plans for Louisiana and France, see F. Todd Smith, *Louisiana*, 78–80; Surrey, *Commerce of Louisiana*, 159–60; Lugan, *Histoire de la Louisiane*, 78–80. For a book-length discussion of Law and his project, see Giraud, *Histoire de la Louisiane Française*, vol. 3, *L'Époque de John Law (1717–1720)*, esp. 3–59 for the Company of the West. See also Winsor, *Mississippi Basin*, 99–110; Moen, "John Law and the Mississippi Bubble"; Buchan, *John Law.* For documents from 1717–19 that present different perspectives on Louisiana in the context of Law's project, see Waggoner, *Plus Beau Païs du Monde.*

2. On the calumet and the fleur-de-lis and their importance for French-Indian relations in lower Louisiana, see Ian W. Brown, "Calumet Ceremony"; Ian W. Brown, "Certain Aspects of French-Indian Interaction." See also Lankford, *Looking for Lost Lore*, 99, 115–18, 122–23, 126, 130, For La Salle's encounters with groups in Arkansas during his 1682 journey, see Sabo, "Rituals of Encounter."

3. Patricia Galloway, "Formation of Historic Tribes and French Colonial Period," in *Native, European, and African Cultures*, ed Galloway, 57; Lankford, *Looking for Lost Lore*, 98–126; Axtell, *Natives and Newcomers*, 24–27.

4. Lankford, *Looking for Lost Lore*, 116.

5. Ian W. Brown, "Calumet Ceremony," 312; Lankford, *Looking for Lost Lore*, 114–15; Leavelle, *Catholic Calumet*; Rushforth, *Bonds of Alliance*, 29–35. In his discussion of place-names in Louisiana, including a "Bayou Calumet," Read, *Louisiana*, 195–96, says that *calumet* derives from the Norman-Picard *chalumet.* On the calumet ceremony as a means to create fictive kinship ties, see Galloway, *Practicing Ethnohistory*, 230–31; Sabo, "Rituals of Encounter," 54. See also Barnett, "Yamasee War," 7–8. The events of 1729 in the Natchez Country that resulted in the deaths of more than two hundred Europeans provide perhaps the most notable use of the calumet and the ceremonies associated with it for purposes of war. For the French governor's account of what happened, see Périer to Maurepas, *MPA-FD*, 1:61–70; Barnett, *Natchez Indians*, 101–25; Lankford, *Looking for Lost Lore*, 116.

6. See Giraud, *History of French Louisiana*, 1:3–13; Waggoner, *Plus Beau Païs du Monde*, 19.

7. Sadler and Christensen, "Jean Philippe Rameau," 780–83; Sadler, "Jean Philippe Rameau"; Jean Philippe Rameau, *Les Indes Galantes*, in Kobbé, *New Kobbé's Complete Opera Book*, 617–20. The title of the final *entrée* of *Les Indes Galantes* is "Les Sauvages." It concludes with the "Danse du Grand Calumet de la Paix." On Amerindians in Europe, especially from early French Canada, see Dickason, *Myth of the Savage*, 205–29; for the eighteenth century, with a focus on "kings," see Shoemaker, *Strange Likeness*, 35–39.

8. Kenneth J. Banks, *Chasing Empire*, 14–42; Allain, *"Not Worth a Straw,"* 1–31, esp. 1, 46; Brasseaux, "La Délaissée"; Knapton, *France*, 153–75, 179–87. Two wars that had both continental and colonial dimensions are the War of the League of Augsburg (1688–97) and the War of the Spanish Succession (1702–13), both of which found France and England opposing each other. See Wallerstein, *Modern World System II*, esp. 28, for the point that between 1450 and 1750, "a world capitalist economy" was created, and 37–71, on an "age of mercantilism." See also R. R. Palmer and Colton, *History of the Modern World*, 190–97; Wolf, *Emergence of the Great Powers*, 15–96; Friedrich, *Age of the Baroque*, 1–31.

9. Giraud, *History of French Louisiana*, 1:3–25; Bekkers, "Catholic Church in Mississippi." On the cartography of early contact in the region, see Galloway, *Choctaw Genesis*, 205–63, esp. 232–43 for Claude Delisle and his sons, one of whom was Guillaume. For more on cartography and "geopolitical competition," see Strang, *Frontiers of Science*, 23, 32, 46–61. Many maps for this period are reproduced in Cumming, *Southeast in Early Maps*.

10. Giraud, *History of French Louisiana*, 1:3–15; Ekberg, *Colonial Ste. Genevieve*, 49–50. For a Spanish perspective on La Salle, see Leonard, "Spanish Re-Exploration." See also Faye, "Contest for Pensacola Bay, Part I"; Faye, "Contest for Pensacola Bay, Part II."

11. Giraud, *History of French Louisiana*, 1:14–16, 48–49; M. de Rémonville, "*Memoir*, Addressed to Count of Pontchartrain, on the Importance of Establishing a Colony in Louisiana," in *Historical Collections of Louisiana and Florida*, pt. 6, 2–3. Richebourg Gaillard McWilliams identifies Pierre-Charles Le Sueur as having been sent to Louisiana "so that he could go up the Mississippi to work or to discover mines in the Sioux Country." See Pénicaut, *Fleur de Lys and Calumet*, 32 n.31. Pénicault describes the "Cioux" as "a nation of nomadic savages more than nine hundred leagues from the mouth of the Missicipy, as far up as the Saut de St. Anthoine." McWilliams identifies that location as "the head of navigation on the Mississippi River, in Minnesota." Pénicaut, *Fleur de Lys and Calumet*, 32 n.32.

12. Giraud, *History of French Louisiana*, 1:6. Tonti, or Tonty, had been born Enrico di Tonti in Italy to Neapolitan parents who moved with their young son to France to seek refuge after an abortive revolt against the Spanish viceroy. Tonti lost his right hand when serving in the military. The hook intrigued Indians, enhanced his status, and endeared him to them. Jay Higginbotham, *Old Mobile*, 54–55; Lugan, *Histoire de la Louisiane*, 37–39; Falconer, *On the Discovery of the Mississippi*, 2–45. For an English translation of Tonti's memoir of the La Salle expedition, see *Historical Collections of Louisiana*, ed. French, pt. 1, 52–78.

13. Giraud, *History of French Louisiana*, 1:8–10; Samuel Wilson Jr., "Colonial Fortifications and Military Architecture in the Mississippi Valley," in *French in the Mississippi Valley*, ed. McDermott, 106–7; Din, "Arkansas Post," 4; Arnold, "Significance of the Arkansas Colonial Experience," 70. During the Spanish occupation, the post assumed the name Fort Carlos III in honor of the Spanish king. Faye, "Arkansas Post of Louisiana: Spanish Domination," 641.

14. Giraud, *History of French Louisiana*, 1:14–34; Lugan, *Histoire de la Louisiane*, 47–56; Moogk, *Nouvelle France*, 81–85; Kenneth J. Banks, *Chasing Empire*, 27–28, 29–30. Allain, *"Not Worth a Straw,"* 46, also sees Iberville as a "would-be Talon," the French intendant in Canada

eager to establish French institutions there. One of thirteen children of Charles Le Moyne, Iberville came to Canada as an indentured servant, had no formal education, and suffered the social stigma of a paternity suit. Iberville, *Iberville's Gulf Journals*, 1–5. Jean-Baptiste acquired the seignorial name *Bienville*, which is used in this book. See Iberville, *Iberville's Gulf Journals*, 37 n.43. According to Coker, "English Reaction to La Salle," 131, the French action produced "hardly a ripple in the English pond." In his *Description of the English Province of Carolana*, however, the English proprietor, Daniel Coxe, included Florida and French Louisiana. For a discussion of Coxe and a reproduction of his map of "Carolana," see Winsor, *Mississippi Basin*, 43–48. For a full discussion of Jérôme Phélypeaux, see John C. Rule, "Jérôme Phélypeaux, Comte de Pontchartrain, and the Establishment of Louisiana, 1696–1715," in *Frenchmen and French Ways*, ed. McDermott, 179–97. For short biographical sketches of Iberville and his brother, Bienville, see Jack D. L. Holmes, "Pierre Lemoyne, Sieur d'Iberville et d'Ardilléres," in *Louisiana Governors*, ed. Dawson, 1–3; Jack D. L. Holmes, "Jean Baptiste Lemoyne, Sieur de Bienville," in *Louisiana Governors*, ed. Dawson, 7–13. For Sauvole, the de facto governor from 1699–1700 while Iberville returned to France after his first expedition, see Patricia K. Galloway, "Sieur de Sauvole," in *Louisiana Governors*, ed. Dawson, 4–7.

15. Axtell, *Natives and Newcomers*, 301. For variations in the spelling of Pénicault's name and a discussion of him as a writer, see Pénicaut, *Fleur de Lys and Calumet*, 5, xxxi–xxxviii. Milne, *Natchez Country*, 13, 19, 28, 141, identifies Pénicault as a "Huguenot journalist" and hence one of the estimated 10 percent of the colony's population that were not communicants of the established Roman Catholic Church despite an attempt through law to exclude non–Roman Catholics.

16. Giraud, *History of French Louisiana*, 1:31–47; Jay Higginbotham, *Fort Maurepas*, 15–64; Samuel Wilson Jr., "Colonial Fortifications and Military Architecture," 107–9; Faye, "Contest for Pensacola Bay, Part I"; Faye, "Contest for Pensacola Bay, Part II"; Zitomersky, *French Americans*, 363; F. Todd Smith, *Louisiana*, 57–60.

17. Moogk, *Nouvelle France*, 12–50. Moogk points out that "wild peoples of the forest" derived from the basic meaning of *les sauvages* in French. For Indian groups identified and others, see the Iberville and Pénicault narratives; Galloway, *Choctaw Genesis*, 309–11. For more on the Biloxis, Pascagoulas, Mobiliens, and many other small Indian groups in the lower Mississippi Valley and Gulf Coast that came to be referred to by the French as *petites nations*, see Ellis, "Many Ties of the Petites Nations."

18. Iberville, *Iberville's Gulf Journals*, 38, 45–48. These Bayagoula and Mougougulasha (Mugulasha) lived in the same village on the west bank of the Mississippi sixty-four leagues from its mouth: Iberville, *Iberville's Gulf Journals*, 45 n.59; Giraud, *History of French Louisiana*, 1:32. For a detailed representation of Massacre Island and an explanation of its name by Antoine Simon Le Page du Pratz, who arrived in the region in 1718, see his *Histoire de la Louisiane* (1758), written after his return to France in 1734 and translated into English as *The History of Louisiana*, which was published in London in 1763 with a different title and deleted and altered text as a way to claim, as Gordon Sayre puts it, Louisiana and its history for the English. The English translation provides a description of Massacre Island on pages 14–15. Sayre, "Plotting the Natchez Massacre," 385–86.

19. Pénicaut, *Fleur de Lys and Calumet*, 5, 28. See also Kenneth J. Banks, *Chasing Empire*, 101–26.

20. Axtell, *Natives and Newcomers*, 32.

21. Shoemaker, *Strange Likeness*, 11; Shoemaker, "How the Indians Got to Be Red." See also Nash, *Red, White, and Black*, 104–11. Milne, *Natchez Country*, 2, finds "discourse of racial categories" useful as a focal argument. His book expands "on Shoemaker's work by exploring

why the Indians decided to become 'red' in Natchez Country and why they decided to do so in that particular place with such determination."

22. Galloway, "Talking with Indians"; Axtell, *Natives and Newcomers*, 46–78; Iberville, *Iberville's Gulf Journals*, 93; Galloway, "Talking with Indians," 111–13. According to Rule, "Jérôme Phélypeaux," 187, Father Anastase Douay, better known as Père Anastase, was "a very pious man" but "offended" Iberville, who found the more worldly Jesuits better able to learn quickly native languages and thereby help spread the Pax Gallica among them. On the importance of gift exchange, see Khalil Saadani, "Gift Exchange between the French and Native Americans in Louisiana," trans. Joanne Burnett, in *French Colonial Louisiana and the Atlantic World*, ed. Bond, 43–64; Lewis Hyde, *Gift*, 1–5.

23. Zitomersky, *French Americans*, 363; Pénicaut, *Fleur de Lys and Calumet*, 29–30; Axtell, *Natives and Newcomers*, 69–70.

24. Pénicaut, *Fleur de Lys and Calumet*, 68 n.15. According to Pénicaut, *Fleur de Lys and Calumet*, 79, "Little St. Michel, who already spoke the language of these savages quite well, was kept at home" after another visit with "these savages" in 1703. Iberville, *Iberville's Gulf Journals*, 176. See Galloway, "Talking with Indians," 14; Maduell, *Census Tables*, 6. Ethridge, *From Chicaza to Chickasaw*, 203, says the boy given to the Chickasaws had been with the Houmas to learn some of their language. He may have been the "little French boy" left with the Bayagoula in 1700 just before Iberville departed to continue on to the Houmas on the Mississippi River. Pénicaut, *Fleur de Lys and Calumet*, 25.

25. Galloway, *Practicing Ethnohistory*, 225–44; Galloway, "Talking with Indians"; Galloway, *Choctaw Genesis*, 322.

26. St. Jean, "Squirrel King," 343.

27. Samuel Wilson Jr., "Colonial Fortifications and Military Architecture," 103.

28. Zitomersky, *French-Americans*, 366. For an assessment that Iberville's Canadian background led him to value Native support in the choice of a site for an effective post, see O'Neill, *Church and State*, 22.

29. O'Neill, *Church and State*, 369–71; Burton and Smith, *Colonial Natchitoches*, 1–19; Rule, "Jérôme Phélypeaux," 188. The French occupation of the western third of the Caribbean island that Columbus had chosen for his first settlement had been effectively established by 1659 but was not acknowledged by the Spanish until the Treaty of Ryswick of 1697 that ended the War of the League of Augsburg. The French called their portion *Saint-Domingue*. R. R. Palmer and Colton, *History of the Modern World*, 192; Weber, *Spanish Frontier*, 156; Hubert Herring, *History of Latin America*, 423.

30. Jack D. Elliott Jr., "Fort of Natchez," esp. 164–65; Meinig, "Continuous Shaping of America," 1186–87, 1190.

31. Calloway, *New Worlds for All*, 178–94. For more on the phrase and concept *New World* applied specifically to the Catawbas, see Merrell, *Indians' New World*.

32. On Fort de Mississippi, see Giraud, *History of French Louisiana*, 1:40–41, 46–47; Pénicaut, *Fleur de Lys and Calumet*, 23, 30–31; Iberville, *Iberville's Gulf Journals*, 120. An account of the meeting with the English ship opens Powell, *Accidental City*, 1. Iberville died in the summer of 1706 of yellow fever in Havana, Cuba. Jay Higginbotham, *Old Mobile*, 284–85. For more insight into the Spanish-French rivalry on the Gulf Coast, see Weddle, *La Salle, the Mississippi, and the Gulf*; Weddle, *French Thorn*; Weddle, *Wilderness Manhunt*; Weddle, *Spanish Sea*.

33. Samuel Wilson Jr., "Colonial Fortifications and Military Architecture," 109; Jay Higginbotham, *Old Mobile*, 26–52; Blitz and Mann, *Fisherfolk, Farmers, and Frenchmen*, 64; Faye, "Contest for Pensacola Bay, Part I," 176–77; Zitomersky, *French Americans*, 366.

34. Zitomersky, *French Americans*, 366; Richard White, *Roots of Dependency*, 29. Faye, "Contest for Pensacola Bay, Part I," 176–77, points out that despite rivalry for territory, French Mobile and Spanish Pensacola maintained "personal relations of friendly character throughout the War of the Spanish Succession."

35. Faye, "Contest for Pensacola Bay, Part I."

36. Richard White, *Roots of Dependency*, 442–48.

37. D'Artaguette to Pontchartrain, Louisiana, August 18, 1708, in *MPA-FD*, 2:33–37. D'Artaguette told Pontchartrain that he prohibited the Canadian soldiers from going. For more information about D'Artaguette, see *MPA-FD*, 1:56 n.1; for more information with his complete name spelled differently, see Giraud, *History of French Louisiana*, 1:126. For a lengthy discussion of hostile English and Indian activity directed against both the French and the Spanish, see Ethridge, *From Chicaza to Chickasaw*, 204–31. The dauphin, who became Louis XV of France in 1715, was born in 1710. Fort Louis on the Mobile River replaced Maurepas as the Louisiana capital from 1702 to 1711 but was then abandoned and replaced by Fort Condé on Mobile Bay, where the present city of Mobile is located, until 1719. According to Blitz and Mann, *Fisherfolk, Farmers and Frenchmen*, 64, storms and flood damage then led the French to reestablish the "old fort" on Biloxi Bay as a capital. In 1721, a site across the bay was chosen to be Nouveau Biloxi and construction begun, and the following year the capital was moved to New Orleans. *MPA-FD*, 3:18–19 n.2.

38. See F. Todd Smith, *Louisiana*. For specific forts and communities associated with them, see Faye, "Arkansas Post of Louisiana: French Domination"; Faye, "Arkansas Post of Louisiana: Spanish Domination"; Arnold, *Arkansas Post*; Jack D. Elliott Jr., "Fort of Natchez"; Barnett, "Yamasee War." For Fort St. Pierre, see Jack D. Elliott Jr., *Comprehensive Plan*, 29–42; Ian W. Brown, "Certain Aspects of French-Indian Interaction," 22–24. For Fort Toulouse, see Daniel H. Thomas, *Fort Toulouse*. For Natchitoches, see Burton and Smith, *Colonial Natchitoches*. For Fort Tombecbé, see Richard White, *Roots of Dependency*, 60, 75; *MPA-FD*, 4:158 n.3.

39. For more detailed and varied accounts of this enterprise, see Crane, *Southern Frontier*, 68–74; Crouse, *Lemoyne d'Iberville*, 168–79; Jay Higginbotham, *Old Mobile*, 53–80; Patricia Galloway, "Henri de Tonti du Village des Chacta, 1702: The Beginning of the French Alliance," in *La Salle and His Legacy*, ed. Galloway, 146–75; Mary Ann Wells, *Native Land*, 76–79; Etheridge, *From Chicaza to Chickasaw*, 146–204.

40. Galloway, "Henri de Tonti"; Crane, *Southern Frontier*, 68–74; Crouse, *Lemoyne d'Iberville*, 235–41; TePaske, "French, Spanish, and English Indian Policy," 24–26; Jay Higginbotham, *Old Mobile*, 57, 60–68. Ethridge, *From Chicaza to Chickasaw*, 200–201, sees evidence of what Richard White, *Roots of Dependency*, 34–68, describes as a "playoff" system working in Tonti's negotiations for the release of the Choctaw boy. The boy was probably destined to be sent to Charleston, which in the words of Steven Deyle, *Carry Me Back*, 22, had emerged by the end of the eighteenth century as "the slave-trading center of North America."

41. Jay Higginbotham, *Old Mobile*, 76–80; Ethridge, *From Chicaza to Chickasaw*, 202–4. The boy may have been the St. Michel mentioned earlier. See Iberville, *Iberville's Gulf Journals*, 97, 176; Pénicaut, *Fleur de Lys and Calumet*, 68, 71–76, 79.

42. Pontchartrain to Bienville, Versailles, January 30, 1704, and Bienville to Pontchartrain, Fort Louis of Louisiana, September 6, 1704, *MPA-FD*, 3:15, 18–24. On the efforts to create a Pax Gallica, see Jay Higginbotham, *Old Mobile*, 53–68. On threats coming from the Carolinas, see Crane, *Southern Frontier*, 45–46, 68, 70–72; Giraud, *History of French Louisiana*, 1:76–78, 200–201.

43. Crane, *Southern Frontier*, 71–107; Giraud, *History of French Louisiana*, 1:103–245. On the War of the Spanish Succession, see R. R. Palmer and Colton, *History of the Modern World*, 192–97. On what might be seen as almost continuous warfare beginning with the French war with the Dutch in 1688 and continuing into the eighteenth century, see Wallerstein, *Modern World System II*, 244.

44. R. R. Palmer and Colton, *History of the Modern World*, 171.

45. R. R. Palmer and Colton, *History of the Modern World*, 105.

46. R. R. Palmer and Colton, *History of the Modern World*, 108–12. Surrey, *Commerce of Louisiana*, 155, writes that between 1702 and 1706 "colonial officials, without royal orders, took out of" the warehouse built on Dauphin Island "47,807 livres, eleven sols, eight deniers worth of merchandise, some of which sold at a profit on the cost in France of 600 per cent." For more on how Iberville, Bienville, and their two brothers used Queen Anne's War for personal profit and gain, see Barnett, "Yamasee War," 5–6. For a general discussion of the movement, licit and illicit, of people and goods into and out of French Louisiana, see Alexandre Dubé, "The Seller King: Revisiting Control and Authority in French Louisiana," in *European Empires in the American South*, ed. Ward, 87–121.

47. Pontchartrain to Bienville, Versailles, June 30, 1707, and Pontchartrain to de La Salle, Versailles, June 20, 1707, *MPA-FD*, 3:67–71.

48. The perspectives of Marcel Giraud and Daniel Usner differ somewhat on the interaction that took place between the newcomers from Europe and Canada. For this early period, see, for example, Giraud, *History of French Louisiana*, 1:232–35; Usner, *Indians, Settlers, and Slaves*, esp. 24–27. For a negative view of the colony in 1718, see Le Page du Pratz, *History of Louisiana*, 5: "The colony had but a scanty measure of commodities, and money scarcer yet: it was rather in a state of languor, than of vigorous activity, in one of the finest countries in the world; because impossible for it to do the laborious works, and make the first advances, always requisite in the best lands."

49. Usner, "From African Captivity to American Slavery," 25; Moogk, "Reluctant Exiles," 504.

50. Moogk, "Reluctant Exiles." For detailed discussions of women in early colonial Louisiana, see Allain, *"Not Worth a Straw,"* 83–88; Baker, "Cherchez les Femmes"; Hawthorne, "That Certain Piece of Furniture"; Gould, "Bienville's Brides."

51. "Census of Louisiana by de La Salle," *MPA-FD*, 2:31–32. For more census data see Maduell, *Census Tables*. For French land policy, see Galloway, *Private Land Cessions*, 5–9.

52. Giraud, *History of French Louisiana*, 1:146–67, esp. 164–67.

53. Caillot, *Company Man*, xxv; Baker, "Cherchez les Femmes," 23. For a Canadian perspective on France's varied ethnicities, provinces, and regions and the difficulty in finding settlers, see Moogk, *Nouvelle France*, 53–54, 87–120. For the regional patois of the French and Spanish newcomers, see Axtell, *Natives and Newcomers*, 47–49.

54. Pontchartrain to Bienville, Marly, November 4, 1705 and Bienville to Pontchartrain, Louisiana, April 10, 1706, *MPA-FD*, 3:25–35.

55. Pontchartrain to Bienville, Versailles, January 30, 1704, *MPA-FD*, 3:15–16. According to Bienville, the *Pélican* arrived in July with twenty girls aboard, and all of them married the Canadians "in a position to support them." He also reported that the *Pélican* also brought from Havana "the plague" that resulted in the deaths of "two officers and twenty men and two women of our fort." Bienville to Pontchartrain, Fort Louis of Louisiana, September 6, 1704, *MPA-FD*, 3:24. Baker, "Cherchez les Femmes," 25, says that the *Pélican* brought twenty-three women accompanied by two families. See also Barnett, *Natchez Indians*, 58; Barnett, "Yamasee War," 5–6; Milne, *Natchez Country*, 54–55; Surrey, *Commerce of Louisiana*, 157.

56. Pontchartrain to Bienville, Versailles, January 30, 1704, *MPA-FD*, 3:17.

57. Pritchard, *In Search of Empire*, 381, 421–22. See also Allain, *"Not Worth a Straw,"* 1.

58. "The Letters Patent Granted by the King of France to M. Crozat," in Joutel, *Joutel's Journal* (1896). To persuade Crozat to accept the offer, the king turned to Cadillac, founder of the French post at Detroit. His memorandum and another report of Louisiana painted for Crozat an attractive picture of the commercial opportunities and mining resources awaiting successful exploitation. Giraud, *History of French Louisiana*, 1:249. See also Allain, *"Not Worth a Straw,"* 60–61; Lugan, *Histoire de la Louisiane*, 73–78.

59. For Louisiana as a "company colony," with particular focus on the Company of the Indies after Crozat, see Greenwald, *Marc-Antoine Caillot*, esp. chapter 5.

60. Giraud, *History of French Louisiana*, 1:250–55; Pontchartrain to Bienville, Versailles, December 21, 1712, *MPA-FD*, 3:173–74. For more on Crozat, see Milne, *Natchez Country*, 54–55. For the limited modification of prices he charged and a progression in his thinking about population, see Giraud, *History of French Louisiana*, 2:46–49, 64–66. For the terms of Crozat's grant, see Surrey, *Commerce of Louisiana*, 157. Cadillac found at least one occasion to express reservations about Crozat. See Cadillac to Pontchartrain, Dauphin Island, February 2, 1716, *MPA-FD*, 3:201–3; "Abstracts of Letters from Cadillac, Dirigoin, and Bienville to Crozat," Louisiana, October 1713, *MPA-FD*, 3:174–78. In 1713, Dirigoin, or Pierre Deregoin, was a director and a controller of the Company of Louisiana, one of the complex of companies that ultimately became the Company of the Indies. Giraud, *History of French Louisiana*, 1:305. Allain, *"Not Worth a Straw,"* 61–62. For the evolution of Crozat's thinking and actions, see Giraud, *History of French Louisiana*, 2:38–49. According to Mathé Allain, "Antoine de Lamothe, Sieur de Cadillac," in *Louisiana Governors*, ed. Dawson, 13–17, Cadillac, who served from 1713 to 1716 as governor and concluded that Louisiana was "not worth a straw," "carefully engineered his own social ascension, with the help of shady dealings, falsified credentials, and bald-faced lies." See also Havard, *Great Peace of Montreal*, 191–92. For a more positive assessment of Cadillac, see Barnett, "Yamasee War," 7. The word *ordonnateur* in the term *commissaire ordonnateur* comes from *ordonnance*, meaning "rational political decrees that led to the regimentation of life under Louis XIV." Bernard Bosanquet quoted in Westfall, *Architecture, Liberty, and Civic Order*, 85. Another term for this official was *intendant*, a "person drawn from the noblesse de robe," in the words of Allain, *"Not Worth a Straw,"* 70, "who administered the finances and supervised the courts of law." The Spanish had a similar official. See also Guenin-Lelle, *Story of French New Orleans*, 19.

61. Jack D. Elliott Jr., *Comprehensive Plan*, 25–38; Jack D. Elliott Jr., "Fort of Natchez," 167–69; Usner, *Indians, Settlers, and Slaves*, 28; Milne, *Natchez Country*, 56. See "The Origin of Rosalie?" Jack Elliott to Stanley Nelson, August 24, 2009, in "Fort Rosalie," Subject File, MDAH. For more on the Phélypeaux de Pontchartrain family, see Chapman, *Private Ambition and Political Alliances*.

62. Giraud, *History of French Louisiana*, 2:155–56; Giraud, *Histoire de la Louisiane Française*, 366–69. See also Samuel Wilson Jr., "French Fortification at Fort Rosalie, Natchez," in *La Salle and His Legacy*, ed. Galloway, 199–201.

63. Greenwald, *Marc-Antoine Caillot*, 130–32.

64. See Barnett, *Natchez Indians*, 65–72; Barnett, "Yamasee War," 4–12; Milne, *Natchez Country*, 60–68. Swanton, *Indian Tribes of the Lower Mississippi Valley*, 193–205, uses an older translation of Pénicault's account of the First Natchez War. For the more recent translation, see Pénicaut, *Fleur de Lys and Calumet*, 168–82.

65. For Crozat's *mémoire* and related documents leading to the creation of a Company of the West, along with the decision to grant Crozat his request for termination, see Giraud, *Histoire de la Louisiane Française*, 3–15; Allain, *"Not Worth a Straw,"* 66. For a slightly different description of the evolution of what eventually became the Company of the Indies, see Waggoner, *Plus Beau Païs du Monde*, 3; Guenin-Lelle, *Story of New Orleans*, 17–22. Louis XIV died in 1715, when his successor, Louis XV, was only five years old. Louis XIV's will provided for a regency council until the king came of age in 1723. For perspectives on this time of transition and what followed, see R. R. Palmer and Colton, *History of the Modern World*, 265–66; Douglas Johnson, *Concise History of France*, 96.

66. See Giraud, *Histoire de la Louisiane Française*; F. Todd Smith, *Louisiana*, 78–80; Baker, "Cherchez les Femmes," 25; Winsor, *Mississippi Basin*, 99–110.

67. For advertisements, see Waggoner, *Plus Beau Païs du Monde*, 35–87.

68. Winsor, *Mississippi Basin*, 110.

69. Winsor, *Mississippi Basin*, 110; Giraud, *Histoire de la Louisiane Française*, 60–87; Moen, "John Law and the Mississippi Bubble"; Kindelberger, *Financial History of Western Europe*, 98–100. Milne, *Natchez Country*, 81, describes Law's direction as central to the new plan, including the enlargement of the Company of the West into the Company of the Indies. Villiers, du Terrage, "History of the Foundation," 171, describes Law as director of the bank of the company and lists other officials who included Diron d'Artaguette. See also Allain, *"Not Worth a Straw,"* 67. For more detail on Law's intervention, his letters patent, and the metamorphosis of the Company of the West into the Company of the Indies, see Giraud, *Histoire de la Louisiane Française*, 16–59.

70. Merchants in such Atlantic ports as La Rochelle had generally supported Law's monopolistic company as a way to revive a French economy, but after the company's collapse, that support turned to opposition. John G. Clark, *La Rochelle*, 15. The collapse of Law's venture may help to explain the assessment made by another Scotsman, Adam Smith, some fifty years later: "The government of an exclusive company of merchants is, perhaps, the worst of all governments for any country whatever." Adam Smith, *Inquiry into the Causes of the Wealth of Nations*, book 4, 81.

71. Kondert, *Germans of Colonial Louisiana*, 22–23; Kondert, *Charles Frederick D'Arensbourg*, 12–15.

72. "Gentlemen of the Council of Louisiana," May 25, 1725, *MPA-FD*, 2:465. See also Giraud, *Histoire de la Louisiane Française*, 129–53; Deiler, *Settlement of the German Coast*; Le Conte and Conrad, "Germans in Louisiana"; Kondert, *Charles Frederick D'Arensbourg*.

73. Giraud, *Histoire de la Louisiane Française*, 221–81; Gould, "Bienville's Brides," 389.

74. Caillot, *Company Man*, xxv. According to one estimate, just over 7,000 immigrants arrived between 1717 and 1721, including 1,215 women and 502 children, but Barker, "'Cherchez les Femmes,'" 26, argues that those numbers are high. Conrad, *First Families of Louisiana*, 1:ii, concludes that between 1717, when Crozat abandoned his concession, and 1731, "there occurred a most significant migration to Louisiana": "thousands of Europeans, mainly Frenchmen and Germans but also Englishmen, Irishmen, and Bohemians, quit their native land in search of a new life." Faber, *Building the Land of Dreams*, 27–28, estimates that in 1732 there were "about 6,000 people living in French Louisiana," about two-thirds of them enslaved. Most lived in or near New Orleans. Population stagnated throughout the remainder of the French period. For women migrants, see Hawthorne, "That Certain Piece of Furniture."

75. Powell, *Accidental City*, 4, describes the establishment of New Orleans as an "unintended consequence" of the collapse of Law's venture. Villiers du Terrage, "History of the

Foundation," 169. On "the founding of the capital of Louisiana," see Guenin-Lelle, *Story of New Orleans*, 22–31; Cécile Vidal, "The Founding of New Orleans in Imperial and Atlantic Perspectives: A Caribbean Port City," in *New Orleans*, ed. Greenwald, 30–43, esp. 33 for Louisiana coming to be referred to more often as "le Mississippi."

76. Greenwald, *New Orleans*, 163; Iberville, *Iberville's Gulf Journals*, 57; Powell, *Accidental City*, 1.

77. Villiers du Terrage, "History of the Foundation," 173; Bienville to the Navy Council, Fort Louis of Louisiana, June 12, 1718, *MPA-FD*, 3:228; Faye, "Contest for Pensacola Bay, Part II," 312.

78. On concerns about flooding and the need for levees, see Pickett, *History of Alabama*, 221; Bénard de La Harpe, *Historical Journal*, 161, 165. Some evidence suggests that Bénard de La Harpe was not the author of the *Historical Journal* (Bénard de La Harpe, *Historical Journal*, 1). See also Jack D. Elliott Jr., *Comprehensive Plan*, 11.

79. Dumont de Montigny, *Memoir of Lieutenant Dumont*, 167–68; Bienville to the Council, New Orleans, February 1, 1723, *MPA-FD*, 3:343.

80. Caillot, *Company Man*, 78. For more description of the city in the context of Caillot's arrival, see Greenwald, *Marc-Antoine Caillot*, esp. 115–18.

81. Quoted in Guenin-Lelle, *Story of French New Orleans*, 78.

82. Guenin-Lelle, *Story of French New Orleans*, 78; Dawdy, *Building the Devil's Empire*, 1–2. On the Ursulines, see Emily Clark, *Masterless Mistresses*.

83. Giraud, *Histoire de la Louisiane Française*, 201, uses the word *bourgade* to describe the built-up areas of both Mobile and New Orleans during the time of the new *régie*, from 1723, when Louis XV replaced the regency, until 1731, when the Company of the Indies withdrew from Louisiana. See also Vidal, "Founding of New Orleans," 33.

84. Bénard de La Harpe, *Historical Journal*, 194, reports this division as one of the regulations for the governance of Louisiana that arrived in the province in April 1722. The parts of Louisiana as defined by the French administrators were New Orleans, Biloxi, Mobile, Alibamons, the Natchez, Yazoos, the Natchitoches, the Arkansas, the Illinois.

85. See Jack D. Elliott Jr., "Fort of Natchez," esp. 165; Meinig, "Continuous Shaping of America," 1186–87. For the transformation of Natchez into a city as part of a Spanish empire, see Jack D. Elliott Jr., "City and Empire."

86. Jack D. Elliott Jr., "The Fort of Natchez," 165; Meinig, *Shaping of America*, 65–76.

87. Milne, *Natchez Country*, 7.

88. *Pipe Dreams*; Milne, *Natchez Country*, 158–59. Layton, "Indian Country to Slave Country," 29–30, focuses on the failure of this interaction, caused mainly by the newcomers and their eagerness to seize land from the Natchez Indians to use for the production of tobacco, foodstuffs, and pasture for livestock.

89. Iberville, *Iberville's Gulf Journals*, 126; du Ru, *Journal of Paul du Ru*, 14; Milne, *Natchez Country*, 15.

90. Barnett, *Natchez Indians*, 75.

91. Barnett, *Natchez Indians*, 77.

92. Prévost, *Histoire*; Prévost, *Manon Lescaut*. *Manon Lescaut* was published four years before the first performance of Rameau's *Les Indes Galantes*. The novel is set between 1717 and 1722 (Prévost, *Manon Lescaut*, xiii). See also Gould, "Bienville's Brides," 392–94. According to Brereton, *Short History of French Literature*, 122–24, the story of des Grieux and Manon formed part of the seventh volume of a collection of stories by Prévost, *Mémoires d'un homme de qualité*, but is now the only one for which he is remembered. Prévost describes New Orleans as not much more than rows of miserable huts, a sharp contrast with

the town described by Dumont, who arrived at about the same time, and by Caillot, who arrived ten years later. See Dumont, *Memoir of Lieutenant Dumont*, 167–69; Caillot, *Company Man*, 77–84. For the deportation of women and Prévost's 1731 eighteenth-century best seller, see Yeven Terrien, "Forced European Migrants and Soldiers in French Colonial New Orleans," in *New Orleans*, ed. Greenwald, 84–88. On Puccini's use of the Prévost story for his opera *Manon Lescaut*, which was first performed in Turin in 1893, see Kobbé, *New Kobbé's Complete Opera Book*, 1154–57.

93. Milne, *Natchez Country*, 83–85.

94. Milne, *Natchez Country*, 85–86.

95. For the African slave trade and Louisiana, see Gwendolyn Midlo Hall, *Africans in Colonial Louisiana*, 381–97. For a critical assessment of slave origins as reported by Hall, see Din, *Spaniards, Planters, and Slaves*, 3–6. On the Code Noir of 1724, a revision of Colbert's Code Noir of 1685 designed to control slaves and free people of color in French colonies, and its implications for Louisiana, including what became the Natchez District, see Pinnen, "Slavery and Empire," 5, 35, 39, 50–51; Pinnen, *Complexion of Empire*, chapter 1; Spear, *Race, Sex, and Social Order*, 33; Layton, "Indian Country to Slave Country," 29–30.

96. Milne, *Natchez Country*, 93.

97. For different accounts of the "crisis" or "war," see Milne, *Natchez Country*, 93–106; Barnett, *Natchez Indians*, 84–90. For extracts from accounts written by people living at the time of the events, some in the Natchez Country, see Swanton, *Indian Tribes of the Lower Mississippi Valley*, 207–11.

98. Gwendolyn Midlo Hall, *Africans in Colonial Louisiana*, 100.

99. For more detail, see Milne, *Natchez Country*, 106–19; Barnett, *Natchez Indians*, 90–98. Swanton, *Indian Tribes of the Lower Mississippi Valley*, 211–17, contains lengthy extracts from accounts of contemporaries. Milne, *Natchez Country*, 160, describes the Tattooed Serpent as the "veteran headman" of the Natchez and observes that the Great Sun "had limited political capital to expend with the older, more experienced leaders from the outlying villages."

100. Chépart is also referred to as Detchéparre, Etchepar, Chepare, and Chepar. His given name is unknown. See Dumont, *Memoir of Lieutenant Dumont*, 421. See also Milne, *Natchez Country*, 119, 159–63; F. Todd Smith, *Louisiana*, 97–101; Giraud, *History of French Louisiana*, V, 396; Caillot, *Company Man*, xxvii n. 20.

101. Giraud, *History of French Louisiana*, 5:397; Milne, *Natchez Country*, 159, 162.

102. Milne, *Natchez Country*, 161.

103. Barnett, *Natchez Indians*, 102.

104. Milne, *Natchez Country*, 149–57. See also Din, *Spaniards, Planters, and Slaves*, 15.

105. Din, *Spaniards and Planters, and Slaves*, 157–59; "At a Conference of the Headmen of the Cherokees and the Lower Creeks in the Presence of Both Houses of the assembly, January 26, 1726," PRO, CO 5, America and the West Indies, vol. 387, folio 137. For the Charles Town meeting, see Crane, *Southern Frontier*, 268–70. For a general discussion of the language of race and color and its limitations as it played out in the colonial Southeast and elsewhere, see Shoemaker, *Strange Likeness*, 125–40. She cites Father Raphael to Abbé Raguet, New Orleans, May 15, 1725, *MPA-FD*, 2:470–492, esp. 485–86 for a fable recounted by the "oldest" Taensa chiefs in attendance at a meeting near Mobile with the Mobile Indians and Father Raphael. Sleeper-Smith, *Indian Women and French Men*, focuses on Native-French intermarriage in the western Great Lakes.

106. Diron d'Artaguette to Maurepas, Mobile, February 10, 1730, *MPA-FD*, 1:56–61. Father Philibert provided a detailed list of 144 men, 35 women, and 56 children. "From Father

Philibert," onboard the Duc de Bourbon, June 9, 1730, *MPA-FD*, 1:122–26. See also Barker, "'*Cherchez les Femmes*,'" 28.

107. Périer to Maurepas, New Orleans, December 5, 1728, *MPA-FD*, 1:54–56. For opposition from "the Stung Arm" or "Tattooed Arm," see Le Page du Pratz, *History of Louisiana*, 73–87, esp. 79–81. For more accounts of the events of November 28, 1729, see Swanton, *Indian Tribes of the Lower Mississippi Valley*, 217–30; Caughey, "Natchez Rebellion"; Grant, "Natchez Revolt"; Barnett, Natchez Indians, 101–9; Milne, *Natchez Country*, 172–82; Giraud, *History of French Louisiana*, 5:398–400; Mary Ann Wells, *Native Land*, 119–31. See also Sophie White, "Massacre, Mardi Gras, and Torture," 498, for the argument that thanks to Marc-Antoine Caillot and others, the Natchez uprising became a permanent part of the political and literary imagination in France.

108. Giraud, *History of French Louisiana*, 5:399.

109. On the fate of the Yazoo fort and settlement, see Milne, *Natchez Country*, 185. For a contemporary perspective, see Lusser to Maurepas, Chickasawhays, March 26, 1730, *MPA-FD*, 1:99–100.

110. Diron d'Artaguette to Maurepas, Mobile, February 10, 1730, *MPA-FD*, 1:56–61.

111. Galloway, "Colonial Transformations," 244. The term *genocide* also frames a discussion of what happened to a group of Native Americans more than a century later in California. See Madley, *American Genocide*. For another perspective on the events of 1729 and what followed, see Lugan, *Histoire de la Louisiane*, 116–21.

112. Baudouin to Salmon, Chickasawhay, November 23, 1732, *MPA-FD*, 1:155–56. Of some relevance is Dawdy's observation in *Building the Devil's Empire*, 154–55, that early eighteenth-century French travel writing and philosophical texts "still tended to discuss groups as 'nations,' a category closer to the modern idea of ethnicity than race."

113. Caillot, *Company Man*, 123–24; Barnett, *Natchez Indians*, 125–26; Milne, *Natchez Country*, 212; *Pipe Dreams*, 15–16.

114. Périer to Maurepas, in *MPA-FD*, 1:71–76; Usner, "From African Captivity to American Slavery," 45; Milne, *Natchez Country*, 188–89. Using evidence provided by anthropologists, Din, *Spaniards, Planters, and Slaves*, 16 n.43, concludes that Périer's claim that he had exterminated the Chaoucha was false.

115. For one view of the particular role of Alibamon Mingo, see Diron d'Artaguette to Maurepas, Mobile, March 20, 1730, *MPA-FD*, 1:78–81. See also Galloway, "Four Ages of Alibamon Mingo," 325–27; Milne, *Natchez Country*, 189–97; Barnett, *Natchez Indians*, 116–18.

116. Mary Ann Wells, *Native Land*, 130; Barnett, *Natchez Indians*, 126–27; Milne, *Natchez Country*, 199–202.

117. Winsor, *Mississippi Basin*, 187–89; Richard White, *Roots of Dependency*, 52–61. Barnett, *Mississippi's American Indians*, 114–16, 128–29, uses the phrase "Choctaw-Chickasaw War" to frame a brief discussion of efforts by Bienville to solicit Choctaw support for the French effort to end English influence among the Chickasaws. For a full description of how the play-off system worked or did not work from the 1730s through the French and Indian War of 1754–63, see Richard White, *Roots of Dependency*, 34–68. On Choctaw factionalism and civil war, see Galloway, *Practicing Ethnohistory*, 259–91.

118. Richard White, *Roots of Dependency*, 130–35. See also Arrell M. Gibson, *Chickasaws*, 49–56; Mary Ann Wells, *Native Land*, 134–41. For the fullest account of these campaigns against the Chickasaws, see James R. Atkinson, *Splendid Land, Splendid People*, 9–18, 36–73. Atkinson criticizes Gibson and others for relying too much on "a poorly documented" older book, Cushman's 1899 *History of the Choctaw, Chickasaw, and Natchez Indians*. In Atkinson's

view, that reliance led, at least in the case of Gibson, to the presentation of a "highly errone-
ous" location for the early Chickasaw villages.

119. Patricia Galloway, *Practicing Ethnohistory*, 245; Donald J. Lemieux, "Pierre François
de Rigaud, Marquis de Vaudreuil," in *Louisiana Governors*, ed. Dawson, 29–32; Donald J.
Lemieux, "Louis Billouart, Chevalier de Kerlérec," in *Louisiana Governors*, ed. Dawson, 33–37
; Carl A. Brasseaux, "Jean-Jacques-Blaise d'Abbadie," in *Louisiana Governors*, ed. Dawson,
37–40}; Carl A. Brasseaux, "Charles Philippe Aubry," in *Louisiana Governors*, ed. Dawson,
41–44}; Villiers du Terrage, *Last Years of French Louisiana*, 191–377. For more on Vaudreuil
and Kerlérec, see *MPA-FD*, 4:210 n.1, 5:124 n.1. For d'Abbadie, see Brasseaux, *Comparative
View of French Louisiana*, 84–138; Pusch, "Jean-Jacques-Blaise d'Abbadie."

120. Chickasaw chiefs to Vaudreuil, *MPA-FD*, 4:211–12.

121. Vaudreuil to Maurepas, *MPA-FD*, 4:214–16.

122. On the American phase of the War of the Austrian Succession, see Mary Ann Wells,
Native Land, 143–44. On Red Shoe, see Vaudreuil to Maurepas, *MPA-FD*, 4:297–304.

123. The most complete study of this conflict is Galloway, *Practicing Ethnohistory*, 259–91.
See also Galloway, "Choctaw Factionalism and Civil War," esp. 121, which characterizes it
as perhaps "the most momentous happening in Choctaw history from the beginning of
European conflict until removal." On the death of Red Shoe, see Vaudreuil to Maurepas,
MPA-FD, 4:297–304; Galloway, *Practicing Ethnohistory*, 280. On the Choctaw civil war, see
Louboey to Maurepas, *MPA-FD*, 4:312–15; "Memoir for the King of the Choctaws," *MPA-
FD*, 4:324–25; Bobè Descloseaux to Maurepas, *MPA-FD*, 4:328–32; Vaudreuil to Maurepas,
MPA-FD, 4:332–40; Galloway, "Four Ages of Alibamon Mingo," 332–25; James R. Atkinson,
Splendid Land, Splendid People, 79–82; Mary Ann Wells, *Native Land*, 142–52; Barnett, *Missis-
sippi's American Indians*, 139–42.

124. See Kerlérec's messages to Jean Baptiste de Machault d'Arnouville, 1754–57, *MPA-FD*,
5:142–82; Mary Ann Wells, *Native Land*, 141.

125. Taylor, *American Colonies*, 428–33; Calloway, *Indian World of George Washington*, 49,
63–65, 102–23, 124, 191.

126. Kerlérec to de Machault d'Arnouville, New Orleans, December 12, 1756, *MPA-FD*,
5:179.

127. For more on these and other problems, see Mary Ann Wells, *Native Land*, 153–64.

128. For a full discussion, with particular emphasis on French geographic conceptions, of
the decision by the French in late 1762 to offer Spain all of Louisiana west of the Mississippi
with the inclusion of New Orleans and the Spanish decision to accept the offer, see Mapp,
Elusive West, 359–412. For a discussion of the peace settlement and the transfers of territory
that occurred with particular focus on Florida, see Gold, *Borderland Empires*. See also Usner,
Indians, Settlers, and Slaves, 105; Narrett, *Adventurism and Empire*, 11–20.

129. Villiers du Terrage, *Last Years of French Louisiana*, 191–377; John Preston Moore,
Revolt in Louisiana, xi, 38–41, 151–83, 196–209; Kerlérec to Choiseul, New Orleans, May 2,
1763, *MPA-FD*, 5:283–86.

130. *MPA-FD*, 5:284.

131. Brasseaux, *Comparative View of French Louisiana*, 96. See also Narrett, *Adventurism
and Empire*, 15.

132. d'Abbadie arrived in New Orleans with his wife and children in late June 1763, but it
was not until October that, as he put it in his journal, "Kerlérec remitted the colony's government to me." "The d'Abbadie Journal," in Broussard, *Comparative View*, 103. John Preston
Moore, *Revolt in Louisiana*, 38–41; Brasseaux, *Comparative View*, 39.

133. d'Abbadie to Kerlérec, Mobile, November 6, 1763, *MPA-FD*, 5:291–93.

Chapter 3: Masters of the World? The British in Mississippi, 1763–1779

1. "d'Abbadie Journal," 89–138; Ellis, "Petite Nation with Powerful Networks," 135; Captain Charles Philippe Aubry to Duc de Choiseul-Stainville, February 4, 1765, in Broussard, *Comparative View of French Louisiana*, 139–42.

2. For a distinction between imperialism and colonialism, see Narrett, *Adventurism and Empire*, 1–8.

3. Alvord, *Mississippi Valley in British Politics*, 1:183–210; Anderson, *Crucible of War*, 565–69. Calloway, *Scratch of a Pen*, 92–100, summarizes varied interpretations of the proclamation with regard what some see in it as "the Indians' 'Bill of Rights.'" See also Calloway, *Indian World of George Washington*, 181–84. Taylor, *Divided Ground*, 40–41, notes that in Pennsylvania and Virginia, the proclamation initially proved unenforceable. Narrett, *Adventurism and Empire*, 15. On Pontiac, see Peckham, *Pontiac and the Indian Uprising*; Winsor, *Mississippi Basin*, 414, 432–57; Anderson, *Crucible of War*, 535–46, 617–37; Dowd, *War under Heaven*, 1–9, 177–79, 233–34; Calloway, *Indian World of George Washington*, 176–77, 180–81; J. H. Elliott, *Empires of the Atlantic World*, 305; Cecil Johnson, *British West Florida*, 5, 113–29; Cecil Johnson, "West Florida Revisited." Fabel, "Eighteenth Colony," 648, notes the exemption of West Florida as a British colony.

4. See Alvord, *Mississippi Valley in British Politics*, 1:211–28. The "List of Indian Tribes in the Southern District of North America" included the Cherokees, Creeks, Chickasaws, Choctaws, Catawbas, "Beluxis," Houmas, "Attacapas," "Bayuglas," Tunicas, "Peluches," "Ofugulas," "Querphas." PRO, CO 5, LC transcripts, vol. 65, 605. For the office of superintendent and Stuart's role in that office, see Alden, *John Stuart*, 139–337.

5. Alden, *John Stuart*, 210–11; Montault de Monbéraut, *Mémoire Justificatif*, 7–58; Calloway, *Scratch of the Pen*, 129–30.

6. See Cecil Johnson *British West Florida*. See also Fabel, *Bombast and Broadsides*, 16–57; Carter, "Beginnings of British West Florida."

7. Cecil Johnson, *British West Florida*, 8–12; Broussard, *Comparative View*, 102–3; Rea, *Major Robert Farmar*, 36–37; Montault de Monbéraut, *Mémoire Justificatif*, 15–28; "Minutes of Council with Choctaws," November 14, 1763, *MPA-FD*, 5:294–301. The minutes, including the speech, were translated by Simon Favre. Other groups that received the same message at separate meetings were, from the region of the Alabamas: the "*Kawitas*," *Abihkas, Chicachas, Kasihtas*, and other dependents of *Kawitas*, and "finally the *Talapoosas* and *Alabamas*" (294).

8. For Stuart's account of his planning for the meeting, see John Stuart to the Earl of Egremont, Charles Town, June 1, 1763, PRO, CO 5, LC transcripts, vol. 65. For different perspectives on the meeting itself, see Alden, *John Stuart*, 178–91; Hahn, *Invention of the Creek Nation*, 266–69; Calloway, *Scratch of the Pen*, 100–111.

9. Rowland, *Mississippi Provincial Archives: English Dominion*, 184–215 (Creeks), 216–55 (Choctaws and Chickasaws). Richard White, *Roots of Dependency*, 69–88, discusses these meetings and others, focusing particularly on the Choctaws.

10. Fabel, *Bombast and Broadsides*, 40–41; Johnstone speech, March 26, 1765, Rowland, *Mississippi Provincial Archives: English Dominion*, 217.

11. Fabel, *Bombast and Broadsides*, 41–42; Rowland, *Mississippi Provincial Archives: English Dominion*, 184–215. For more insight into the Creeks at this time, see Piker, "White and Clean."

12. Greg O'Brien, "Supplying Our Wants: Choctaws and Chickasaws Reassess the Trade Relationship with Britain, 1771–72," in *Coastal Encounters*, ed. Richmond F. Brown, 59; Cecil Johnson, *British West Florida*, 80–82; PRO, CO 5, LC transcripts, vol. 73. The account of the Choctaw-Chickasaw congress includes "A List of Towns in the Choctaw Nation with the

names of the Indians in each Town receiving presents at the Congress 1771–1772." A total of 719 Choctaws had received presents.

13. John Stuart to Lord George Germain, Pensacola, June 14, 1777, PRO, CO 5, LC transcripts, box 81. For more on colonial-Indian relations in 1763–75, see Narrett, *Adventurism and Empire*, 31–35, 58–62.

14. Charles Stuart to John Stuart, Mobile, July 1, 1778: PRO, CO 5, LC transcripts, vol. 79; Alden, *John Stuart*, 212 n.87; Narrett, *Adventurism and Empire*, 31–35, 58–62. On the problem of alcohol, see Mancall, *Deadly Medicine*; Mancall, "Bewitching Tyranny of Custom"; Richard White, *Roots of Dependency*, 85; Wallace, *Long and Bitter Trail*, 23; Calloway, *American Revolution in Indian Country*, 221–22.

15. Anderson, *Crucible of War*, 566. Meinig, *Shaping of America*, 284, describes the proclamation as "an emergency measure designed to quiet the fears of Indians and to block the advance of land seekers until more detailed empirical policies could be put in place."

16. See Fabel, *Economy of British West Florida*, 2, 157–58; Fabel, "Eighteenth Colony," 648; Narrett, *Adventurism and Empire*, 26–27.

17. See Calloway, *Scratch of the Pen*, 102; Calloway, *Indian World of George Washington*, 102. See also Howard, "Early Settlers," 46.

18. For the Natchez District of West Florida and efforts to populate it, see Grant, "They Stayed On," 27–28, summarizing three waves of immigration: the first in 1763–70, the second under Chester, 1770–75, and the third from 1775 to 1778.

19. Fabel, *Economy of British West Florida*, 6–21. For a somewhat different perspective on immigration, see Cecil Johnson, *British West Florida*, 132–49. On Chester's land grants in what became Warren County, Mississippi, see Bragg, "British Land Grants."

20. See the last of the "Letters of R," *New York Gazette*, October 18, 1773, reproduced in Fabel, "Letters of R," 421–27. The anonymous author refers to the Iberville River as the River Manchac. For a map showing an inside route bypassing the Mississippi River delta, see Meinig, *Shaping of America*, 196. Engineer and surveyor Elias Durnford's 1770 "Plan of the River Mississippi from the Indian Village of the Tonicas to the River Ibberville Showing the Lands Surveyed Thereon as also the Rivers Ibberville, Amit, and Comit with the Situation of the New Town Proposed on the Ibberville," PRO, Board of Trade, Maps, and MDAH, Map 98.0114(c), shows a grant of land to Johnston of 100,000 acres as well as "Lieut. Gov. Brown's Land of 17,400 acres." On the project, see Fabel, *Bombast and Broadsides*, 25–27, 42–45; Cecil Johnson, *British West Florida*, 7, 33–36; Brown, "Iberville Canal Project." On Durnford, see Fabel, "Elias Durnford."

21. Cecil Johnson, *British West Florida*, 67–69, 123, 151–52.

22. For a map showing the route to the Mississippi River bypassing New Orleans and the Mississippi River delta, see Meinig, *Shaping of America*, 196. Kimberly M. Welch, *Black Litigants*, 15, defines the "Natchez District" as "the plantation region along the Mississippi River between Vicksburg, Mississippi and Baton Rouge, Louisiana." It began to emerge as a plantation region in the late 1760s. Milne, *Natchez Country*, esp. 1–14, uses the term *Natchez Country* for the smaller area around the French fort as the focus of his book. John Eliot had been appointed to succeed Johnstone early in 1767 but did not arrive in the province until April 2, 1769. After a month of trying to sort out the problems he inherited from Browne, who had been controversial and had acquired enemies, Eliot committed suicide. Cecil Johnson, *British West Florida*, 69–70. On Browne, see Fabel, "Eighteenth Colony"; Narrett, *Adventurism and Empire*, 49–58.

23. Montfort Browne to Hillsborough, July 6, 1768, PRO, CO 5, 577, MDAH, microfilm 3868. For similar language, see Fabel, "Letters of R," 414–20. The contemporary descriptions

of Johnstone, Browne, and others illustrate what Shoemaker, *Strange Likeness*, 29, discusses as Euro-American views of land related to economic potential rather than the historic attachment important to Indians.

24. Romans, *Concise Natural History*, 82. See also Bartram, *Travels of William Bartram*; and a study of the Florida travels of William Bartram's father, John, a Quaker farmer and botanist: Robert Olwell, "Incidental Imperialist: John Bartram's Florida Travels, 1765–1766," in *European Empires in the American South*, ed. Ward, 188–217.

25. The region became, beginning with the British, one of plantations. Kimberly M. Welch, *Black Litigants*, 15.

26. George Washington to Thomas Lewis, February 17, 1774, in *Writings of George Washington*, 3:184; Fabel, *Economy of British West Florida*, 156.

27. On the Mississippi Company and Washington as land speculator, see Anderson, *Crucible of War*, 106–7, 593–94, 738–41; Calloway, *Indian World of George Washington*, 178–79, 191, 211.

28. Layton, "Indian Country to Slave Country," 33–34. For yet another map, see William G. Wilton, "A Manuscript Map of British Land Grants along the Mississippi River 1774," Mississippi River Commission, Vicksburg, copy in MDAH.

29. For more specific information that Browne held 17,400 acres of land, see "Land Grants and Other Land Transactions"; Durnford, "Plan of the River Mississippi"; Wilton, "Manuscript Map of British Land Grants"; Cecil Johnson, *British West Florida*, 67–69, 151–52; Haynes, *Natchez District*, 20–21; Fabel, *Economy of British West Florida*, 12–14. Narrett, *Adventurism and Empire*, 49–50, quotes a Pensacola critic as describing Browne as "avaricious, ignorant, and notorious for saying what he should not say and for denying what he doth say." Cecil Johnson, *British West Florida*, 123, blames the failure of the project at Campbell Town and its abandonment on the unhealthy environment of the place, erratic leadership by the French pastor, and settlers' lack of skills.

30. Bate, *Two Putnams*, 3–46; Fabel, *Economy of British West Florida*, 153–59; Fabel, "Eighteenth Colony," 665. See also Christopher Morris, *Becoming Southern*, 7–37. For one of those who went and the challenges faced, see Matthew Phelps, *Memoirs and Adventures*.

31. Christopher Morris, *Becoming Southern*, 15; Fitzpatrick, *Merchant of Manchac*, 3–4, 11, 162, 180–81, 267, 347–53, 369. For Price, see Inglis, "Searching for Free People of Color," 100–103; Pinnen, *Complexion of Empire*. For more on Turnbull and other traders, see Charles A. Weeks, *Paths to a Middle Ground*, 96–97 n.53.

32. See Howard, *British Development of West Florida*, 50–106. See also Cummins, "Enduring Community"; Gordon M. Wells, "British Land Grants."

33. Cummins, "Enduring Community," esp. 144 for Eglinton as absentee landowner and "drinking companion"; Howard, "Colonial Natchez," 161–63; Fabel, "Eighteenth Colony," 658.

34. Fabel, *Economy of British West Florida*, 6–20; Starr, *Tories, Dons, and Rebels*, 231; Elias Durnford, "Description of West Florida, January 15, 1774," PRO, CO 5/591:24. Wilton's 1774 map records the names of 247 people who received grants along the Mississippi River between Baton Rouge and Natchez and along the Iberville and Amite Rivers. See Gordon M. Wells, "British Land Grants"; Cummins, "Enduring Community," 135; Milton B. Newman Jr., "Mapping the Foundations of the Old Natchez District: The William Wilton Map of 1774," in *Natchez before 1830*, ed. Polk, 81–84. For additional perspective on the nonnative population, see Haynes, *Natchez District*, 12–16; Johnston to Pownall, April 1, 1766, PRO, CO 5/583:433.

35. Hafner, "Major Arthur Loftus' Journal"; Cecil Johnson, *British West Florida*, 50 n.65; Rea, *Major Robert Farmar*, 45; Alden, *John Stuart*, 196. For more on the diversity of Indian responses, in particular those of the Choctaws, during the American Revolution,

see O'Brien, *Pre-Removal Choctaw History*. For a discussion of the Houmas who lived in the region during the early French period, see d'Oney, "Houma Nation." The heights on the eastern side of the Mississippi in the vicinity of the attack on Loftus came to be called Loftus Heights. For more on Loftus and his expedition, see Narrett, *Adventurism and Empire*, 34–35.

36. Rea, *Major Robert Farmar*, 63–68; O'Brien, *Choctaws in a Revolutionary Age*, 70–73.

37. Farmar remained at Fort Chartres for some time. According to Rea, *Major Robert Farmar*, 71–75, Farmar found it a "gem of military architecture" and renamed it Fort Cavendish.

38. Alden, *John Stuart*, 316–17. See also Fitzpatrick, *Merchant of Manchac*, 83–85.

39. Cecil Johnson, *British West Florida*, 136–41; Haynes, *Natchez District*, 13–14; Peter Chester to the Earl of Hillsborough, Pensacola, September 6, 1770, PRO, CO 5/578:59–68.

40. To quote Cecil Johnson, *British West Florida*, 142, "Governors . . . were ordered, under pain of the king's highest displeasure, to issue no more warrants nor to pass any additional grants, except under authority of a royal order of the Proclamation of 1763." See also Haynes, *Natchez District*, 14–17.

41. Christopher Morris, *Becoming Southern*, 18.

42. Coker, "Luke Collins Senior and Family," 141. See also Cecil Johnson, "Distribution of Land." On Natchez settlers who remained nominally loyal "out of a desire to avoid the war," see Layton, "Indian Country to Slave Country," 27. See also Siebert, "Loyalists in West Florida."

43. Cecil Johnson, *British West Florida*, 145–46. See Haynes, *Natchez District*, 3–26, esp. 14–20 on the creation of a "town" of Natchez.

44. PRO, CO 5: America and the West Indies, 78: 301/151–303/154, typescript Huntington Library, San Marino, CA. See also transcript PRO, CO 5, LC, box 81.

45. PRO, CO 5, LC, box/vol. 81. For more on the "Natchez District" after 1763, see Jack D. Elliott Jr., *Comprehensive Plan*, 54–62.

46. "The Superintendent's Speech to the Choctaws & Chickasaws at Mobile in Congress the 14th of May 1777," PRO, CO 5, LC, box/vol. 81.

47. John Stuart to Lord George Germain, Pensacola , June 14, 1777, PRO, CO 5, LC, box/vol. 81.

48. PRO, CO 5, LC, box/vol. 81. On Bethune, see O'Brien, "We Are behind You," 110.

49. Haynes, *Natchez District*, 63. For a full account of the Willing expedition, see Haynes, *Natchez District*, 51–75; Haynes, "James Willing." On Hutchins, see Inglis, "Anthony Hutchins." See also Narrett, *Adventurism and Empire*, 79–88; Siebert, "Loyalists in West Florida," 471; Faye, "Arkansas Post of Louisiana: Spanish Domination," 655–58.

50. For British measures, see Haynes, *Natchez District*, 77–100.

51. For the short Choctaw occupation of Natchez, see O'Brien, "We Are behind You," 116.

52. Gershoy, *From Despotism to Revolution*, 167–71; Medina Rojas, *José de Ezpeleta*, xlii, 3; J. H. Elliott, *Empires of the Atlantic World*, 353–68; Weber, *Spanish Frontier*, 236–30, 265–66; Ekberg, *Colonial Ste. Genevieve*, 58–59. For a book-length discussion of Gálvez's career, see Caughey, *Bernardo de Gálvez*. For an older discussion of "Three Nations on the Mississippi" (France, Britain, Spain), see Faye, "Arkansas Post of Louisiana: Spanish Domination," 654–70.

53. Caughey, *Bernardo de Gálvez*, 135–48; Haynes, *Natchez District*, 105–12; Weber, *Spanish Frontier*, 236–39, 265–70; F. Todd Smith, *Louisiana*, 160; Medina Rojas, *José de Ezpeleta*, xlii–xliii. For more on Pollock, see Narrett, *Adventurism and Empire*, 63; Cummins, "Oliver Pollock"; James Alton James, *Oliver Pollock*.

54. Caughey, *Bernardo de Gálvez*, 163. On the Acadians in Louisiana, see Brasseaux, *Founding of New Acadia*; Brasseaux, *"Scattered to the Wind."* On the Acadians and other peoples who came to make up the population of the region, see F. Todd Smith, *Louisiana*, 146–47.

55. Haynes, *Natchez District*, 113–24; Din, *Spaniards, Planters, and Slaves*, 82–83; McConnell, *Negro Troops of Antebellum Louisiana*, 18; Martín Navarro to Gálvez, New Orleans, August 28, 1779, AGI, PC, file 82. See also F. Todd Smith, *Louisiana*, 160–61.

56. Haynes, *Natchez District*, 124 n.41.

57. Holmes, "Juan de la Villebeuvre," 102–6, 113–14; Haynes, *Natchez District*, 123–26.

58. Caughey, *Bernardo de Gálvez*, 140–42; Abraham P. Nasatir, "The Legacy of Spain," in *Anglo-Spanish Confrontation*, ed. Coker and Rea, 4; Jacinto Panis to Bernardo de Gálvez, New Orleans, April 29, 1779, in Kinnaird, *Spain in the Mississippi Valley*, 336–38.

59. For the campaigns to secure Mobile and Pensacola, see Medina Rojas, *José de Ezpeleta*, 3–42. See also Weber, *Spanish Frontier*, 268. For the Pensacola campaign, see Beerman, "Arturo O'Neill." On the role of both the Choctaws and the Creeks during the Mobile and Pensacola campaigns, see Medina Rojas, *José de Ezpeleta*, 54–135; Carson, *Searching for the Bright Path*, 38–39; O'Brien, *Choctaws in a Revolutionary Age*, 49; Kathryn Holland, "The Anglo-Spanish Contest for the Gulf Coast as Viewed from the Townsquare," in *Anglo-Spanish Confrontation*, ed. Coker and Rea, 97–101; Michael D. Green, "The Creek Confederacy in the American Revolution: Cautious Participants," in *Anglo-Spanish Confrontation*, ed. Coker and Rea, 68–72. For a discussion of the effects of the loss of Pensacola by the British and their withdrawal from the Gulf Coast, see J. Leitch Wright Jr., "The Queen's Redoubt Explosion in the Lives of William A. Bowles, John Miller, and William Panton," in *Anglo-Spanish Confrontation*, ed. Coker and Rea, 177. For Ezpeleta's role in these events, see Francisco de Borja Medina Rojas, "José de Ezpeleta and the Siege of Pensacola," in *Anglo-Spanish Confrontation*, ed. Coker and Rea, 106–24. See also Haynes, *Natchez District*, 131–33.

60. On the 1781 Natchez revolt, see Caughey, "Natchez Rebellion"; Scott, "Britain Loses Natchez," 45–46; Haynes, *Natchez District*, 131–52; Grant, "Natchez Revolt." In addition to Blommart and Winfree, Layton, "Indian Country to Slave Country," 45, identifies John Alston, Philip Alston, John Turner, and Anthony Hutchins as leaders of several hundred residents, thirty western division Choctaws, and one Chickasaw as having compelled Villebeuvre to surrender Fort Panmure on April 22, 1781. According to Faye, "Arkansas Post of Louisiana: Spanish Dominion," 631, John or Jean Blommart had come to Natchez from Pensacola, where he was a successful merchant. He was a native of Geneva, Switzerland, who had obtained a substantial grant of land along the Mississippi. For more on James Colbert and Loyalist resistance after the fall of Pensacola, see "Declaration of Labbadie, July 5, 1782," in Kinnaird, *Spain in the Mississippi Valley*, 21–34. For a description of Colbert's background and role as a Chickasaw, see Gilbert C. Din, "Loyalist Resistance after Pensacola: The Case of James Colbert," in *Anglo-Spanish Confrontation*, ed. Coker and Rea, 158–75.

61. Din, "Loyalist Resistance."

62. Din, "Loyalist Resistance"; "Natchez Rebellion," 65; Haynes, *Natchez District*, 141; "Robberies on the Mississippi—Madame Cruzat Captured—Her Account—1782," in *Spanish Regime in Missouri*, ed. Houck, 1:211–34; Din, "Arkansas Post." See "Declaration of Labbadie." For added perspective that characterizes the Arkansas Post as different from most during the Spanish period, see F. Todd Smith, *Louisiana*, 152–53. For a discussion of the Chickasaws in relation to the American Revolution, see James R. Atkinson, *Splendid Land, Splendid People*, 100–119; Du Val, *Independence Lost*, 11–23, 238–45.

63. Bemis, *Pinckney's Treaty*, 41–42. Bemis observes that "the impartial student must admit that abundantly unimpeachable evidence proves that the northern boundary of West Florida under British dominion from 1764 until the Spanish conquest had been the latitude of the mouth of the Yazoo River from the Mississippi to the Chattahooche."

64. For a discussion of the diplomacy associated with these peace settlements, see Narrett, *Adventurism and Empire*, 109–13.

65. For an older study with focus on Spanish-American conflict as a legacy of the 1783 settlements, see Whitaker, *Spanish-American Frontier*, 1–14.

Chapter 4: Resurgence of Empire? A "Spanish" Mississippi, 1779–1798

1. The Spanish king's minister of state, the Conde de Floridablanca, asserted the claim for West Florida's boundary in 1784. That claim was followed in the same year by the appointment of Diego de Gardoqui as Spain's minister to the United States. Coker and Watson, *Indian Traders*, 2; Din, *Francisco Bouligny*, 128–29.

2. Du Val, *Independence Lost*, 217.

3. Colin G. Calloway, "The Continuing Revolution in Indian Country," in *Native Americans and the Early Republic*, ed. Hoxie, Hoffman, and Albert, 23–25; Calloway, *Indian World of George Washington*, 283; Medina Rojas, *José de Ezpeleta*, 51–135. At the November 1763 Mobile meeting with Choctaws after the "Great War for Empire," both the British governor, Farmar, and the French director-general, d'Abbadie, reported that the Choctaws "will probably object strongly to their lands' and even their persons' being disposed of without their cooperation." "Minutes of Council with the Choctaws," *MPA-FD*, 5:295.

4. Whitaker, *Spanish-American Frontier*, 10–11. North Carolina, too, delayed ceding its western claims. Reginald Horsman, "The Indian Policy of an 'Empire for Liberty,'" in *Native Americans and the Early Republic*, ed. Hoxie, Hoffman, and Albert, 38. For more on the complexities and ambiguities regarding the 1783 treaties, see Du Val, *Independence Lost*, 229–38; Bemis, *Pinckney's Treaty*, esp. 37–45. See also Whitaker, *Spanish-American Frontier*, 13–14; Weber, *Spanish Frontier*, 275–79; Narrett, *Adventurism and Empire*, 109–14; Calloway, *Indian World of George Washington*, 280–81, 283, 348, 437.

5. Narrett, *Adventurism and Empire*, 120–22. Din, "Troubled Seven Years," discusses those border disputes with particular focus on the so-called Florida parishes of Louisiana and points east after 1803.

6. Whitaker, *Spanish-American Frontier*, 8; Haring, *Spanish Empire in America*, 69–81.

7. Narrett, *Adventurism and Empire*, 115–17.

8. Calloway, *Indian World of George Washington*, 283–85.

9. Abernethy, *South in the New Nation*, 69–70; Alan Taylor, "Remaking Americans: Louisiana, Upper Canada, and Texas," in *Contested Spaces of Early America*, ed. Barr and Countryman, 208.

10. Din, *Spaniards, Planters, and Slaves*, 124. Din notes further that the 1780s witnessed the rapid arrival in Louisiana of many immigrants, both white and Black. By comparing the 1785 and 1788 censuses, he found that about six thousand slaves became part of Louisiana's workforce during those three years.

11. Holmes, *Gayoso*, 16 n.41. The census document used by Holmes is the *Padrón general del Distrito de Natchez, 1784*, AGI, PC, file 116.

12. Holmes, *Gayoso*, 113–17. A microfilm copy of the *Padrón del Distrito de Natchez del Año 1792* can be found in MDAH, microfilm roll 2528. It uses the categories *blanco* (white),

mulato (mixed), and *negro* for the population. A total of five censuses were carried out between 1784 and 1794. See Inglis, "Character and Some Characteristics," 37, which gives Natchez's total population as 1,628 in 1784 and 4,698 in 1792. See also Din, "Empires Too Far."

13. Din, *Populating the Barrera*, 39–78, 122–51; Haring, *Spanish Empire in America*, 321.

14. On religious policies and activities, see Holmes, "Irish Priests in Spanish Natchez"; Holmes, *Gayoso*, 68–85; Inglis, "Character and Some Characteristics," 25–27. For the Jersey settlement and Gayoso's attempt to regulate Baptist activity, see Sparks, *On Jordan's Stormy Banks*, 7–9. See also Forman, *Narrative*, 58. On trade, particularly the use of the Mississippi River, see Article IV of Treaty of 1795; Bemis, *Pinckney's Treaty*, 546–47. On both trade and religious policy, see Whitaker, *Spanish-American Frontier*, 65, 68–70, 81, 101–102, 161. Narrett, *Adventurism and Empire*, 177, notes that "one cannot easily over-state the degree to which Miró's plans for Louisiana emphasized lawful Anglo-American colonization."

15. Those "frontier areas" were only nominally American in the sense that Indians still regarded much of the land as theirs and some Spanish argued that it was part of Louisiana. Sánchez-Fabrés Mirat, *Situación Histórica*, 87; Charles A. Weeks, *Paths to a Middle Ground*, 15; *Federalist*, 38–39; Whitaker, *Spanish-American Frontier*, 26.

16. Whitaker, *Spanish-American Frontier*, 51; Abernethy, *South in the New Nation*, 49, 59; Narrett, *Adventurism and Empire*, 166–67. Taylor "Introduction," 627, observes that "eastern leaders feared that western settlers would soon reject American rule to seek association with the British or Spanish empires."

17. Ulysses S. Ricard Jr., "African Slavery in Provincial Mississippi," in *Native, European, and African Cultures*, ed. Galloway, 88.

18. Grant, "They Stayed On"; Haring, *Spanish Empire in America*, 79.

19. McMichael, *Atlantic Loyalties*, 22–23; Din, *Francisco Bouligny*, 2–6. Din points out that for Bouligny and his siblings, there was never any question of *patria* (fatherland): it was Spain. For Villebeuvre, see Holmes, "Juan de la Villebeuvre." For Minor, who came down the Mississippi River during the American Revolution and joined the service of Spain, see Holmes, "Stephen Minor"; Holmes, *Gayoso*, 51.

20. Coker, "Brief History of Mississippi," 199. For the most complete discussion of Spanish population policy for the whole of Louisiana, including the Natchez area, see Din, *Populating the Barrera*. For another perspective, see Gitlin, "Crossroads on the Chinaberry Coast," 365. See also the older Hamilton, "Southwestern Frontier," 390, which focuses on an 1801 census of the Natchez District that found a total population of 7,500, of whom a "negli-gible number" were Spanish, many were of British and Central and West African origin, and others were French: the author thus characterizes the population as "cosmopolitan."

21. Inglis, "Character and Some Characteristics," 28–29; "Asiento de Manuel García de Texada," June 15, 1782, AGI, PC, file 538-A (28 n.31). Well after his death, Tejada became an "honored ancestor" as Manuel Garcia de Texada of the Order of the First Families of Missis-sippi, 1699–1817. See "Manuel Garcia de Texada," Order of the First Families of Mississippi, 1699–1817, http://www.offms.org/ancestors/texada_manuel.html, accessed June 4, 2020.

22. Alfred E. Lemmon, "Some Sources of Pre-1830 Natchez History in Spanish Archives," in *Natchez before 1830*, ed. Polk, 43–44; Jack D. Elliott Jr., "City and Empire," 271–74. Elliott, "Comprehensive Plan for Historic Preservation," 54–127, identifies and describes in some of "three major areas of settlement and defense" in the Natchez District: Natchez, Villa Gayoso, and Los Nogales. For more on the general theory and structure of Spanish colonial govern-ment, see Charles Gibson, *Spain in America*, 90–111; Haring, *Spanish Empire in America*, 69–81, 128–38; Hubert Herring, *History of Latin America*, 157–68; Bourne, *Spain in America*,

220–42. For Cuba, Louisiana, and the Floridas, see Whitaker, *Spanish-American Frontier*, 8; Whitaker, *Mississippi Question*, 29–32.

23. Villebeuvre generally signed his name on Spanish documents *Juan Delavillebeuvre*. Grand-Pré used the Spanish *Carlos* for *Charles*. Manuel Gayoso de Lemos, also a military man, was appointed to be both military commandant and civil governor of an upgraded and more independent Natchez District within Louisiana and West Florida in 1787 but did not arrive until 1789. See Holmes, *Gayoso*, 3–18.

24. Bouligny to Miró, August 22, 1785, in Kinnaird, *Spain in the Mississippi Valley*, 136–42. Bouligny's letter to Miró is reproduced and discussed in "Commandant Francisco Bouligny and the Problems of a Frontier District—1785," in Sarah J. Banks and Weeks, *Mississippi's Spanish Heritage*, 82–91. See also Din, *Francisco Bouligny*, 145–48. The length of the "league" varied according to time and place. In general, the English league was about three miles. Spanish officials recorded an increase in the population of cattle from between 3,100 and 3,400 in 1784 to 18,301 in 1794. Thomas D. Clark and Guice, *Frontiers in Conflict*, 103.

25. Holmes, *Gayoso*, 49–56; Haring, *Spanish Empire in America*, 147–65. On the *cabildo*, see John Preston Moore, *Revolt in Louisiana*, 217–18.

26. Din, *Francisco Bouligny*, 132; Din, *Spaniards, Planters, and Slaves*, 42–47, 222. O'Reilly abolished enslavement of Indians, but little was done to enforce that decree. See Kinnaird, *Spain in the Mississippi Valley*, 108–61; Webre, "Problem of Indian Slavery," 122. For particular focus on the Cane River region, see Mills, *Forgotten People*.

27. The legal documents were bound and became the property of the Chancery Court of Adams County. They were filmed in the 1950s, and the collection of microfilm can be accessed at the MDAH. Charles A. Weeks, "Voices from Mississippi's Past," 174–75; Sarah J. Banks and Weeks, *Mississippi's Spanish Heritage*, 92–107; McBee, *Natchez Court Records*. For more on sacramental or ecclesiastical records for the Natchez Country, see Beers, *French and Spanish Records*, 208–9.

28. "Negro James v. Clement Dyson and John Staybraker, Natchez, October 21, 1781," Original Spanish Records, book 1, Natchez Court Records, Adams County Chancery Court Records, Natchez; Pinnen, "Slavery, Race, and Freedom," 551; Spanish Records at Natchez, microfilm 5323, MDAH.

29. For a discussion of some of these cases and others, see Pinnen, "Slavery, Race, and Freedom"; Inglis, "Searching for Free People of Color." For Betty, see "Le Memorial de La Negresse Betty contre Jacques Willing," November 27, 1783, Original Spanish Records, 1783, September, Adams County Chancery Court Records, MDAH, microfilm 5327; Grant, "They Stayed On," 186. For Jeannette's efforts to secure the "enfranchisement" of her son, beginning with purchasing him from his father, Grand-Pré, see Grant, "They Stayed On," 246; Pinnen, *Complexion of Empire*.

30. Pinnen, "Slavery, Race, and Freedom," 558–61.

31. Sarah J. Banks and Gail Buzhardt, eds. and trans., "Sacramental Records from the Parish of San Salvador, Natchez, Mississippi and the Parish of the Virgin Mary of Sorrows, Baton Rouge, Louisiana (1788–1818) and Transferred to the Archive of the Roman Catholic Diocese of Jackson, Jackson, Mississippi" (2007, 2011), 34, MDAH. For a critical assessment of Father Lennan's work in Natchez, see Holmes, "Irish Priests in Spanish Natchez," 178–79. For discussion of more such cases, see Pinnen, "Slavery, Race, and Freedom."

32. For full discussion of a Spanish perspective on slavery, the legal aspect, runaway slaves, and slave revolts, see Din, *Spanish, Planters, and Slaves*, 94–107. On complexion and liberty, see Pinnen, "Slavery, Race, and Freedom," 554; Pinnen, *Complexion of Empire*. See

also Saunt, *New Order of Things*, 51–54, 124–29; Ethridge, *Creek Country*, 115–19; James R. Atkinson, *Splendid Land, Splendid People*, 23–24. Nash, *Red, White, and Black*, 295, concludes that "at no time in the colonial period did Creeks, Cherokees, and other Southern tribes work in a concerted way to unite with slaves."

33. Bouligny to Miró, August 22, 1785, in Kinnaird, *Spain in the Mississippi Valley*, 136–42. For Bouligny and the 1776 *memoria*, see Bouligny, *Louisiana in 1776*; Din, *Francisco Bouligny*, 67–69; Narrett, *Adventurism and Empire*, 120–22; "An Act Creating Bourbon County," February 7, 1785, in Kinnaird, *Spain in the Mississippi Valley*, 120–22; Whitaker, *Spanish-American Frontier*, 55–58.

34. Burnett, "Papers Relating to Bourbon County," 72–75, 82; Narrett, *Adventurism and Empire*, 120–23; Din, "War Clouds on the Mississippi"; Din, *Francisco Bouligny*, 141–47. For more insight into post-1780 Georgia and Georgians, see Nichols, "Land, Republicans, and Indians."

35. "Ellis, Gaillard, and Banks to the Citizens of Natchez, June —, 1785," in Burnett, "Papers Relating to Bourbon County," 77; Din, "War Clouds on the Mississippi," 56.

36. Din, "War Clouds on the Mississippi," 56–76. Arthur Whitaker cites two other colonial schemes emanating from the new United States: a scheme by North Carolinians to establish a settlement at Chickasaw Bluffs on the Mississippi River and a plan by a number of prominent Americans to create a settlement at Muscle Shoals on the Tennessee River. Whitaker, *Spanish-American Frontier*, 54–57; Din, *Francisco Bouligny*, 147–48; Pinnen, "Slavery and Empire," 200.

37. See Cava Mesa and Cava Mesa, *Diego de Gardoquí*; Whitaker, *Spanish American Frontier*, 77, 78. For Gardoqui's role in attracting colonists, see Din, *Populating the Barrera*, 66–78. For Wouves d'Argès, see Whitaker, *Spanish-American Frontier*, 77–79; Din, *Populating the Barrera*, 79–103.

38. Din, *Francisco Bouligny*, 147–53. Whitaker, *Spanish American Frontier*, 9–14.

39. Whitaker, *Spanish-American Frontier*, 126–29.

40. Weber, *Bárbaros*, 214; Weber, *Spanish Frontier*, 277–79; Whitaker, *Spanish-American Frontier*, 33–41; Coker and Watson, *Indian Traders*, 58; Charles A. Weeks, *Paths to a Middle Ground*, 40–41; F. Todd Smith, *Louisiana*, 167; Richard White, *Roots of Dependency*, 90.

41. For more on Alexander McGillivray, Lachlan McGillivray, and the many other Scots Highlanders who came to America, see Calloway, *White People, Indians, and Highlanders*, 118–19, 147–56; Saunt, *New Order of Things*, 67–89. Calloway, *American Revolution in Indian Country*, 276, quotes McGillivray as expressing doubts about placing too much confidence in either the Americans or the Spanish in this ambiguous context: "To find ourselves and country betrayed to our enemies and divided between the Spanish and Americans is cruel and ungenerous." See also Calloway, *Indian World of George Washington*, 346–77; Richter, *Facing East*, 223–24.

42. Green, "Alexander Mc Gillivray," 46–47; Braund, *Deerskins and Duffels*, 21; Saunt, *New Order of Things*, 67–89; Ethridge, *Creek Country*, 11–12; Du Val, *Independence Lost*, 24–34, 246–55.

43. O'Brien, *Choctaws in a Revolutionary Age*, 71–73, 85–87

44. "Simon Favre—His Indian Family," in Heitzmann with Cassibry, *Favre Family*, 35–37; Heitzmann, "Favre Family," 63–80. Samuel James Wells, "Choctaw Mixed Bloods and the Advent of Removal," 48–49, describes the Favre family as having "some of the deepest roots in Choctaw country." For Favre as interpreter, see *MPA-FD*, 5:299, 301.

45. Favre to Tugean, Mobile, December 4, 1783, in Kinnaird, *Spain in the Mississippi Valley*, 92; Coker and Watson, *Indian Traders*, 8–14; Din and Harkins, *New Orleans Cabildo*, 90; Caughey, *Bernardo de Gálvez*, 14, 17–18.

46. O'Brien, *Choctaws in a Revolutionary Age*, 51, 85; De Fina, "Rivalidades y Contactos," 1:256–74.

47. Sánchez-Fabrés Mirat, *Situación Histórica*, 52–54; Whitaker, *Spanish-American Frontier*, 65; Weber, *Spanish Frontier*, 279. Whitaker, *Spanish-American Frontier*, 101.

48. De Fina, "Rivalidades y Contactos, 1:256–74. Din and Harkins, *New Orleans Cabildo*, 84 n.2, 93–95.

49. O'Brien, *Choctaws in a Revolutionary Age*, 73–74; Du Val, *Independence Lost*, 240–41, 304–6; Dowd, *Spirited Resistance*, 90–95.

50. Charles A. Weeks, *Paths to a Middle Ground*, 41.

51. Charles A. Weeks, *Paths to a Middle Ground*, 41; Martín Navarro to José de Gálvez, New Orleans, July 27, 1784, no. 239, AGI, Santo Domingo, file 2611.

52. Charles A. Weeks, *Paths to a Middle Ground*, 41–42; Braund, *Deerskins and Duffels*, 170–71, 173; Coker and Watson, *Indian Traders*, 58–61. Panton died in early 1801. For a characterization of Panton as maintaining a "form of hybrid political loyalty" by pledging "fidelity to the Spanish crown" as well as "reserving national allegiance to Great Britain," see Narrett, "William Panton," 139.

53. James R. Atkinson, *Splendid Land, Splendid People*, 124. Atkinson says that there were six Chickasaw villages. See also Charles A. Weeks, *Paths to a Middle Ground*, 42. Contemporary Chickasaw usage prefers *Piominko* to *Piomingo*.

54. On the Choctaws at Hopewell, see, O'Brien, "Conqueror Meets the Unconquered." On the Chickasaws, see James R. Atkinson, *Splendid Land, Splendid People*, 126–33

55. On the subjects of both war and reform, see J. H. Elliott, *Empires of the Atlantic World*, 293–324; Lynch, *España*, 295–336. Charles A. Weeks, *Paths to a Middle Ground*, focuses on a culture of diplomacy, with particular emphasis on four meetings between Spanish and Natives: Natchez in 1792, Boukfouka and Nogales in 1793, and San Fernando de las Barrancas in 1795. On the Nootka Sound controversy, see Whitaker, *Spanish-American Frontier*, 140–52.

56. Din, *Populating the Barrera*, 63–78. Din concludes that efforts "to counter-colonize with American settlers in Louisiana and West Florida resulted largely in failure." In April 1791, the commandant at the newly created post at Nogales, at the mouth of the Yazoo River, received instructions that new settlers were to be guaranteed freedom of religion, although only Roman Catholics could be employed by the state in either a military or civil capacity. In addition, settlers could sell any goods they brought free of duty. "Instrucciones para la Admission de Pobladores," Natchez, April 1, 1791, AGI, PC, file 2352.

57. See Din, *Populating the Barrera*," 153–77.

58. Galloway, *Practicing Ethnohistory*, 112.

59. Holmes, *Gayoso*, 86–108. On tobacco, cotton, and other crops, see Whitaker, *Mississippi Question*, 63, 130; Adam Rothman, *Slave Country*, 45–49. Carlos de Grand-Pré to Estevan Miró, March 2, 1790, AGI, PC, file 16, lists the names of 363 people in Natchez who produced tobacco and the amount each produced. See Kinnaird, *Spain in the Mississippi Valley*, 305–11.

60. Adam Rothman, *Slave Country*, 45–49. On the cotton gin, see Holmes, "Cotton Gins,"; Holmes, *Gayoso*, 63, 130. See also Pinnen, "Slavery and Empire," 196–223. On the 1795 Treaty of San Lorenzo, which opened the Mississippi River and New Orleans to free trade, see Abernethy, *South in the New Nation*, 150–51; Calloway, *Indian World of George Washington*, 445.

61. Narrett, "Geopolitics and Intrigue," 103, 106. Historian Walter Johnson, *River of Dark Dreams*, 26, identifies Wilkinson as a "paid agent of the government of Spain."

62. Abernethy, *South in the New Nation*, 49. For more on the fluidity of loyalties, see Strang, *Frontiers of Science*, 1–6.

63. Remini, "Andrew Jackson Takes an Oath"; "Juramento de Fidelidad," July 15, 1789, AGI, PC, file 2321; Remini, *Andrew Jackson and His Indian Wars*, 19–26, 31–33.

64. Holmes, *Gayoso*, 3–10, 110. See also Jack D. Elliott Jr., "City and Empire," 286.

65. Din, *War on the Gulf Coast*, 45. Whitaker, *Spanish-American Frontier*, 153–70, characterizes the appointment of Carondelet as "deplorable." For a thorough study of Carondelet, see Fiehrer, "Baron de Carondelet."

66. Pedro Olivier was appointed commissary or commissioner to the Creeks, Juan Delavillebeuvre commissioner to the Choctaws, and Benjamin Fooy commissioner to the Chickasaws. John McDonald, a former British agent among the Cherokees, was offered the position of commissioner to Cherokee towns. Pate, "Fort of the Confederation," 172–73. On the fleet, see Nasatir, *Spanish War Vessels*.

67. Jack D. Elliott Jr., "City and Empire," 273. For a full discussion of the emergence of the city of Natchez, see Jack D. Elliott Jr., "City and Empire." According to Holmes, *Gayoso*, 40–41, Grand-Pré initiated a town plan before Gayoso arrived in 1788. On the *cabildo*, see Holmes, *Gayoso*, 49–50. On Irish priests, see Din, *Populating the Barrera*, 133–51; Holmes, "Irish Priests in Spanish Natchez," 170.

68. Forman, *Narrative*, 53–56. Forman also mentions Anthony Hutchins, "a wealthy planter" and brother of Thomas, "the geographer-general of the United States"; "Mr. Bernard Lintot"; "Mr. Moore"; and "Mr. Ellis," a "wealthy planter." He also recalls a Spanish Jewish couple, "Monsieur and Madam Mansanto," who were "the most kind and hospitable of people." For more on both Samuel and Ezekiel Forman, see Holmes, *Gayoso*, 37, 42–43, 64, 79, 119, 126–27.

69. Conlin, "American Mission," 502–3. Narrett, *Adventurism and Empire*, 234–35, describes the mission as one of "espionage and conspiracy." See also Kyte, "Spy on the Western Waters." On Jay's mission to Britain and the resulting treaty, ratified by the US Senate in 1795 despite substantial opposition in the American South, see Abernethy, *South in the New Nation*, 129–35. Calloway, *Indian World of George Washington*, 444–45, describes the treaty as creating something of a "firestorm" in the United States.

70. Collot, *Journey in North America*, 2:62. For a translation of Collot's plan and objectives for his journey, see Echeverria, "General Collot's Plan." See also Weddle, *Changing Tides*, 223–27.

71. Cruzat, "General Collot's Reconnoitering Trip," 314. For an older view of how Americans, particularly those of the Federalist Party, viewed Collot's mission, see Whitaker, *Mississippi Question*, 119–20.

72. Baily, *Journal of a Tour*, 148–58, xxv–xxvi, 151. John Francis McDermott describes Baily as the "twenty-one-year-old son of an English banker, who, for reasons not known to us, made this grand tour of inland America down the Ohio and the Mississippi to New Orleans and return[ed] by way of the Natchez Trace in the winter of 1796–97." Baily, *Journal of a Tour*, vii.

73. For the estimate of twenty-five million acres in grants, see Abernethy, *South in the New Nation*, 74–101. Din, *War on the Gulf Coast*, 31, puts the total at fifteen million acres. See also Nichols, "Land, Republicanism, and Indians," 207. On the illegality of the land acquisitions and their liquidation when Georgia finally ceded its western claims, see Wallace, *Long and Bitter Trail*, 63–64. For an emphasis on the South Carolina Company, see Narrett,

Adventurism and Empire, 188–95. President Washington and the US government opposed the grants. Calloway *Indian World of George Washington*, 364–65.

74. Din, *War on the Gulf Coast*, 31; Abernethy, *South in the New Nation*, 76; O'Brien, "Conqueror Meets the Unconquered," 39, 44–45; Charles A. Weeks, *Paths to a Middle Ground*, 49. *Nogal* is Spanish for "walnut."

75. O'Fallon to Miró, Lexington, Kentucky, July 1790, in Kinnaird, *Spain in the Mississippi Valley*, 357–64.

76. For an older general discussion of Nogales, see Kinnaird and Kinnaird, "Nogales." See also Charles A. Weeks, *Paths to a Middle Ground*, 49–80, 118–25, esp. 60 for the map and 146–49 for an English translation of Gayoso's diary of the trip to Nogales in March and April 1791. Gayoso found in Girault another valuable assistant. For a full discussion of Girault, see Pineda, "Preserving Good Order."

77. Charles A. Weeks, *Paths to a Middle Ground*, 63–80, 146–202. Holmes describes Minor and José (Joseph) Vidal as the two most helpful associates of Gayoso. Like Gayoso, Minor had acquired knowledge of many languages including some Native American. See Holmes, "Stephen Minor"; Holmes, *Gayoso*, 51. For a description of the ball game, see Charles M. Hudson, *Southeastern Indians*, 408–21; Mooney, "Cherokee Ball Play."

78. Estevan Miró to Antonio Valdés, New Orleans, May 20, 1789, no. 38, Archivo Histórico Nacional, Madrid, Spain, file 3887; Holmes, "Notes on the Spanish Fort," 281–82; Charles A. Weeks, *Paths to a Middle Ground*, 47–48.

79. Pate, "Fort of the Confederation," 173–78; Charles A. Weeks, *Paths to a Middle Ground*, 81–102. Boukfouka (Boucfouca), somewhere near the boundary between Leake and Neshoba Counties, was where Regis du Roullet began his 1732 trip down the Pearl River. See "Journal of Regis du Roullet" with "Map of the Course of the Pearl River from Boucfouca to Its Mouth Which Is at the Pass à Dion Opposite Goose Island, Drawn up by Reckoning on the 14th of July, 1732, by Mr. Régis du Roullet, an Officer in the Colony," *MPA-FD*, 1:136–54.

80. Kinnaird and Kinnaird, "Nogales," 2–4; Charles A. Weeks, *Paths to a Middle Ground*, 101, 118–25, 209–32; Adam Rothman, *Slave Country*, 15.

81. For a discussion the French Revolution and "American filibustering," see Narrett, *Adventurism and Empire*, 195–203. For more on Genet and his appeal in the United States, see Abernethy, *South in the New Nation*, 102–28. Genet remained in the United States, married the daughter of Governor George Clinton of New York, and settled on Long Island

82. Charles A. Weeks, *Paths to a Middle Ground*, 123–24. For Gayoso's full report of the meeting, see Charles A. Weeks, *Paths to a Middle Ground*, 207–29.

83. Abernethy, *South in the New Nation*, 136–68; Richter, *Facing East*, 227–28.

84. Charles A. Weeks, *Paths to a Middle Ground*, 126–40, 233–35.

85. Crabb, "George Washington and the Chickasaw Nation"; Calloway, *Indian World of George Washington*, 431.

86. For a detailed discussion of Pinckney's treaty along with a bilingual text of the document, see Bemis, *Pinckney's Treaty*. See also Whitaker, *Spanish-American Frontier*, 205–7; F. Todd Smith, *Louisiana*, 170–71. For more insight into Manuel de Godoy, first minister to Spain's King Charles IV and his principal negotiator for this treaty, see Lynch, *España*, 343–66. See also Bemis, *Pinckney's Treaty*, 219, 267–68, 272–73; Weddle, *Changing Tides*, 223.

87. F. Todd Smith, *Louisiana*, 171.

88. Carson, *Searching for the Bright Path*, 47–48. Historian Richard White, *Roots of Dependency*, 68, argues that the "Choctaw play-off system" began to decline with the withdrawal of the French in 1763.

89. Charles A. Weeks, "Of Rattlesnakes, Wolves, and Tigers," 487–88, 511–13; Calloway, *One Vast Winter Count*, 374–75.

90. Holmes, *Documentos Inéditos*, 306; Charles A. Weeks, "Of Rattlesnakes, Wolves, and Tigers," 501–2; Ellicott, *Journal of Andrew Ellicott*, 43–46. For biographical information about Ellicott, see the editor's introduction to Ellicott, *Surveying the Early Republic*. For more on the Choctaw response, see Carson, *Searching for the Bright Path*, 48–50; Van Horne, "Andrew Ellicott's Mission to Natchez."

91. Calloway, *One Vast Winter Count*, 375–76. Although initially opposed by Miró but supported by Gardoqui, New Madrid was established in the late 1780s by a George Morgan on a generous grant of land on the west side of the Mississippi River south of the mouth of the Ohio River. Abernethy, *South in the New Nation*, 80; Narrett, *Adventurism and Empire*, 178–86. For translated Spanish documents on the creation of New Madrid, see Houck, *Spanish Regime in Missouri*, 1:275–309. For more insight into the Osages and the Spanish, see Din and Nasatir, *Imperial Osages*; Calloway, *One Vast Winter Count*, 361–65, 379–82.

92. According to Holmes, *Documentos Inéditos*, 305–15, both Ellicott and Pierce S. Pope, the commander of American soldiers accompanying the border commission, also took advantage of the sentiment of many in the Natchez District, especially debtors, who saw a change to US dominion as a way to avoid payment. See also Holmes, "Barton Hannon"; Sparks, *On Jordan's Stormy Banks*, 9–10; Sparks, *Religion in Mississippi*, 21.

93. Coker and Watson, *Indian Traders*, 199–200; Narrett, "William Panton," 167–68; Holmes, *Gayoso*, 198–99; Holmes, "Stephen Minor," 20–21. For more on the commission, which included Spain's "leading scientist in the initial westernmost phase," Natchez planter William Dunbar, and its work, see Holmes, "William Dunbar's Correspondence"; Riley, "Sir William Dunbar"; Dunbar, "Report of Sir William Dunbar"; John, "Riddle of Mapmaker Juan Pedro Walker," 104–7.

94. On Vidal, "Concordia," and "Vidalia," see Holmes, *Gayoso*, 50, 102, 196, 228, 260; Calhoun, "History of Concordia Parish"; Holmes, "Stephen Minor," 22; F. Todd Smith, *Louisiana*, 171.

Chapter 5: A Gulf Coast, 1779–1821

1. J. H. Elliott, *Empires of the Atlantic World*, 372–73. Knapton, *France*, 343–44. On the importance of Saint-Domingue, which " produced more sugar than all of the islands of the British West Indies combined" and the decision of Napoleon to sell Louisiana, see Walter Johnson, *River of Dark Dreams*, 22–23.

2. Weddle, *La Salle, the Mississippi, and the Gulf*, 8, suggests that view derived, in part at least, from La Salle and his "pretensions" that the Texas coast could be open to the settlement he attempted. On Jefferson and his thoughts on American expansion, see Onuf, *Jefferson's Empire*, 1–17, 53; Nugent, *Habits of Empire*, xiii, 69–72, 103, 130, 316, 243.

3. Cox, *West Florida Controversy*. Cox used both Spanish and American primary sources extensively, and his book remains the best general treatment of the subject, at least to 1813. For a discussion of the 1803–19 period, see Sánchez-Fabrés Mirat, *Situación Histórica*, 245–316. See also Thomas D. Clark and Guice, *Frontiers in Conflict*, 41–65, 67–68; Weber, *Spanish Frontier*, 290–301; Kastor, *Nation's Crucible*, 33–45, 70–78, 120–34, 156–59, 196–97; F. Todd Smith, *Louisiana*, 177–78, 186 (map), 192–95, 215–24, 239–42; Din, *War on the Gulf Coast*, 99, 100 (maps). An earlier eastern boundary for West Florida was the Perdido River,

deriving from the French acceptance of that line that excluded Pensacola already occupied by Spanish. After 1783, all of Florida became politically Spanish, and it was divided into East Florida and West Florida at Apalachicola and Chattahoochee Rivers. Haynes, *Mississippi Territory*, 241, and others identify those two rivers as the effective eastern boundary of West Florida. See also Cox, *West Florida Controversy*, 11–12; Richter, *Facing East*, 227–28.

4. Din, "Troubled Seven Years," 409, 418; Haynes, *Mississippi Territory*, 241–43; Weddle, *Changing Tides,* 262–63; Jared William Bradley, "Vicente Folch y Juan," in W. C. C. Claiborne, *Interim Appointment*, 499–532, esp. 503; David Hart White, *Vicente Folch*. The eight Florida parishes are East Baton Rouge, West Feliciana, East Feliciana, St. Helena, Livingston, Tangipahoa, Washington, and St. Tammany. Tangipahoa was not formed until 1869. See Samuel C. Hyde Jr., *Pistols and Politics*, 2.

5. For more on this region and period with particular focus on coastal waterways, see Weddle, *Changing Tides*; Napier, *Lower Pearl River's Piney Woods*, 21.

6. For a full discussion of this trip and a translation of Villebeuvre's journal and addenda listing names of villages of the Large Party, Small Party, and Six Villages of the Choctaws, see Charles A. Weeks, "Politics of Trade." For the description of the waterway from Mobile to New Orleans, see Medina Rojas, *José de Ezpeleta*, 44.

7. Charles A. Weeks, "Politics of Trade," 38 (map), 63–64, 69. For a more complete description of this coastal area, see the 1784 account of geographer Hutchins, *Historical Narrative*, 63–70.

8. Charles A. Weeks, "Politics of Trade," 64 n.71

9. Giraud, *History of French Louisiana*, 1:25; Weber, *Spanish Frontier*, 267–68. At the conclusion of the French and Indian War in 1763, the British organized four new colonial governments. According to Cox, *West Florida Controversy*, 11–12, "East Florida, the second mentioned in the [1763] proclamation, was 'bounded to the westward by the Gulph of Mexico and the Appalachicola river.' The third colony, West Florida, was to be 'bounded to the Southward by the Gulph of Mexico, including all islands within six leagues of the coast, the river Appalachicola to Lake Pontchartrain,' and to the westward by the line laid down in the treaty. Its northern limit was a 'line drawn due East from that part of the Mississippi, which lies in the 31st degree of North latitude, to the river Appalachicola, or the Catahouchee,' which was its eastern limit." For the Perdido River boundary, see Cox, *West Florida Controversy*, 7–9. See also Thomas D. Clark and Guice, *Frontiers in Conflict*, 41–65, esp. 43–45, which stresses the artificiality of such borders as the one defined by the Treaty of San Lorenzo, a socially, politically, and economically "unrealistic" treaty given the "heterogeneity of the inhabitants" and their settlement patterns and interests.

10. Holmes, "Juan de la Villebeuvre," 392–93, 398–99.

11. Greenwell, *Twelve Flags*; Greenwell, *D'Iberville and St. Martin*; Gail Buzhardt, personal communication, September 22, 2017. For a visual representation of the coast and islands, see Giraud, *History of French Louisiana*, 1:35.

12. Maduell, *Census Tables*, v–ix.

13. "Noticia, y Nombres de los Habitantes en General, de la Plaza y Jurisdicción de la Mobila," signed Pedro de Favrot, Mobile, January 1, 1786, AGI, PC, file 2360; "Noticia y Nombres de los Blancos, Pardos y Negros Libres; Pardos y Negros Esclavos; de la Jurisdicción de la Mobila; con Expecificación de los Artículos de su Producto; y Número de Ganado que cada uno posee," signed Pedro Favrot, Mobile, [1787], AGI, PC, file 2361; "Padrón del Distrito y Jurisdicción de la Mobila, para el año de mil setecientos ochenta y ocho, con expresión de Cosechas, y Piezas de Esclavos, &a.," Mobile, 1788, AGI, PC, file 202; "Copia de la Sta. Visita de la Plaza de Panzacola, y Ciudad de la Movila, efectuado en el año 1791, por el Ylmo. Ser.

Dn. Fray Cirilo de Barcelona," including "Padrón General de los havitantes de la Jurisdición de la Ciudad de la Movila con sus cabezas de Familia, edades Niños, esclavos Negros y Mulatos Libres y edades de estos," signed Fr. Manuel García, Mobile, April 30, 1791, AGI, Santo Domingo, file 1436; "Autos de la Sta. Visita de Panzacola y de la Movila por Ylmo Sor. Dn. Fray Cirilo de Barcelona," including "Extracto del Plan General de vecinos y Havitantes existentes en la Parroquía de la Ynmaculada Concepción e N. S. de la Movila comprehensiba de las edades que se expresan," n.d., AGI, Santo Domingo, file 2673; Lista de los Habitantes de esta Plaza, &a. qe. Tienen Esclavos," signed Pedro Olivier, Mobile, December 31, 1795, AGI, PC, file 212-B. Inglis, "Forgotten but Not Lost," 9–10 nn.16–17.

14. *Ladner* may have originated as *Ladnier* and been anglicized. The 1786 census for a "District of Mobile" has subdivisions labeled "Gulf Coast," "Mobile," "French Mobile," "Tombigbee-Tensaw," and "Mobile District" with a total population of 3,066 for the region stretching roughly from Bay St. Louis to the Mobile. Only 238 of those people resided along the Gulf Coast, and that number was the highest recorded in all of the censuses. Inglis, "Forgotten but Not Lost," 26. Napier, *Lower Pearl River's Piney Woods*, 28, offers the much smaller figure of 746 for what he says became a district of Mobile beginning east of the Pearl River.

15. Napier, *Lower Pearl River's Piney Woods*, 10–12.

16. Napier, *Lower Pearl River's Piney Woods*, 13–14, 26; Charles A. Weeks, *Paths to a Middle Ground*, 47–48.

17. Inglis, "Forgotten But Not Lost," 15–19; for population tables, 26.

18. Both Dunbar and Ellicott recorded extensively their impressions of the natural landscape. See Ellicott, *Journal of Andrew Ellicott*, 285–89; Dunbar, "Report of Sir William Dunbar."

19. For an extended discussion of "vernacular landscape," see John Brinckerhoff Jackson, *Discovering the Vernacular Landscape*, 149–51. For added perspective, especially with regard to the relationship between verbal descriptions of landscape and territory and pictorial representation in the form of maps, see Valverde and Lafuente, "Space Production and Spanish Imperial Geopolitics."

20. Inglis, "Forgotten but Not Lost," 20–21, concludes that "skin color, ethnicity, outside worldly status and wealth meant little" in this region.

21. Inglis, "Forgotten but Not Lost," 21–22. All of the documents including the "Proceso formado contra Andres Brè, Pedro Danguy, Pedro Grelié, Mc. Gonagle, Loudy Bennett, Juez fiscal el The. Dn. Juan Bautista Pellerín Comandante. Militar del distrito de la Bahia de Sn Luis año de 1806," Pass Christian, June 15, 1806, can be found in AGI, PC, file 61.

22. Joseph Collins, Pascagoula, to Vicente Folch y Juan, July 7, 1806, AGI, PC, file 2369. For documentation regarding the attempt to land and sell "negros ladinos," see "Testimonio de autos sobre la detención de la goleta anglo-americano 'Nancy,'" Pensacola, January 8, 1807, AGI, PC, file 62; Testimonio," AGI, PC, file 697; AGI, PC, file 267. Inglis, "Forgotten but Not Lost," 22–24, 39. On smuggling and contraband, see Cox, *West Florida Controversy*, 171, 585; Weber, *Spanish Frontier*, 280; Din, *War on the Gulf Coast*, 9–10.

23. Inglis, "Forgotten but Not Lost," 1.

24. Weddle, *Spanish Sea*, 223–27; Ellicott, *Journal of Andrew Ellicott*; John, "Riddle of Mapmaker Juan Pedro Walker," 103–6. See also Holmes, "William Dunbar's Correspondence"; Dungan, "'Sir' William Dunbar of Natchez," 216–18. For discussion of the scientific talent and interests of such people as Ellicott, Power, and Dunbar who were involved in surveying the boundary, see Strang, *Frontiers of Science*, 131–44, 164–92.

25. Ellicott, *Journal of Andrew Ellicott*, 236–37. Weddle discusses Ellicott's trip in *Changing Tides*, 227–34.

26. Ellicott, *Journal of Andrew Ellicott*, 281–82.

27. Sánchez-Fabrés Mirat, *Situación Histórica*, 245.

28. Weber, *Spanish Frontier*, 297–99; Meyer and Sherman, *Course of Mexican History*, 281, 285–97; Villoro, "Revolución de Independencia," 316. For one older discussion of "the independence of Spanish South America," see Hubert Herring, *History of Latin America*, 260–86.

29. Knapton, *France*, 343.

30. See Knapton, *France*, 343–49.

31. Knapton, *France*, 348–49; Herr, *Historical Essay*, 69–72.

32. Lynch, *España*, 222, 337–77; J. H. Elliott, *Empires of the Atlantic World*, 372–74; 399; Weber, *Spanish Frontier*, 296; Herr, *Historical Essay*, 65–69.

33. Weber, *Spanish Frontier*, 290–91; J. H. Elliott, *Empires of the Atlantic World*, 353–68, 371–91.

34. Thomas D. Clark and Guice, *Frontiers in Conflict*, 49; McMichael, *Atlantic Loyalties*, 22–23; David Hart White, *Vicente Folch*; Bradley, "Vicente Folch y Juan," in W. C. C. Claiborne, *Interim Appointment*, 499–32; Din, "Troubled Seven Years." Haynes, *Mississippi Territory*, 244, sees the Spanish government of West Florida as "weak, generally inefficient, and often corrupt." Bradley, at least for the period of the interim appointment of Claiborne, uses the word *chauvinism* to characterize the mentality of some of its officials, among them Juan Ventura Morales, intendant for much of the period between 1784 and 1812, whom Bradley characterizes as "the most unpopular Spanish official along the Gulf Coast in the late eighteenth and early nineteenth centuries." See W. C. C. Claiborne, *Interim Appointment*, 12, 495. Gayoso found Folch arrogant, too independent, and arbitrary. W. C. C. Claiborne, *Interim Appointment*, 499.

35. Padrón, *Spacious Word*, 1–44.

36. Charles A. Weeks, unpublished essay on "Plan de una Parte de la Provincia de la Luisiana y de Otra de la Florida Occidental y de la Provincia de Texas" (Map of a Part of the Province of Louisiana and the Other of West Florida and the Province of Texas), ca. 1803–6, ink and watercolor wash on paper, 21½″ × 41¼″. The map is held by the Arader Galleries. See also O'Gorman, *Invención de América*. On maps, see Buisseret, *Monarchs, Ministers, and Maps*. The document does not identify any specific cartographers or include any dates.

37. Charles A. Weeks, unpublished essay on "Plan de una Parte de la Provincia de la Luisiana."

38. Charles A. Weeks, unpublished essay on "Plan de una Parte de la Provincia de la Luisiana." See also F. Todd Smith, *Louisiana*, 73–74. For Loftus Heights, see chapter 4.

39. McMichael, *Atlantic Loyalties*, 17–20, 22–23, 77–78, 149, 155–56; Haynes, *Mississippi Territory*, 243; Din, "Troubled Seven Years," 418. Cox, *West Florida Controversy*, 150–51, sees Grand-Pré's "mild administration" as effective in keeping the Anglo-American population "under nominal Spanish sway."

40. The phrases "perimeter of conflict" and "land of speculation" are titles of chapters in Thomas D. Clark and Guice, *Frontiers in Conflict*. See also Samuel Watson, "Conquerors, Peacekeepers, or Both?," 69.

41. Charles de Grand-Pré to Robert Williams, Baton Rouge, September 9, 1805, RG 2, Series 488, Doc. 519, Box 16722, MDAH; Haynes, *Mississippi Territory*, 109–17, 241–43; McMichael, *Atlantic Loyalties*, 77–78; Cox, *West Florida Controversy*, 152–68; Din, "Troubled Seven Years," 432–39. Kemper County in Mississippi is named for Reuben Kemper. Louis Farmer, *Kemper County*, 187. See also William Horace Brown, *Glory Seekers*, 161–78, which describes Reuben Kemper as "a buccaneer." On the Kempers and other "bandits and bands

of Americans who disliked the Spanish" and "roamed the border area south of Natchez," see McCain, "Administrations of David Holmes," 334. For an American republican "empire for liberty," see Onuf, *Jefferson's Empire*, 2–8, 53–79. Reuben Kemper later went to New Orleans as a pawn of Clark and others, including the Spanish intendant, Juan Ventura Morales. The American Historical Association concluded that in his article on Holmes, McCain had "violated approved scholarly usage" by taking sixty of sixty-five paragraphs almost verbatim from Frances Melton Racine's Emory University master's thesis without acknowledging their source. W. F. Minor, "McCain Article Hit by AHA Unit," *New Orleans Times-Picayune*, February 12, 1972, William D. McCain Subject File, MDAH. See also Bond, "'Unmitigated Thievery.'"

42. Din, "William Augustus Bowles"; Narrett, *Adventurism and Empire*, 6.

43. See Din, *War on the Gulf Coast*, 204–13; Narrett, *Adventurism and Empire*, 139, 211–28, 254–55, 259–60. For an older account of Bowles, which, in the view of Din, incorrectly depicts him as the "genuine director general of the Creeks," see J. Leitch Wright Jr., *William Augustus Bowles*. See also Din, *War on the Gulf Coast*, xii; David Hart White, *Vicente Folch*, 47–69.

44. Owsley and Smith, *Filibusters and Expansionists*, 32,38, 62–63; Sánchez Fabrés-Mirat, *Situación Histórica*, 258–61; Isenberg, *Fallen Founder*, 288–92; Onuf, *Jefferson's Empire*, 131–37; Din, "Troubled Seven Years," 439–40; Walter Johnson, *River of Dark Dreams*, 26. For more on Burr and Wilkinson, see Faber, *Building the Land of Dreams*, 253–58.

45. Haynes, *Mississippi Territory*, 139–66; Owsley and Smith, *Filibusters and Expansionists*, 62; Tucker and Hendrickson, *Empire of Liberty*, 150–51; Abernethy, *Burr Conspiracy*, 37.

46. Abernethy, *Burr Conspiracy*, 53–54, 117–18, 199–211.

47. Abernethy, *Burr Conspiracy*, 217–49; Haynes, *Mississippi Territory*, 164–68.

48. Haynes, *Mississippi Territory*, 247–49; Sánchez Fabrés-Mirat, *Situación Histórica*, 258–67; McMichael, *Atlantic Loyalties*, 149–57.

49. McMichael, *Atlantic Loyalties*, 157; Haynes, *Mississippi Territory*, 248; Cox, *West Florida Controversy*, 313–15.

50. Haynes, *Mississippi Territory*, 250–52; McMichael, *Atlantic Loyalties*, 159–68; David Hart White, *Vicente Folch*, 92–94, 99–102; Sánchez-Fabrés Mirat, *Situación Histórica*, 267–69; McCain, "Administrations of David Holmes," 335–39; Faber, *Building the Land of Dreams*, 293–95. The "lone star" reflects the failure to have an uprising in East Florida and hence no Republic of Florida. See Din, "Troubled Seven Years," 450–51.

51. Sánchez-Fabrés Mirat, *Situación Histórica*, 267–68; Haynes, *Mississippi Territory*, 267–68; Owsley and Smith, *Filibusters and Expansionists*, 7–13; Samuel Watson, "Conquerors, Peacekeepers, or Both?"

52. Cox, *West Florida Controversy*, 413–36; Sánchez-Fabrés Mirat, *Situación Histórica*, 269–72; Haynes, *Mississippi Territory*, 250–55. Located near Cape Trafalgar in southwest Spain, Cádiz was serving at this time as a kind of de facto capital of Spain and its empire. The Central Junta had fled there from Seville in January 1810 and before dissolving itself decreed that all the king's subjects in America would no longer be colonists but equal to *peninsulares* (Spaniards) and called for the creation of the Cortes to represent all of the empire. Herr, *Historical Essay*, 71–75. For the Onís's perspective, see Onís, *Memoria*.

53. Sánchez-Fabrés Mirat, *Situación Histórica*, 273–74; McCain, "Administrations of David Holmes," 336–40; Samuel Watson, "Conquerors, Peacekeepers, or Both?," 73.

54. F. Todd Smith, *Louisiana*, 225; Din, "Troubled Seven Years," 426–52; Sánchez-Fabrés Mirat, *Situación Histórica*, 278–84; Owsley and Smith, *Filibusters and Expansionists*, 63–81.

Andrew K. Frank, "Taking the State," 10, argues that Florida was essentially stateless in that between 1750 and 1810 the Muskogee Indians "held the upper hand in intercolonial affairs and made Florida 'Indian country.'"

55. Haynes, *Mississippi Territory*, 282; McCain, "Administrations of David Holmes," 338–41.

56. Sánchez-Fabrés Mirat, *Situación Histórica*, 284–85.

57. Sánchez-Fabrés Mirat, *Situación Histórica*, 287.

58. Sánchez-Fabrés Mirat, *Situación Histórica*, 287–88. For the treaty, see Brooks, *Diplomacy and the Borderlands*, 205–14. The United States did give up its claim to the Rio Bravo as the southern boundary of the Louisiana Purchase. See also Onís, *Memoria*; Sánchez-Fabrés Mirat, Situación Histórica, 289–316.

59. Sánchez-Fabrés Mirat, *Situación Histórica*, 289; Owsley and Smith, *Filibusters and Expansionists*, 103–13.

60. Brooks, *Diplomacy of the Borderlands*, 205–14. For more on San Marcos, see David Hart White, *Vicente Folch*, 95.

Chapter 6: From Borrowed Land to Possessed Land, 1798 and Beyond

1. Lyon, *Louisiana in French Diplomacy*, 232–50. For a brief summary of the successful slave revolt on the island of Saint-Domingue that led to an independent Haiti in 1804, see Trouillot, *Silencing the Past*, 37–40. See also Houck, *Boundaries of the Louisiana Purchase*, 5–17; Tucker and Hendrickson, *Empire of Liberty*, 101–7, 137–71; William Earl Weeks, *Building the Continental Empire*, 24–28, 59–85. "Liberty," for some, meant liberty to own slaves, leading to the emergence by 1819 of what historian Hammond, *Slavery, Freedom, and Expansion*, 3, calls "an 'empire for slavery' in the West."

2. Burns, *History of Brazil*, 100–101; Worcester, *Brazil*, 56, 124–26.

3. Meyer and Sherman, *Course of Mexican History*, 294–96; 387–401; Simpson, *Many Mexicos*, 283–85; Charles A. Weeks, *Juárez Myth*, 12–13, 93, 115.

4. Wallace, *Jefferson and the Indians*, 161. Wallace's earlier *Long and Bitter Trail*, 26–27, offers a more critical view of the ordinance, interpreting it as Congress's way to get land to use to pay back wages to veterans of the American Revolution and meet other financial obligations. He sees it as a means to sell public lands to "hungrily waiting land companies." For more on "empire of liberty," especially as it played out in Louisiana after the Northwest Ordinance, see Faber, *Building the Land of Dreams*, 4–5. On an "imperial republic," see Calloway, *Indian World of George Washington*, 283–318. On "imperial-revolutionaries," see Griffin, *Experiencing Empire*, 6.

5. Hammond, *Slavery, Freedom, and Expansion*, 13–14.

6. Joshua D. Rothman, *Flush Times and Fever Dreams*, 10.

7. Ellicott, *Journal of Andrew Ellicott*, 134–76. For a full discussion of the personalities, politics, and issues of this transition, see Haynes, *Mississippi Territory*, 7–26.

8. Ellicott, *Journal of Andrew Ellicott*, v.

9. Thomas D. Clark and Guice, *Frontiers in Conflict*, 85.

10. "Plan de una Parte de la Provincia de la Luisiana y de Otra de la Florida Occidental y de la Provincia de Texas" (Map of a Part of the Province of Louisiana and the Other of West Florida and the Province of Texas), ca. 1803–6, ink and watercolor wash on paper, 21½" × 41¼".

11. Jack D. Elliott Jr., "Paving the Trace," 199–201; Haynes, *Mississippi Territory*, 119–33; Thomas D. Clark and Guice, *Frontiers in Conflict*, 85–86; Hawkins, *Collected Works*, 359–412; James R. Atkinson, *Splendid Land, Splendid People*, 189–91; O'Brien, *Choctaws in a Revolutionary Age*, 104–6; Carson, *Searching for the Bright Path*, 48–49; Wallace, *Jefferson and the Indians*, 189; Barnett, *Mississippi's American Indians*, 164–65.

12. Robert B. Ferguson, "Treaties between the United States and the Choctaw Nation," in *Choctaw before Removal*, ed. Reeves, 214–30; O'Brien, *Choctaws in a Revolutionary Age*, 66–67; Abbott, "Indian Policy and Management," 161, 168.

13. Waselkov, *Conquering Spirit*, 56–71; Dowd, *Spirited Resistance*, 152–54; Grivno, "Antebellum Mississippi"; Gitlin, "Crossroads on the Chinaberry Coast"; Angela Pulley Hudson, *Creek Paths and Federal Roads*.

14. Holmes, "Cotton Gins"; Abernethy, *South in the New Nation*, 444–75; Calloway, *Indian World of George Washington*, 448. According to census figures, in 1810, 31,306 people, including 14,523 slaves, lived in counties that became the state of Mississippi; 9,046, including 2,565 bondspeople, lived in the counties that became Alabama. In 1820, Mississippi's population increased to 75,448, while Alabama's grew to 144,317. Thomas D. Clark and Guice, *Frontiers in Conflict*, 164. See also Grivno, "Antebellum Mississippi." The term *white gold* served as a key phrase to describe the interactive exhibit concluding the Mississippi Museum of Art's major exhibition, *Picturing Mississippi, 1817–2017: Land of Plenty, Pain, and Promise*, as part of the 2017 commemoration of Mississippi's bicentennial. See *Picturing Mississippi, 1817–2017*. On "flush times," see Joshua D. Rothman, *Flush Times and Fever Dreams*.

15. Southerland and Brown, *Federal Road through Georgia*; Jack D. Elliott Jr., *Three Chopped Way*; Remini, *Andrew Jackson and His Indian Wars*, 100–101, 116–17, 188, 272; Thomas D. Clark and Guice, *Frontiers in Conflict*, 175–77; Haynes, *Mississippi Territory*, 128–29. For Cotton Gin Port, see Jack D. Elliott Jr., "Buried City," 118–19. For George Strother Gaines's role in the creation of that road, see Gaines, *Reminiscences*, 46–49. For a general discussion of these roads and their relation to the growth of population, including enslaved people, and the consequences of both on Native peoples, in particular the Creeks, see Angela Pulley Hudson, *Creek Paths and Federal Roads*, 121–44.

16. Sparks, *On Jordan's Stormy Banks*, esp. 19–40 on camp meetings; Kidwell, *Choctaws and Missionaries*, 24–25. For an older discussion of the advent of various Protestant Christian denominations in Mississippi, especially Presbyterians, see Haman, "Beginnings of Presbyterianism"; Sparks, *Religion in Mississippi*, xi; Sparks, "Mississippi's Apostle of Slavery." On Bullen and Ugulayacabé, see Dawson A. Phelps, "Excerpts from the Journal," 270–73.

17. The secretary of war bore responsibility for the management of Indian affairs. Wallace, *Jefferson and the Indians*, 161–240. See also Calloway, *Indian World of George Washington*, 422–92. For further insight into Jefferson's thoughts on Indians, see Onuf, *Jefferson's Empire*, 23–33. On Indian "fighters" and "haters," see Onuf, *Jefferson's Empire*, 191–98; Melville, *Confidence Man*, 131–38; Takaki, *Iron Cages*, 80–107; McBee, *Life and Times of David Smith*. On the use of debt to secure Indian lands, see Takaki, *Iron Cages*, 221; Garrison, *Legal Ideology of Removal*, 13. For the Removal Act of 1830, see Wallace, *Long and Bitter Trail*, 50–72; Remini, *Andrew Jackson and His Indian Wars*, 226–38.

18. Barnett, *Mississippi's American Indians*, 166–67. On Hawkins as Indian agent and promoter of "civilization," see Wallace, *Jefferson and the Indians*; Hawkins, *Collected Works*, vii; Ethridge, *Creek Country*, 12, 128, 140–94; Calloway, *White People, Indians, and Highlanders*, 15–56; Saunt, *New Order of Things*, 1–7.

19. Ethridge, *Creek Country*, 238.

20. On divisions among the Creeks and the Red Sticks, see Ethridge, *Creek Country*, 20–21, 240–41; Dowd, *Spirited Resistance*, 154–57; Braund, *Deerskins and Duffels*, 185–88; Saunt, *New Order of Things*, 249–72; Richter, *Facing East*, 227–30, 232–34; Waselkov, *Conquering Spirit*, 72–115; Remini, *Andrew Jackson and His Indian Wars*, 5, 63–79. For divisions among the Cherokees, see Dowd, *Spirited Resistance*, 157–66.

21. Richard White, *Roots of Dependency*, 97–118.

22. Dowd, *Spirited Resistance*, 159–60.

23. "From the Governor to Judge Rodney, Washington, [Mississippi Territory], April 5, 1806," MDAH, RG 2, Territorial Papers, Series 483: Indian Affairs—Superintendent's Journal, 1803–1808; Dawson A. Phelps, "Excerpts from the Journal," 270–73; Charles A. Weeks, "Of Rattlesnakes, Wolves, and Tigers," 508; James Hall, *Brief History*, 5–6; Barnett, *Mississippi's American Indians*, 166.

24. On removal generally, see Wallace, *Long and Bitter Trail*, 50–72. For Mississippi in particular, see Barnett, *Mississippi's American Indians*, 164–207. See also Guice, "Face to Face"; Samuel J. Wells, "Federal Indian Policy: From Accommodation to Removal," in *Choctaws before Removal*, ed. Reeves, 157–213.

25. Carson, "Greenwood LeFlore," 369.

26. Remini, *Andrew Jackson and His Indian Wars*, 239–53, 245; Carson, "Greenwood LeFlore," 369. See also Samuel James Wells, "Choctaw Mixed Bloods and the Advent of Removal," 49–50.

27. Richter, *Facing East*, 235–36.

28. Greenwood LeFlore's father was Louis LeFleur, a French trader from Canada who worked for Panton, Leslie & Company of Pensacola. His mother was the daughter of Choctaw chief Pushmataha. Pate, "LeFlore, Greenwood"; Carson, "Greenwood LeFlore," 360. O'Brien, *Choctaws in a Revolutionary Age*, 90, notes that "well into the nineteenth century, Choctaws considered the children of Choctaw mothers and Euro-American fathers to be Choctaw, as well as elite." See also O'Brien, "Mushulatubbee and Choctaw Removal."

29. Kidwell, *Choctaws and Missionaries*, 176–83. For the Treaty of Dancing Rabbit Creek, see Halbert, "Story of the Treaty"; Dillard, *Treaty of Dancing Rabbit Creek*, 25–31 (based on information provided by George S. Gaines). Dillard puts the number of Choctaws attending at three thousand. Carson, "Greenwood LeFlore," 370–72; Halbert, "Story of the Treaty," 376. For more on Mushulatubbee, see O'Brien, "Mushulatubbee and Choctaw Removal." For a more recent and thorough account of the treaty proceedings, see Barnett, *Mississippi's American Indians*, 195–98.

30. Halbert, "Story of the Treaty," 377.

31. Halbert, "Story of the Treaty," 379.

32. Halbert, "Story of the Treaty"; Remini, *Andrew Jackson and His Indian Wars*, 249–50; Barnett, *Mississippi's American Indians*, 195–98; Wallace, *Long and Bitter Trail*, 78–79. For other perspectives, see Kidwell, *Choctaws and Missionaries*, 116–46; Richard White, *Roots of Dependency*, 142–46.

33. Halbert, "Story of the Treaty," 396; Barnett, *Mississippi's American Indians*, 398.

34. Barnett, *Mississippi's American Indians*, 203; for a full text of the treaty, see 214–23.

35. James Culberson, "Tushpa Crosses the Mississippi," in *Native American Testimony*, ed. Nabokov, 152–57. See also Sawyer, *Tushpa's Story*; O'Brien, "Mushulatubbee and Choctaw Removal."

36. For the encounter with the Choctaws at the Mississippi, see Tocqueville, *Democracy in America*, 1:352–53.

37. Kidwell, *Choctaws and Missionaries*, 169, puts the number of Choctaws who remained at about five thousand, a number that dropped to just over twenty-two hundred by 1855. See also Clara Sue Kidwell, "Mississippi Choctaws in the Nineteenth Century," in *Ethnic Heritage in Mississippi*, ed. Carpenter, 63; Carson, "Greenwood LeFlore," 372; Pate, "LeFlore, Greenwood."

38. On the "Choctaw miracle," see Osburn, *Choctaw Resurgence in Mississippi*. See also Kidwell, "Mississippi Choctaws in the Nineteenth Century"; Kidwell, *Choctaws and Missionaries*; Tom Mould, "'Chahta Siyah Ókih': Ethnicity in the Oral Tradition of the Mississippi Band of Choctaw Indians," in *Ethnic Heritage in Mississippi*, ed. Walton, 219–60.

39. Barnett, *Mississippi's American Indians*, 164–207. On debt, see Garrison, *Legal Ideology of Removal*, 13; Coker and Watson, *Indian Traders*, 243–72; Wallace, *Long and Bitter Trail*, 75, 81–83; James R. Atkinson, *Splendid Land, Splendid People*, 228–35; Remini, *Andrew Jackson and His Indian Wars*, 242–47, 251–52. On Dinsmoor, who served first as Washington's agent to the Cherokees and later as Jefferson's agent to the Choctaws, see Calloway, *Indian World of George Washington*, 464–65; Wallace, *Jefferson and the Indians*, 210.

40. Smaller indigenous groups, the "petites nations," also found ways to survive, as they had during the seventeenth and eighteenth centuries. They relied on strategies of networking, adapted economically, and learned to live in joint settlements. According to historian Elizabeth Ellis, as of 2010, Louisiana had fourteen state-recognized Indian tribes and more than fifty thousand people who identified themselves as Native Americans. Ellis, "Many Ties of the Petites Nations," 257–60.

Chapter 7: Remembering, Recovering, and Representing a Mississippi Past, 1500–1800

1. Padrón, *Spacious Word*, 1–44; O'Gorman, *Invención de América*, 124–36. On Vespucci, Waldseemüller, and the naming of America, see Fernández-Armesto, *Amerigo*, esp. 117–23, 144–46, 184–88, 190–91. See also Markham, *Letters of Amerigo Vespucci*, xvii, xliii. For more context on Waldseemüller and cartography in the late fifteenth and early sixteenth centuries, see Gilmore, *World of Humanism*, 255–56; Durand, *Vienna-Klosterneuburg Map Corpus*; Cumming, *Southeast in Early Maps*, 106–7. In 1500, Spanish cartographer Juan de la Cosa created a world map that includes a northern continent with a long coastline marked by English flags and a note that it had been discovered by English people from Bristol. Evan T. Jones and Condon, *Cabot and Bristol's Age of Discovery*, 1–2. The map is held by the Museo Naval in Madrid.

2. Well before 1500, Europeans had reached America by water and Africa and Asia by both land and water. Much of this section derives from Parry, *Establishment of European Hegemony*; Parry, *Age of Reconnaissance*; Worcester, *Brazil*, 15–17. Much of the ideological content of this expansionism is the subject of books by Pagden, esp. *Lords of All the World*. The concept of "new world" is explored from an American Indianist perspective in Merrell, *Indians' New World*, and is further elaborated with specific reference to the South in Axtell, *Indians' New South*.

3. O'Gorman, *Invención de América*; Padrón, *Spacious Word*, 12–32. Galloway, *Practicing Ethnohistory*, 175–77. On narrative and emplotment, see Hayden White, *Content of the Form*, esp. 20–57; Hayden White, *Metahistory*, 7–11; Hayden White, *Probing the Limits of Representation*, 37–53. For some insight into varieties of emplotment and interpretation with regard to the so-called Natchez Massacre, see Sayre, "Plotting the Natchez Massacre." On Indian

maps and Indian assistance to European newcomers beginning with Columbus, see De Vorsey, "Silent Witnesses"; Cumming, *Southeast in Early Maps*, 65–98.

4. Daniel H. Usner Jr., "Between Creoles and Yankees: The Discursive Representation of Colonial Louisiana in American History," in *French Colonial Louisiana and the Atlantic World*, ed. Bond, 1–21. On remembering, recovering, and representing, with particular focus on the Native American dimension, see Galloway, *Practicing Ethnohistory*, esp. 1–30, 33–42. For a more general discussion of "landscape and memory," see Schama, *Landscape and Memory*.

5. A member of the Cortés expedition, Bernal Díaz del Castillo, *Conquest of Mexico*, 214, expressed awe in his account of that expedition when he and his companions encountered the valley of Mexico: "And when we saw all those cities and villages built in the water, and other great towns on dry land, and that straight and level causeway leading to Mexico, we were astounded. These great towns and cues and buildings rising from the water, all made of stone, seemed like an enchanted vision from the tale of Amadís." See also Hugh Thomas's account of the first Spanish encounter with the valley of Mexico and its cities, especially Tenochtitlán, in *Conquest, Cortés, and the Fall of Old Mexico*, 265–85; Leonard, *Books of the Brave*. For more on Mexico, see Peterson, *Ancient Mexico*, 259–78; Lockhart, *Nahuatl as Written*; Lockhart, *We People Here*.

6. Galloway, *Practicing Ethnohistory*, 175–201; Barr, "There's No Such Thing as 'Prehistory'"; Gardner, *Gardner's Art through the Ages*, 502–34; Baca, *Native American Place Names*. On place-names and words other than French (Indian, German, English, African, Spanish, and Italian) for Louisiana, see Read, *Louisiana*.

7. Cooper, *Looking Back Mississippi*, 169–75, 111–17. Cooper also notes that many of the county seats took their names from such Revolutionary War figures as John Stark from New Hampshire (Starkville) and Polish general Thaddeus Kosciusko (Tadeusz Andrzei Bonawentura Kosciuszko). See also Chateaubriand, *Atala; René*; Chateaubriand, *Atala*. Sayre, "Plotting the Natchez Massacre," 381, argues that the "epic" was not *Atala* but *Les Natchez*. For more on Chateaubriand and the "massacre," see Milne, *Natchez Country*, 3, 175–82.

8. Asher Miller, "The Act of Looking in Delacroix's Early Narrative Paintings," in Allard and Fabre, *Delacroix*, esp. 225, 229–30.

9. Williamson, *William Faulkner and Southern History*, 11–14.

10. See Williamson, *William Faulkner and Southern History*, 355–64, 399–426. With the caveat that Faulkner had "no experience to draw from" and an "aversion to research," Howell, "William Faulkner," 386–87, discusses what he identifies as Faulkner's Indian stories: "Red Leaves," "A Justice," "Lo!," and "A Courtship." See also Jay Watson, Trefzer, and Thomas, *Faulkner and the Native South*, esp. Le Anne Howe, "Faulkner Didn't Invent Yoknapatawpha, Everybody Knows That: So What Other Stories Do Chickasaws and Choctaws Know about Our Homelands?," 3–14. On Faulkner and memory, see Spiller, *Cycle of American Literature*, 208–28.

11. Sayre, introduction, 15.

12. James Hall, *Brief History*, 5–6. For Hall's sources, see Haynes, "Historians and the Mississippi Territory," 411–12. See also Todd Ashley Herring, "Natchez, 1795–1830," 101–38, for a listing (106 n.1) and some discussion of writings of "traveler-journalists," with particular focus on how they represented Natchez-under-the Hill.

13. Pickett, *History of Alabama*, 10–14, 209–25, 236–67, 484–86, 505, 507–8. Three years before the publication of Pickett's book, Harper & Brothers had published Monette's *History of the Discovery and Settlement of the Valley of the Mississippi*.

14. Haynes, "Historians and the Mississippi Territory," 413–16. For Claiborne's political proclivities and activities, see Williams, "Career of J. F. H. Claiborne."

15. J. F. H. Claiborne, *Mississippi*, 1–4

16. J. F. H. Claiborne, *Mississippi*, vii–ix.

17. Halbert, "Some Inaccuracies," 101. See also Henry S. Halbert to Prof. Sims, Crawford. Lowndes County, Miss., June 6, 1872, in Halbert (Henry S.) Manuscript, File Z1616f, MDAH; Halbert and Ball, *Creek War*, 40–57. On records of Tecumseh's speeches, see Dowd, *Spirited Resistance*, 146–47. On Halbert and Byington, see Kidwell, *Choctaws and Missionaries*, 59, 88–89, 178, 180.

18. J. F. H. Claiborne, *Mississippi*, vii–ix, 160, 210. For "partisan bias" related to Ellicott and relations between him and Claiborne's maternal grandfather, Anthony Hutchins, see Riley, "Life of J. F. H. Claiborne," 241.

19. Cushman, *History of the Choctaw, Chickasaw, and Natchez Indians*, 152.

20. Cushman, *History of the Choctaw, Chickasaw, and Natchez Indians*, 3.

21. Cushman, *History of the Choctaw, Chickasaw, and Natchez Indians*, 22, 36–42.

22. Cushman, *History of the Choctaw, Chickasaw, and Natchez Indians*, 13, 36, 131–35, 178–85, 237–38, 486–88. In his brief discussion of the Soto expedition, Axtell, *Indians' New South*, 9, notes that in addition to some 700 Spaniards and slaves, 220 horses, and assorted "war dogs," the "army" consisted of "a proliferating drove of pigs."

23. Cushman, *History of the Choctaw, Chickasaw, and Natchez Indians*, 131–36, 152–53.

24. Cushman, *History of the Choctaw, Chickasaw, and Natchez Indians*, 242–63; "Tecumseh's Visit to the Choctaw Nation 1811," in Henry Halbert Papers, vol. 1, folder 9, MDAH; Halbert and Ball, *Creek War*, 40–57. Halbert, "Some Inaccuracies," 101, identifies the location of the meeting as Blewett's plantation in Noxubee County. See also Jack D. Elliott Jr., "Plymouth Fort and the Creek War," 341. For more on Tecumseh and his southern journey, see Dowd, *Spirited Resistance*, 144–69.

25. H. G. Jones, *Historical Consciousness in the Early Republic*, 136; Faye Phillips, "Writing Louisiana Colonial History," 164–65; Sydnor, "Historical Activities."

26. Galloway, "Archives, Power, and History," 84–85; Charles Reagan Wilson, *Baptized in Blood*; Tate, "Franklin Riley," 100–101. For a different perspective on motives for the establishment of a state archives in Mississippi, see Rasmussen, "Southern Progressives." For the German influence on historical writing, see Burrow, *History of Histories*, 425–37. For a particular focus on one historian, Bolton, and his *Spanish Borderlands*, see Hurtado, "Parkmanizing the Spanish Borderlands." See also Keen's assessment of Edward Gaylord Bourne in Bourne, *Spain in America*, vii–viii. For a biography of Wailes, see Sydnor, *Gentleman of the Old Natchez Region*.

27. For the report of the Mississippi Historical Commission, see *Publications of the Mississippi Historical Society* 5 (1902), esp. 7, 8. Riley authored many of the sections. See also Galloway, "Archives, Power, and History," 81–86; Charles A. Weeks, "Voices from Mississippi's Past," 152.

28. For two examples of the influence of the Lost Cause on Rowland's treatment of Mississippi's past, see Rowland, "Rise and Fall of Negro Rule"; Rowland, "Plantation Life in Mississippi." On archives and the construction of public memory, particularly with regard to Rowland, see Galloway, "Archives, Power, and History," 81–83.

29. Galloway, "Archives, Power, and History," 83; Charles A. Weeks, "Voices from Mississippi's Past," 152–53. Halbert became identified with Alabama's Department of Archives and History, which had been created in 1901.

30. Galloway, "Archives, Power, and History," 152–54.

31. See Rowland's introduction to *MPA-FD*, 1:1–6. Rowland, *General Correspondence*, includes a reprint of Rowland's 1907 MDAH Annual Report, which describes his work in England and France. See also RG 25, English Provincial Archives, MDAH.

32. *MPA-FD*; RG 24: French Provincial Archives—Introduction, MDAH, 1–3. See also the discussion in RG 24 of Series 679: Archives Nationales, Transcripts—Bound Volumes, 1906; Rowland, *General Correspondence*. For a valuable calendar of French documents for this region, see Surrey, *Calendar of Manuscripts*.

33. Rowland, *Mississippi Provincial Archives: English Dominion*. For an account of Rowland's work in London, including a list of "English Records Relating to Mississippi History," see Rowland, *General Correspondence*, 31–43.

34. Halbert found the collection of great value with respect to researchers focused on southern Indians but observed that "historic facts are often obscured, sometimes made worthless, by the carelessness of copyists": "Extracts from Mississippi's Provincial Archives—English Dominion, 1763–1766," Henry Halbert Papers, MDAH, microfilm 4294, file 64.

35. Charles A. Weeks, "Voices from Mississippi's Past," 166–72. For more detail on the MDAH's holdings, see RG 26: Spanish Provincial Archives. For the provenance of the Panton, Leslie Papers, see Coker and Watson, *Indian Traders*, 371–74.

36. For the state, see Sandra E. Boyd and Young, *Mississippi's Historical Heritage*. On the Center for Louisiana Studies, which had emerged by the late 1970s as one of largest French and Spanish colonial depositories in the country, see Brasseaux, "Colonial Records Collection." Usner, *Indians, Settlers, and Slaves*, 1–9, discusses late-twentieth-century historical literature that has provided a more informed and broader discursive representation of the lower Mississippi Valley.

37. Baca and Gilberti, "Utility and Potential"; Usner, "Between Creoles and Yankees."

38. Bailey and Lowry, *Historic Preservation in Mississippi*; Jack D. Elliott Jr., *Comprehensive Plan*.

39. RG 17: State Historical Commission, MDAH; Galloway and McGahey, *Evidence and Proof*. For the Daughters of the American Revolution, see Jack D. Elliott Jr., "Buried City," 135–36. With regard to locating "Points and Places of Historic Interest in Mississippi" as an objective of the first commission, see Riley, "Extinct Towns and Villages of Mississippi," which is based on what local residents could tell him.

40. Galloway and McGahey, *Evidence and Proof*, 4–5.

41. Galloway and McGahey, *Evidence and Proof*, 4; Winston, *Story of Pontotoc*, 47–56. Described by Jack D. Elliott Jr., "Paving the Trace," 226, as someone "known for his imaginative local history writings," Winston delivered a paper describing a migration of Toltec Indians around 1000 AD from central Mexico to Mississippi. According to Winston, one group settled at Natchez and became what the French encountered as Natchez Indians, while other groups became the Choctaws and the Chickasaws.

42. For a more recent detailed discussion regarding these two sites and the events related to them, see James R. Atkinson, *Splendid Land, Splendid People*, 11–18, 43–73.

43. Dawson A. Phelps, "Vaudreuil Expedition," 483–84, 493.

44. Skates, *Mississippi's Old Capitol*, 141–55. On the architect and his design of the Old Capitol, see Kapp with Sanders, *Architecture of William Nichols*, 185–230.

45. Charlotte Capers, "Diary of a Museum Director," Charlotte Capers Papers, MDAH, Box 51.

46. Photograph of Capers, *Jackson Clarion-Ledger*, March 29, 1961, clipping in Subject File: Civil War—Secession Day, MDAH.

47. "Dedication of the Old Capitol Restoration and State Historical Museum," June 3, 1961, Subject File: Civil War—Secession Day, MDAH; Rolph, *Resisting Equality*, 100; Skates, *Mississippi's Old Capitol*, 166; Bettersworth, *Mississippi*, 287; Capers, "Diary of a Museum

Director." Millsaps College student Richard Pierce played Davis. *Jackson Clarion-Ledger*, March 29, 1961, clipping in Subject File: Civil War—Secession Day, MDAH.

48. Dittmer, *Local People*, 87–88. See also Payton, "Tougaloo Nine."

49. Skates, *Mississippi's Old Capitol*, 171.

50. Capers, "Diary of a Museum Director."

51. Photograph in Subject File: Museum & State History, 1961, MDAH. On the Tombecbé marker, see Charles A. Weeks, *Paths to a Middle Ground*, 103.

52. Galloway, *Practicing Ethnohistory*, 377–87. For the civil rights movement in Mississippi, see Dittmer, *Local People*, 211–337.

53. Galloway, *Hernando de Soto Expedition*, vii. The anthology is Galloway, *La Salle and His Legacy*.

54. Galloway, *Hernando de Soto Expedition*. The University of Alabama, Peru's Universidad de Lima, and Spain's Universidad de Extremadura sponsored an international congress in Cáceres, Spain, devoted to the Soto expedition: Congreso Internacional Hernando de Soto y su Tiempo Barcarrota-Cáceres-Guadalupe, May 15–18, 1991.

55. On discussions and debates regarding the quincentenary of the Columbus trip, see Charles A. Weeks, "The Encounter." See also Axtell, *Natives and Newcomers*, 15. In 1988, the Society for American Archaeology decided that the primary way to observe the Columbus Quincentenary should be a three-volume series, Columbian Consequences, that would include multidisciplinary essays describing the social, demographic, ecological, ideological, and human repercussions of the European–African–Native American encounters across the Spanish borderlands. Two of the volumes dealt with the Spanish borderlands west and east of the Mississippi River, while the third looked at the Spanish borderlands from a pan-American perspective. See David Hurst Thomas, "Retrospective Look"; Charles A. Weeks, review of *Columbian Consequences*.

56. See Galloway, *Native, European, and African Cultures*.

57. Patricia K. Galloway, "Community and History: A New Initiative at the Old Capitol Museum of History," *Mississippi Humanities Council Newsletter*, in Patricia K. Galloway subject file, MDAH; Sherry Lucas, "A Shared History: Mississippi, 1500–1800," *Jackson Clarion-Ledger*, April 10, 1997.

58. Carpenter, *Ethnic Heritage in Mississippi*, vii–x.

59. Carpenter, *Ethnic Heritage in Mississippi*, vii–x. An ethnic heritage volume followed with emphasis on the twentieth century. See Walton, *Ethnic Heritage in Mississippi*.

60. Jeanne Wells Cook and Caroline S. Kelly, preface to *Mississippi's Spanish Heritage*, ed. Sarah J. Banks and Weeks, vi; Buzhardt with Hawthorne, *Mississippi's French Heritage*. The latter began in 1991 as Buzhardt and Hawthorne, *Française le Long du Mississippi* and then was expanded from 51 items to 107 in Buzhardt and Hawthorne, *Rencontres sur le Mississippi*.

61. The cypress canoe may have been the same pirogue displayed in the earlier exhibit.

62. Sherry Lucas, "Mississippi, 1500–1800: A Shared History," *Jackson Clarion-Ledger*, April 11, 1997; Galloway, *Practicing Ethnohistory*, 386–87; Alford, *Prince among Slaves*. Ibrahima served in his father's army and in 1788 was captured in battle and sold to Natchez planter Thomas Foster. Ibrahima gained freedom in 1828, when Natchez printer Andrew Marschalk, US secretary of state Henry Clay, and President John Quincy Adams intervened. See *Picturing Mississippi 1817–2017*, 23; Alford, *Prince among Slaves*.

63. Galloway, *Practicing Ethnohistory*, 387; Sherry Lucas, "Mississippi, 1500–1800: A Shared History," *Jackson Clarion-Ledger*, April 11, 1997.

BIBLIOGRAPHY

Abbott, Martin. "Indian Policy and Management in the Mississippi Territory, 1798–1817." *Journal of Mississippi History* 14 (July 1952): 153–69.

Abernethy, Thomas P. *The Burr Conspiracy.* 1954. Gloucester, Mass.: Smith, 1968.

Abernethy, Thomas P. *The South in the New Nation, 1789–1819.* Baton Rouge: Louisiana State University Press, 1961.

Adelman, Jeremy, and Stephen Aaron. "From Borderlands to Borders: Empires, Nation States, and the Lands between in North American History." *American Historical Review* 104 (June 1999): 814–41.

Adorno, Rolena, and Patrick Charles Pautz. *Álvar Núñez Cabeza de Vaca: His Account, His Life, and the Expedition of Panfilo de Narvaez.* 3 vols. Lincoln: University of Nebraska Press, 1999.

Alden, John Richard. *John Stuart and the Southern Colonial Frontier: A Study of Indian Relations, War, Trade, and Land Problems in the Southern Wilderness, 1754–1775.* 1944. New York: Gordion, 1966.

Alford, Terry. *Prince among Slaves.* New York: Harcourt Brace Jovanovich, 1977.

Allain, Mathé. *"Not Worth a Straw": French Colonial Policy and the Early Years of Louisiana.* Lafayette: Center for Louisiana Studies, University of Southwestern Louisiana, 1988.

Allard, Sébastian, and Côme Fabre. *Delacroix.* New York: Metropolitan Museum of Art, 2018.

Altman, Ida. *Contesting Conquest: Indigenous Perspectives on the Spanish Occupation of Nueva Galicia, 1524–1545.* University Park: Pennsylvania State University Press, 2017.

Alvord, Clarence Walworth. *The Mississippi Valley in British Politics: A Study in Trade, Land Speculation, and Experiments in Imperialism Culminating in the American Revolution.* 2 vols. New York: Russell and Russell, 1959.

Anderson, Fred. *Crucible of War: The Seven Years' War and the Fate of Empire in British North America, 1754–1766.* New York: Knopf, 2000.

Arnold, Morris. *The Arkansas Post in Louisiana.* Fayetteville: University of Arkansas Press, 2017.

Arnold, Morris. "The Significance of the Arkansas Colonial Experience." *Arkansas Historical Quarterly* 51 (Spring 1992): 69–82.

Atkinson, James R. *Splendid Land, Splendid People: The Chickasaw Indians to Removal.* Tuscaloosa: University of Alabama Press, 2004.

Atkinson, William C. *A History of Spain and Portugal.* Baltimore: Penguin, 1960.

Axtell, James. *The Indians' New South: Cultural Change in the Colonial Southeast.* Baton Rouge: Louisiana State University Press, 1997.

Axtell, James. *Natives and Newcomers: The Cultural Origins of North America.* New York, Oxford: Oxford University Press, 2001.

Baca, Keith A. *Native American Place Names in Mississippi*. Jackson: University Press of
   Mississippi, 2007.
Baca, Keith A., and Joseph A. Gilberti. "The Utility and Potential of the Mississippi
   Archaeological Site File." In *Archaeological Site File Management: A Southeastern
   Perspective*, ed. David G. Anderson and Virginia Horak, 54–61. Atlanta: Interagency
   Archaeological Services Division, 1995.
Bailey, Robert J., and Priscilla M. Lowry, eds. *Historic Preservation in Mississippi: A
   Comprehensive Plan*. Jackson: Mississippi Department of Archives and History, 1975.
Baily, Francis. *Journal of a Tour of Unsettled Parts of North America in 1796 and 1797*. Ed.
   Jack D. L. Holmes. Carbondale: Southern Illinois University Press, 1969.
Baker, Vaughan B. "'Cherchez les Femmes': Glimpses of Women in Early Eighteenth Century
   Louisiana." *Louisiana History* 31 (Winter 1990): 21–37.
Banks, Kenneth J. *Chasing Empire across the Sea: Communications and the State in the French
   Atlantic, 1713–1763*. Montreal: McGill-Queen's University Press, 2003.
Banks, Sarah J., and Charles A. Weeks. *Mississippi's Spanish Heritage: Selected Readings,
   1492–1798*. Ed. Caroline S. Kelly. Jackson: Mississippi Department of Education and
   Mississippi Institutions of Higher Learning, 1992.
Barnett, James F., Jr. *Mississippi's American Indians*. Jackson: University Press of Mississippi, 2012.
Barnett, James F., Jr. "The Yamasee War, the Bearded Chief, and the Founding of Fort
   Rosalie." *Journal of Mississippi History* 64 (Spring 2012): 1–24.
Barnett, James F., Jr. *The Natchez Indians: A History to 1735*. Jackson: University Press of
   Mississippi, 2007.
Barr, Juliana. "How Do You Get from Jamestown to Santa Fe? A Colonial Sun Belt." *Journal
   of Southern History* 73 (August 2007): 553–66.
Barr, Juliana. "There's No Such Thing as 'Prehistory': What the Longue Durée of Caddo and
   Pueblo History Tells Us about Colonial America." *William and Mary Quarterly* 74, no. 2
   (April 2017): 203–40.
Barr, Juliana, and Edward Countryman, eds. *Contested Spaces of Early America*. Philadelphia:
   University of Pennsylvania Press, 2014.
Bartram, William. *Travels of William Bartram*. Ed. Mark Van Doren. 1928. New York: Dover,
   1955.
Bate, Albert C., ed. *The Two Putnams, Israel and Rufus, in the Havana Expedition 1762, and in
   the Mississippi River Exploration 1772–73*. Hartford: Connecticut Historical Society, 1930.
Beerman, Eric. "Arturo O'Neill: First Governor of West Florida during the Second Spanish
   Period." *Florida Historical Quarterly* 60 (July 1981): 29–41.
Beers, Henry Putney. *French and Spanish Records of Louisiana: A Bibliographical Guide to
   Archive and Manuscript Sources*. Baton Rouge: Louisiana State University Press, 1989.
Bekkers, B. J. "The Catholic Church in Mississippi during Colonial Times." *Publications of
   the Mississippi Historical Society* 6 (1902): 351–57.
Bemis, Samuel Flagg. *Pinckney's Treaty: America's Advantage from Europe's Distress,
   1783–1800*. Rev. ed. New Haven: Yale University Press, 1960.
Bénard de La Harpe, Jean-Baptiste. *The Historical Journal of the Establishment of the French
   in Louisiana*. Trans. Joan Cain and Virginia Koenig, ed. Glenn R. Conrad. Lafayette:
   University of Southwestern Louisiana, 1971.
Bettersworth, John K. *Mississippi: A History*. Austin, Tex.: Steck, 1959.
Blitz, John H., and C. Baxter Mann. *Fisherfolk, Farmers, and Frenchmen: Archaeological
   Explorations on the Mississippi Gulf Coast*. Jackson: Mississippi Department of Archives
   and History, 2000.

Bolton, Charles. *The Spanish Borderlands: A Chronicle of the Old South*. New Haven: Yale University Press, 1921.

Bond, Bradley G., ed. *French Colonial Louisiana and the Atlantic World*. Baton Rouge: Louisiana State University Press, 2005.

Bond, Bradley G. "'Unmitigated Thievery': The Case against William David McCain." *Journal of Mississippi History* 72 (Summer 2012): 163–97.

Boucher, Philip B. *Les Nouvelles Frances: France in America, 1500–1815, an Imperial Perspective*. Providence, R.I.: John Carter Brown Library, 1989.

Bouligny, Francisco. *Louisiana in 1776: A Memoria of Francisco Bouligny*. Trans. and ed. Gilbert C. Din. New Orleans: Holmes, 1977.

Bourne, Edward Taylor. *Spain in America, 1450–1580*. Ed. Benjamin Keen. 1904. New York: Barnes and Noble, 1962.

Boyd, C. Clifford, and Gerald F. Schroedl. "In Search of Coosa." *American Antiquity* 52, no. 4 (1987): 840–44.

Boyd, Sandra E., and Julia Marks Young. *Mississippi's Historical Heritage: A Directory of Libraries, Archives, and Organizations*. Hattiesburg: Society of Mississippi Archivists, 1990.

Bragg, Marion. "British Land Grants in Warren County, Mississippi." *Journal of Mississippi History* 26 (August 1964): 229–64.

Brain, Jeffrey P. *Winterville: Late Prehistoric Culture Contact in the Lower Mississippi Valley*. Jackson: Mississippi Department of Archives and History, 1989.

Brasseaux, Carl A. "The Colonial Records Collection of the Center for Louisiana Studies." *Louisiana History* 25 (Spring 1984): 181–88.

Brasseaux, Carl A., trans. and ed. *A Comparative View of French Louisiana, 1699 and 1762: The Journals of Pierre Le Moyne d'Iberville and Jean-Jacques-Blaise d'Abbadie*. Rev. ed. Lafayette: Center for Louisiana Studies, University of Southwestern Louisiana, 1981.

Brasseaux, Carl A. "La Délaissée: Louisiana during the Reign of Louis XIV, 1699–1715." In *A Refuge for All Ages: Immigration in Louisiana History*, vol. 10, ed. Carl A. Brasseaux, 13–23. Lafayette: Center for Louisiana Studies, University of Southwestern Louisiana, 1996.

Brasseaux, Carl A. *The Founding of New Acadia: The Beginnings of Acadian Life in Louisiana, 1765–1803*. Baton Rouge: Louisiana State University Press, 1987.

Brasseaux, Carl A. *"Scattered to the Wind": Dispersal and Wanderings of the Acadians, 1755–1809*. Lafayette: Center for Louisiana Studies, University of Southwestern Louisiana, 1991.

Braund, Kathryn E. Holland. *Deerskins and Duffels: Creek Indian Trade with Anglo-America, 1685–1815*. Lincoln: University of Nebraska Press, 1993.

Brereton, Geoffrey. *A Short History of French Literature*. Baltimore: Penguin, 1954.

Brooks, Philip C. *Diplomacy and the Borderlands: The Adams-Onís Treaty of 1819*. New York: Octagon, 1939.

Brown, Douglas Stewart. "The Iberville Canal Project: Its Relations to Anglo-French Commercial Rivalry in the Mississippi Valley." *Mississippi Valley Historical Review* 32 (March 1946): 491–516.

Brown, Ian W. "The Calumet Ceremony in the Southeast and Its Archaeological Manifestations." *American Antiquity* 54 (1989): 311–31.

Brown, Ian W. "Certain Aspects of French-Indian Interaction in Lower Louisiana." In *Calumet and Fleur-de-Lys: Archaeology of Indian and French Contact in the Midcontinent*, ed. John A. Wulthall and Thomas E. Emerson, 17–34. Washington, DC: Smithsonian Institution Press, 1992.

Brown, Ian W. "Functional Group Changes and Acculturation: A Case Study of the French and Indians in the Lower Mississippi Valley." *Mid-Continental Journal of Archaeology* 4 (1979): 147–65.

Brown, Ian W. "The Indians of the Lower Mississippi Valley: An Archaeologist's View." In *Towns and Temples along the Mississippi*, ed David H. Dye and Cheryl Anne Cox, 227–38. Tuscaloosa: University of Alabama Press, 1990.

Brown, Richmond F., ed. *Coastal Encounters: The Transformation of the Gulf South in the Eighteenth Century.* Lincoln: University of Nebraska Press, 2007.

Brown, William Horace. *The Glory Seekers: The Romance of Would-Be Founders of Empire in the Early Days of the Great Southwest.* Chicago: McClurg, 1906.

Buchan, James. *John Law: A Scottish Adventurer of the Eighteenth Century.* London: MacLehose, 2018.

Buisseret, David. *Monarchs, Ministers, and Maps: The Emergence of Cartography as a Tool of Empire in Early Modern Europe.* Chicago: University of Chicago Press, 1992.

Burnett, Edmund C. "Papers Relating to Bourbon County, Georgia, 1785–1786." *American Historical Review* 15 (October 1909): 66–111; (January 1910): 297–353.

Burns, E. Bradford. *A History of Brazil.* New York: Columbia University Press, 1970.

Burrow, John. *A History of Histories: Epics, Chronicles, Romances, and Inquiries from Herodotus and Thucydides to the Twentieth Century.* New York: Vintage, 2007.

Burton, H. Sophie, and Todd Smith. *Colonial Natchitoches: A Creole Community on the Louisiana-Texas Frontier.* College Station: Texas A&M University Press, 2008.

Buzhardt, Gail Alexander, and Margaret Hawthorne. *Les Française le Long du Mississippi au Temps de la Colonie Louisianaise, 1682–1763.* Jackson: Mississippi Department of Archives and History, 1991.

Buzhardt, Gail Alexander, with Margaret Hawthorne. *Mississippi's French Heritage.* Jackson: Mississippi Department of Education and Mississippi Institutions of Higher Learning, 1992.

Buzhardt, Gail Alexander, and Margaret Hawthorne. *Rencontres sur le Mississippi, 1682–1763: A French Language Reader of Historical Texts.* Jackson: University Press of Mississippi for Mississippi State Department of Archives and History, 1993.

Byington, Cyrus. *A Dictionary of the Choctaw Language.* Ed. J. R. Swanton and H. S. Halbert. Washington, D.C.: US Government Printing Office, 1915.

Cabeza de Vaca, Álvar Núñez. *Cabeza de Vaca's Adventures in the Unknown Interior of America.* Albuquerque: University of New Mexico Press, 1992.

Cabeza de Vaca, Álvar Núñez. *Chronicle of the Narváez Expedition.* Trans. Fanny Bandelier. Rev. and ann. Harold Augenbraum. New York: Penguin, 2002.

Caillot, Marc-Antoine. *A Company Man: The Remarkable French-Atlantic Voyage of a Clerk for the Company of the Indies.* Ed. and intro. Erin Greenwald, trans. Teri F. Chalmers. New Orleans: Historic New Orleans Collection, 2013.

Calhoun, Robert Dabney. "A History of Concordia Parish, Louisiana." *Louisiana Historical Quarterly* 15 (January 1932): 44–67; (April 1932): 214–33.

Calloway, Colin G. *The American Revolution in Indian Country: Crisis and Diversity in Native American Communities.* Cambridge: Cambridge University Press, 1995.

Calloway, Colin G. *The Indian World of George Washington: The First President, the First Americans, and the Birth of the Nation.* Oxford: Oxford University Press, 2018.

Calloway, Colin G. *New Worlds for All: Indians, Europeans, and the Remaking of Early America.* Baltimore: Johns Hopkins University Press, 1997.

Calloway, Colin G. *One Vast Winter Count: The Native American World before Lewis and Clark*. Lincoln: University of Nebraska Press, 2003.

Calloway, Colin G. *The Scratch of a Pen: 1763 and the Transformation of North America*. Oxford: Oxford University Press, 2006.

Calloway, Colin G. *White People, Indians, and Highlanders: Tribal Peoples and Colonial Encounters in Scotland and America*. New York: Oxford University Press, 2008.

Carpenter, Barbara, ed. *Ethnic Heritage in Mississippi*. Jackson: University Press of Mississippi for the Mississippi Humanities Council, 1992.

Carson, James Taylor. "Greenwood LeFlore, Southern Creole, Choctaw Chief." *Journal of Mississippi History* 65 (Winter 2003): 355–73.

Carson, James Taylor. *Searching for the Bright Path: The Mississippi Choctaws from Prehistory to Removal*. Lincoln: University of Nebraska Press, 1999.

Carter, Clarence. "The Beginnings of British West Florida." *Mississippi Valley Historical Review* 4 (December 1917): 314–41.

Caughey, John Walker. *Bernardo de Gálvez in Louisiana, 1776–1783*. 1934. Gretna, LA: Pelican, 1972.Caughey, John. "The Natchez Rebellion of 1781 and Its Aftermath." *Louisiana Historical Quarterly* 16 (1933): 57–83.

Cava Mesa, María Jesús, and Begoña Cava Mesa. *Diego María de Gardoqui: Un Bilbaíno en la Diplomacia del Siglo XVIII*. Bilbao: Bilbao Bizkaia Kutxa, 1992.

Cavelier, Jean. *The Journal of Jean Cavelier: The Account of a Survivor of La Salle's Texas Expedition, 1684–1688*. Ed. and annot. Jean Delanglez. Chicago: Institute of Jesuit History, 1938.

Chapman, Sara E. *Private Ambition and Political Alliances: The Phélypeaux de Pontchartrain Family and Louis XIV's Government, 1650–1715*. Rochester, N.Y.: University of Rochester Press, 2004.

Chateaubriand, François-René de. *Atala; or The Love and Constancy of Two Savages in the Desert*. Trans. Caleb Bingham. Boston: Carlisle for Bingham, 1802.

Chateaubriand, François-René de. *Atala; René*. 1801. Paris: Garnier Flammarion, 1964.

Claiborne, J. F. H. *Mississippi, as a Province, Territory, and State, with Biographical Notices of Eminent Citizens*. 1880. Baton Rouge: Louisiana State University Press, 1964.

Claiborne, W. C. C. *Interim Appointment: W. C. C. Claiborne Letter Book, 1804–1805*. Ed. Jared Williams Bradley. Baton Rouge: Louisiana State University Press, 2002.

Clark, Emily. *Masterless Mistresses: The New Orleans Ursulines and the Development of a New World Society, 1727–1834*. Chapel Hill: University of North Carolina Press, 2007.

Clark, John G. *La Rochelle and the Atlantic Economy during the Eighteenth Century*. Baltimore: Johns Hopkins University Press, 1981.

Clark, Thomas D., and John D. W. Guice. *Frontiers in Conflict: The Old Southwest, 1795–1830*. Albuquerque: University of New Mexico Press, 1989.

Clayton, Lawrence A., Vernon James Knight Jr., and Edward C. Moore, eds. *The De Soto Chronicles: The Expedition of Hernando De Soto to North America in 1539–1543*. 2 vols. Tuscaloosa: University of Alabama Press, 1993.

Coker, William S. "A Brief History of Mississippi, 1763–1817." In *Native, European, and African Cultures in Mississippi, 1500–1800*, ed. Patricia K. Galloway, 91–103. Jackson: Mississippi Department of Archives and History, 1991.

Coker, William S. "The English Reaction to La Salle." In *La Salle and His Legacy: Frenchmen and Indians in the Lower Mississippi Valley*, ed. Patricia Galloway, 129–35. Jackson: University Press of Mississippi, 1982.

Coker, William S. "Luke Collins Senior and Family: An Overview." *Louisiana History* 14 (Spring 1973): 137–55.

Coker, William S., ed. *The Military Presence on the Gulf Coast*. Pensacola, Fla.: Gulf Coast History and Humanities Conference, 1978.

Coker, William S., and Robert R. Rea, eds. *Anglo-Spanish Confrontation on the Gulf Coast during the American Revolution*. Pensacola, Fla.: Gulf Coast History and Humanities Conference, 1982.

Coker, William S., and Thomas D. Watson. *Indian Traders of the Southeastern Borderlands: Panton Leslie & Company and John Forbes & Company, 1783–1847.* Pensacola: University of West Florida Press, 1986.

Collot, Victor. *A Journey in North America*. 3 vols. 1924. New York: AMI, 1974.

"Concession Made by the King of Spain to Hernando de Soto of the Government of Cuba and the Conquest of Florida with the Title of *Adelantado* the King, April 20, 1527." Trans. Buckingham Smith. *Florida Historical Quarterly* 16 (January 1938): 179–87.

Conlin, Michael F. "The American Mission of Pierre-August Adet: Revolutionary Chemistry and Diplomacy in the Early Republic." *Pennsylvania Magazine of History and Biography* 124 (October 2000): 489–520.

Conrad, Glenn R., trans. and comp. *The First Families of Louisiana*. 2 vols. Baton Rouge: Claitor's, 1970.

Cooper, Forrest Lamar. *Looking Back Mississippi: Towns and Places*. Jackson: University Press of Mississippi, 2011.

Corbitt, Duvon C., and Roberta Corbitt, trans. and eds. "Papers from the Spanish Archives Relating to Tennessee and the Old Southwest." *East Tennessee Historical Publications* 30 (1958): 96–103.

Corona Werkreihe für Kammerorchester Nr. 100/Telemann/La Bourse. Wolfenbüttel: Möseler, 1967.

Cortés, Hernán. *Letters from Mexico*. Trans. and ed. Anthony Pagden, intro. J. H. Elliott. New Haven: Yale University Press, 1986.

Cox, Isaac Joslin. *The West Florida Controversy, 1798–1813: A Study in American Diplomacy*. 1918. Gloucester, Mass.: Smith, 1967.

Coxe, Daniel. *A Description of the English Province of Carolana: By the Spanish Call'd Florida and by the French La Louisiane*. London: Payne, 1741.

Crabb, A. L., ed. "George Washington and the Chickasaw Nation, 1795." *Mississippi Valley Historical Review* 19 (December 1932): 404–8.

Crane, Verner W. *The Southern Frontier, 1670–1732*. Ann Arbor: University of Michigan Press, 1929.

Crosby, Alfred W. *The Columbian Exchange: Biological and Cultural Consequences of 1492*. Westport, Conn.: Greenwood, 1972.

Crosby, Alfred W. "Reassessing 1492." *American Quarterly* 41 (December 1989): 661–69.

Crouse, Nellis M. *Lemoyne d'Iberville: Soldier of Fortune of New France*. Ithaca: Cornell University Press, 1954.

Cruzat, Heloise Hulse. "General Collot's Reconnoitering Trip down the Mississippi and His Arrest in New Orleans in 1796, by Order of the Baron de Carondelet, Governor of Louisiana." *Louisiana Historical Quarterly* 1 (January 1918): 303–26.

Cumming, William P. *The Southeast in Early Maps*. 3rd ed. Rev. and enl. Louis De Vorsey Jr. Chapel Hill: University of North Carolina Press, 1998

Cummins, Light Townshend. "An Enduring Community: Anglo-American Settlers at Colonial Natchez and the Felicianas, 1774–1810." *Journal of Mississippi History* 55 ((May 1993): 133–54.

Cummins, Light Townshend. "Oliver Pollock and the Creation of an American Identity in Spanish Colonial Louisiana." In *Nexus of Empire: Negotiating Loyalty and Identity in the Revolutionary Borderlands, 1760s-1820s*, ed. Gene Allen Smith and Sylvia L. Hilton, 198–218. Gainesville: University Press of Florida, 2010.

Cushman, H. B. *History of the Choctaw, Chickasaw, and Natchez Indians.* Ed. Angie Debo, intro. Clara Sue Kidwell. 1899. Norman: University of Oklahoma Press, 1999.

Davis, Jack E. *The Gulf: The Making of an American Sea.* New York: Liveright, 2017.

Dawdy, Shannon Lee. *Building the Devil's Empire: French Colonial New Orleans.* Chicago: University of Chicago Press, 2008.

Dawson, Joseph G., III, ed. *The Louisiana Governors: From Iberville to Edwards.* Baton Rouge: Louisiana State University Press, 1990.

De Fina, Frank Paul. "Rivalidades y Contactos entre España, Norte América y las Naciones Chactas, Chicasaws, Cherokis y Criks en la Segunda Mitad del Siglo XVIII." 2 vols. Ph.D. diss., Universidad de Madrid, 1962.

Deiler, J. Hanno. *The Settlement of the German Coast of Louisiana and the Creoles of German Descent.* Philadelphia: Americana Germanica Press, 1908.

Delanglez, Jean. *El Rio del Espíritu Santo: An Essay on the Cartography of the Gulf Coast and the Adjacent Territory during the Sixteenth and Seventeenth Centuries.* New York: US Catholic Historical Society, 1945.

De Rosier, Arthur H. "William Dunbar, Explorer." *Journal of Mississippi History* 25 (July 1963): 165–85.

De Vorsey, Louis, Jr. "Silent Witnesses: Native American Maps." *Georgia Review* 46 (Winter 1992): 709–26.

Deyle, Steven. *Carry Me Back: The Domestic Slave Trade in American Life.* Oxford: Oxford University Press, 2005.

Díaz del Castillo, Bernal. *The Discovery and Conquest of Mexico, 1517–1521.* Trans. and intro. J. M. Cohen. Baltimore: Penguin, 1963.

Dickason, Olivia Patricia. *The Myth of the Savage and the Beginnings of French Colonialism in the Americas.* Edmonton: University of Alberta Press, 1997.

Dillard, Anthony Winston. *The Treaty of Dancing Rabbit Creek between the United States and the Choctaw Indians in 1830.* Birmingham, Ala.: Birmingham Printing, 1928.

Din, Gilbert C. "Arkansas Post in the American Revolution." *Arkansas Historical Quarterly* 40 (Spring 1981): 3–30.

Din, Gilbert C. "Empires Too Far: The Demographic Limitations of Three Imperial Powers in the Eighteenth-Century Mississippi Valley." *Louisiana History* 50 (2009): 261–93.

Din, Gilbert C. *Francisco Bouligny: A Bourbon Soldier in Spanish Louisiana.* Baton Rouge: Louisiana State University Press, 1993.

Din, Gilbert C. *Populating the Barrera: Spanish Immigration Efforts in Colonial Louisiana.* Lafayette: University of Louisiana at Lafayette Press, 2014.

Din, Gilbert C. *Spaniards, Planters, and Slaves: The Spanish Regulation of Slavery in Louisiana, 1763–1803.* College Station: Texas A&M University Press, 1999.

Din, Gilbert C. "A Troubled Seven Years: Spanish Reactions to American Claims and Aggression in 'West Florida,' 1803–1810." *Louisiana History* 59 (Fall 2018): 409–52.

Din, Gilbert C. "War Clouds on the Mississippi: Spain's 1785 Crisis in West Florida." *Florida Historical Quarterly* 68 (July 1981): 51–76.

Din, Gilbert C. *War on the Gulf Coast: The Spanish Fight against William Augustus Bowles.* Gainesville: University Press of Florida, 2012.

Din, Gilbert C. "William Augustus Bowles on the Gulf Coast, 1787–1803: Unraveling a Conundrum." *Florida Historical Quarterly* 89 (Summer 2010): 1–25.

Din, Gilbert C., and John E. Harkins. *The New Orleans Cabildo: Colonial Louisiana's First City Government, 1769–1803.* Baton Rouge: Louisiana State University Press, 1996.

Din, Gilbert C., and A. P. Nasatir, *The Imperial Osages and Spanish Diplomacy.* Norman: University of Oklahoma Press, 1983.

Dittmer, John, *Local People: The Struggle for Civil Rights in Mississippi.* Urbana: University of Illinois Press, 1994.

Dobyns, Henry F. *Their Number Become Thinned: Native American Population Dynamics in Eastern North America.* Knoxville: University of Tennessee Press, 1983.

Domínguez, Virginia R. *White by Definition: Social Characteristics in Creole Louisiana.* New Brunswick: Rutgers University Press, 1993.

d'Oney, Daniel. "The Houma Nation in Mississippi's Early French Colonial Period: Modern Interpretations and Influences." *Journal of Mississippi History* 68 (Spring 2006): 40–64.

Dowd, Gregory Evans. *A Spirited Resistance: The North American Indian Struggle for Unity 1745–1815.* Baltimore: Johns Hopkins University Press, 1992.

Dowd, Gregory Evans. *War under Heaven: Pontiac, the Indian Nations, and the British Empire.* Baltimore: Johns Hopkins University Press, 2002.

Dumont de Montigny, Jean-François-Benjamin. *The Memoir of Lieutenant Dumont, 1715–1747.* Trans. Gordon M. Sayre, ed. Gordon M. Sayre and Carla Zecher. Chapel Hill: University of North Carolina Press, 2012.

Dunbar, William. "Report of Sir William Dunbar to the Spanish Government at the Conclusion of His Service in Locating and Surveying the Thirty-First Degree of Latitude." *Publications of the Mississippi Historical Society* 3 (1900): 185–205.

Duncan, David Ewing. *Hernando de Soto: A Savage Quest in the Americas.* Norman: University of Oklahoma Press, 1996.

Dungan, James R. "'Sir' William Dunbar of Natchez: Planter, Explorer, and Scientist, 1792–1810." *Journal of Mississippi History* 23 (1961): 211–28.

Durand, D. *The Vienna-Klosterneuburg Map Corpus.* Leiden: Brill, 1952.

Du Ru, Paul. *The Journal of Paul du Ru (February 1 to May 8, 1700).* Trans. Ruth Lapham Butler. Chicago: Caxton Club, 1934.

Du Val, Kathleen. *Independence Lost: Lives on the Edge of the American Revolution.* New York: Random House, 2013.

Dye, David H., and Cheryl Anne Cox, eds. *Towns and Temples along the Mississippi.* Tuscaloosa: University of Alabama Press, 1990.

Eccles, W. J. *France in America.* New York: Harper Torchbooks, 1972.

Echeverria, Durand, trans. "General Collot's Plan for Reconnaissance of the Ohio and Mississippi Valleys, 1796." *William and Mary Quarterly* 9 (October 1952): 512–19.

Ekberg, Carl J. *Colonial Ste. Genevieve: An Adventure on the Mississippi Frontier.* Tucson, Ariz.: Patrice, 1996.

Ellicott, Andrew. *The Journal of Andrew Ellicott.* 1803. Chicago: Quadrangle, 1962.

Ellicott, Andrew. *Surveying the Early Republic: The Journal of Andrew Ellicott, U.S. Boundary Commissioner in the Old Southwest, 1796–1800.* Ed. Robert D. Bush. Baton Rouge: Louisiana State University Press, 2016.

Elliott, Jack D., Jr. "The Buried City: A Meditation on History and Place." *Journal of Mississippi History* 66 (Summer 2004): 107–50.

Elliott, Jack D., Jr. "City and Empire: The Spanish Origins of Natchez." *Journal of Mississippi History* 59 (Winter 1997): 271–321.

Elliott, Jack D., Jr. *Comprehensive Plan for Historic Preservation for the Period of European Colonization in Mississippi (Draft).* Jackson: Division of Historic Preservation, Mississippi Department of Archives and History, 1989.

Elliott, Jack D., Jr. "The Fort of Natchez and the Colonial Origins of Mississippi." *Journal of Mississippi History* 52 (August 1990): 159–97.

Elliott, Jack D., Jr. "Paving the Trace." *Journal of Mississippi History* 63 (Spring 2001): 198–233.

Elliott, Jack D., Jr. "The Plymouth Fort and the Creek War: A Mystery Solved." *Journal of Mississippi History* 62 (Winter 2000): 328–70.

Elliott, Jack D., Jr. *Three Chopped Way: The History of an Error.* Jackson: Mississippi Department of Archives and History, Historic Preservation Division, 1998.

Elliott, J. H. *Empires of the Atlantic World: Britain and Spain in America 1492–1830.* New Haven: Yale University Press, 2008.

Elliott, J. H. *Spain and Its World: Selected Essays.* New Haven: Yale University Press, 1989.

Ellis, Elizabeth. "The Many Ties of the Petites Nations: Relationships, Power, and Diplomacy in the Lower Mississippi Valley, 1685–1785." Ph.D. diss., University of North Carolina at Chapel Hill, 2015.

Ellis, Elizabeth. "Petite Nation with Powerful Networks: The Tunicas in the Eighteenth Century." *Louisiana History* 58 (Spring 2017): 133–78.

Ethridge, Robbie Franklyn. *Creek Country: The Creek Indians and Their World.* Chapel Hill: University of North Carolina Press, 2003.

Ethridge, Robbie Franklyn. *From Chicaza to Chickasaw: The European Invasion and the Transformation of the Mississippian World, 1540–1715.* Chapel Hill: University of North Carolina Press, 2010.

Ethridge, Robbie Franklyn, and Charles Hudson, eds. *Transformation of the Southeastern Indians, 1540–1760.* Jackson: University Press of Mississippi, 2002.

Ethridge, Robbie Franklyn, and Sheri Marie Shuck-Hall, eds. *Mapping the Mississippian Shatter Zone: The Colonial Indian Slave Trade and Regional Instability in the American South.* Lincoln: University of Nebraska Press, 2009.

Fabel, Robin F. A. *Bombast and Broadsides: The Lives of George Johnstone.* Tuscaloosa: University of Alabama Press, 1987.

Fabel, Robin F. A. *The Economy of British West Florida, 1763–1783.* Tuscaloosa: University of Alabama Press, 1988.

Fabel, Robin F. A. "Elias Durnford." In *Encyclopedia of Alabama.* 2007. http://www. encyclopediaofalabama.org/article/h-1090.

Fabel, Robin F. A. "An Eighteenth Colony: Dreams for the Mississippi on the Eve of the Revolution." *Journal of Southern History* 59 (November 1993): 647–72.

Fabel, Robin F. A. "The Letters of R: The Lower Mississippi in the Early 1770s." *Louisiana History* 24 (Spring 1983): 402–27.

Faber, Eberhard L. *Building the Land of Dreams: New Orleans and the Transformation of Early America.* Princeton: Princeton University Press, 2016.

Falconer, Thomas. *On the Discovery of the Mississippi, and on the Southwestern, Oregon, and Northwestern Boundary of the United States.* 1844. Austin, Tex.: Shoal, 1975.

Farmer, Louis. *Kemper County: The Pioneer Days.* Livingston, Ala.: Sumter Graphics, 1982.

Faye, Stanley. "The Arkansas Post of Louisiana: French Domination." *Louisiana Historical Quarterly* 26 (July 1943): 633–721.

Faye, Stanley. "The Arkansas Post of Louisiana: Spanish Domination." *Louisiana Historical Quarterly* 27 (July 1944): 629–716.

Faye, Stanley. "The Contest for Pensacola Bay and Other Gulf Ports, 1698–1722, Part I." *Florida Historical Quarterly* 24 (January 1946): 167–95

Faye, Stanley. "The Contest for Pensacola Bay and Other Gulf Ports, 1698–1722, Part II." *Florida Historical Quarterly* 24 (April 1946): 302–28.

The Federalist: A Commentary on the Constitution agreed upon September 17, 1787 by the Federal Convention: From the Original Text of Alexander Hamilton, John Jay, and James Madison. New York: Modern Library, 1941.

Fernández-Armesto, Felipe. *Amerigo: The Man Who Gave His Name to America.* New York: Random House, 2007.

Fernández-Armesto, Felipe. *Columbus.* Oxford: Oxford University Press, 1997.

Fiehrer, Thomas Marc. "The Baron de Carondelet as Agent of Bourbon Reform: A Study in Spanish Colonial Administration in the Years of the French Revolution," Ph.D. diss., Tulane University, 1977.

Fitzpatrick, John. *The Merchant of Manchac: The Letterbooks of John Fitzpatrick, 1768–1790.* Ed. Margaret Fisher Dalrymple. Baton Rouge: Louisiana State University Press, 1978.

Forman, Samuel S. *Narrative of a Journey Down the Ohio and Mississippi in 1789–90 with a Memoir and Illustrative Notes by Lyman C. Draper.* Cincinnati: Clarke, 1888.

Frank, Andrew K. "Taking the State Out: Seminoles and Creeks in Late Eighteenth-Century Florida." *Florida Historical Quarterly* 84 (Summer 2015): 10–27.

French, B. F., ed. *Historical Collections of Louisiana.* Pt. 1 New York: Wiley and Putnam, 1846.

French, B. F., ed. *Historical Collections of Louisiana and Florida.* Pt. 6. New York: Sabin, 1869.

French, B. F., ed. *Historical Collections of Louisiana and Florida.* Pt. 7. New York: Mason, 1875.

Friedrich, Carl J. *The Age of the Baroque, 1610–1660.* New York: Harper and Row, 1952.

Fuson, Robert H. *Juan Ponce de León and the Spanish Discovery of Puerto Rico and Florida.* Blacksburg, Va.: MacDonald and Woodward, 1999.

Gaines, George Strother. *The Reminiscences of George Strother Gaines: Pioneer and Statesman of Early Alabama and Mississippi, 1805–1843.* Ed. James P. Pate. Tuscaloosa: University of Alabama Press, 1998.

Gallay, Allan, ed. *Indian Slavery in Colonial America.* Lincoln: University of Nebraska Press, 2009.

Gallay, Allan. *The Indian Slave Trade: The Rise of the English Empire in the South, 1670–1717.* New Haven: Yale University Press, 2002.

Galloway, Patricia. "Archives, Power, and History: Dunbar Rowland and the Beginning of the State Archives of Mississippi (1902–1936)." *American Archivist* 69 (Spring–Summer 2006): 79–116.

Galloway, Patricia K. "Choctaw Factionalism and Civil War, 1746–1750." In *The Choctaw before Removal,* ed. Carolyn Keller Reeves, 120–56. Jackson: University Press of Mississippi, 1985,

Galloway, Patricia K. *Choctaw Genesis, 1500–1700.* Lincoln: University of Nebraska Press, 1995.

Galloway, Patricia K. "The Four Ages of Alibamon Mingo, fl. 1700–1766." *Journal of Mississippi History* 65 (Winter 2003): 321–42.

Galloway, Patricia K., ed. *The Hernando de Soto Expedition: History, Historiography, and "Discovery" in the American Southeast.* Lincoln: University of Nebraska Press, 1997.

Galloway, Patricia K., ed. *La Salle and His Legacy: Frenchmen and Indians in the Lower Mississippi Valley.* Jackson: University Press of Mississippi, 1982.

Galloway, Patricia K., ed. *Native, European, and African Cultures in Mississippi, 1500–1800.* Jackson: Mississippi Department of Archives and History, 1991.

Galloway, Patricia K. *Practicing Ethnohistory: Mining Archives, Hearing Testimony, Constructing Narrative.* Lincoln: University of Nebraska Press, 2006.

Galloway, Patricia K. *Private Land Cessions in Mississippi: A Documentary History.* Jackson: Mississippi Department of Archives and History, 1984.

Galloway, Patricia K., ed. *The Southeastern Ceremonial Complex: Artifacts and Analysis.* Lincoln: University of Nebraska Press, 1989.

Galloway, Patricia K. "Talking with Indians: Interpreters and Diplomacy in French Louisiana." In *Race and Family in the Colonial South,* ed. Winthrop Jordan and Sheila L. Skemp, 109–29. Jackson: University Press of Mississippi, 1987.

Galloway, Patricia K., and Samuel G. McGahey. *Evidence and Proof in Popular History: The Case of Ougoula Tchetoka.* Jackson: Mississippi Department of Archives and History, 1987.

Gardner, Helen. *Gardner's Art through the Ages.* 9th ed. Ed. Horst de la Croix, Richard G. Tansey, and Diane Kirkpatrick. San Diego: Harcourt Brace Jovanovich, 1991.

Garrison, Tim Alan. *The Legal Ideology of Removal: The Southern Judiciary and the Sovereignty of Native American Nations.* Athens: University of Georgia Press, 2002.

Gershoy, Leo. *From Despotism to Revolution, 1763–1789.* New York: Harper and Row, 1944.

Gibson, Arrell M. *The Chickasaws.* Norman: University of Oklahoma Press, 1971.

Gibson, Charles. "Conquest, *Capitulación,* and Indian Treaties." *American Historical Review* 83 (February 1978): 1–15.

Gibson, Charles. *Spain in America.* New York: Harper Colophon, 1966.

Gilmore, Myron P. *The World of Humanism, 1453–1517.* New York: Harper, 1952.

Giraud, Marcel. *Histoire de la Louisiane Française.* Vol. 3, *L'Époque de John Law (1717–1720).* Paris: Presses Universitaires de France, 1966.

Giraud, Marcel. *A History of French Louisiana.* Vol. 1, *The Reign of Louis XIV, 1698–1715.* Trans. Joseph C. Lambert. Baton Rouge: Louisiana State University Press, 1974.

Giraud, Marcel. *A History of French Louisiana.* Vol. 2, *Years of Transition, 1715–1717.* Trans. Brian Pearce. Baton Rouge: Louisiana State University Press, 1958.

Giraud, Marcel. *A History of French Louisiana.* Vol. 5, *The Company of the Indies, 1723–1731.* Trans. Brian Pearce. Baton Rouge: Louisiana State University Press, 1991.

Gitlin, Jay. *The Bourgeois Frontier: French Towns, French Traders, and American Expansion.* New Haven: Yale University Press, 2010.

Gitlin, Jay. "Crossroads on the Chinaberry Coast: Natchez and the Creole World of the Mississippi Valley." *Journal of Mississippi History* 54 (November 1992): 365–84.

Gold, Robert L. *Borderland Empires in Transition: The Triple-Nation Transfer of Florida* Carbondale: Southern Illinois University Press, 1969.

Gould, Virginia. "Bienville's Brides: Virgins or Prostitutes? 1719–1721." *Louisiana History* 59 (Fall 2018): 389–408.

Grant, Ethan. "The Natchez Revolt of 1781: A Reconsideration." *Journal of Mississippi History* 56 (November 1994): 309–24.

Grant, Ethan. "They Stayed On: The British Settler Community at Natchez, 1765–1800." Ph.D. diss., Auburn University, 1993.

Green, Michael D. "Alexander Mc Gillivray." In *American Indian Leaders: Studies in Diversity*, ed. R. David Edmunds, 41–63. Lincoln: University of Nebraska Press, 1980.

Greenwald, Erin M. *Marc-Antoine Caillot and the Company of the Indies: Trade in the French Atlantic World*. Baton Rouge: Louisiana State University Press, 2016.

Greenwald, Erin M., ed. *New Orleans: The Founding Era*. New Orleans: Historic New Orleans Collection, 2018.

Greenwell, Dale. *D'Iberville and St. Martin*. Charleston, S.C.: Arcadia, 2013.

Greenwell, Dale. *Twelve Flags: Triumphs and Tragedies*. Vol. 1. Ocean Springs, Miss.: n.p., 1968.

Griffin, Patrick, ed. *Experiencing Empire: Power, People, and Revolution in Early America*. Charlottesville: University of Virginia Press, 2017.

Grivno, Max. "Antebellum Mississippi." *Mississippi History Now*, July 2015. http://www.ms historynow.mdah.ms.gov/articles/395/antebellum-mississippi.

Guenin-Lelle, Dianne. *The Story of French New Orleans: History of a Creole City*. Jackson: University Press of Mississippi, 2016.

Guice, John D. W. "Face to Face in Mississippi Territory, 1798–1817." In *The Choctaw before Removal*, ed. Carolyn Keller Reeves, 157–80. Jackson: University Press of Mississippi, 1985.

Hafner, Gerald O. "Major Arthur Loftus' Journal of the Proceedings of His Majesty's Twenty-Second Regiment up the River Mississippi in 1764." *Louisiana History* 20 (Summer 1979): 325–34.

Hahn, Steven C. *The Invention of the Creek Nation, 1670–1763*. Lincoln: University of Nebraska Press, 2004.

Halbert, Henry S. "Some Inaccuracies in Claiborne's History in Regard to Tecumseh." *Publications of the Mississippi Historical Society* 1 (June 1898): 101–3.

Halbert, Henry S. "Story of the Treaty of Dancing Rabbit Creek." *Publications of the Mississippi Historical Society* 6 (1920): 373–402.

Halbert, Henry S., and T. H. Ball. *The Creek War of 1813 and 1814*. Chicago: Donahue and Hennberry, Montgomery, Ala.: White, Woodruff and Fowler, 1895.

Hall, Gwendolyn Midlo. *Africans in Colonial Louisiana: The Development of Afro-Creole Culture in the Eighteenth Century*. Baton Rouge: Louisiana State University Press, 1992.

Hall, James. *A Brief History of the Mississippi Territory to Which Is Attached a Summary View of the Country between the Settlements on the Cumberland River and the Territory*. 1801. Spartanburg, S.C.: Reprint Company, 1976.

Hall, Joseph M., Jr. *Zamumo's Gifts: Indian-European Exchange in the Colonial Southeast*. Philadelphia: University of Pennsylvania Press, 2009.

Hämäläinen, Pekka. *The Comanche Empire*. New Haven: Yale University Press, 2008.

Haman, Rev. T. L. "Beginnings of Presbyterianism in Mississippi." *Publications of the Mississippi Historical Society* 10 (1909): 203–21.

Hamilton, William B. "The Southwestern Frontier, 1795–1817: An Essay in Social History." *Journal of Southern History* 10 (November 1944): 389–403.

Hammond, John Craig. *Slavery, Freedom, and Expansion in the Early American West*. Charlottesville: University of Virginia Press, 2007.

Hanke, Lewis. *The Spanish Struggle for Justice in the Conquest of America*. Boston: Little, Brown, 1965.

Haring, C. H. *The Spanish Empire in America*. Rev. ed. New York: Oxford University Press, 1952.

Havard, Gilles. *The Great Peace of Montreal of 1701: French-Native Diplomacy in the Seventeenth Century.* Trans. Phyllis Aronoff and Howard Scott. Montreal: McGill-Queen's University Press, 2001.

Havard, Gilles. *Histoire des Coureurs de Bois: Amérique du Nord, 1600–1840.* Paris: Les Indes Savantes, 2016.

Hawkins, Benjamin. *The Collected Works of Benjamin Hawkins, 1796–1810.* Ed. Thomas Foster. Tuscaloosa: University of Alabama Press, 2003.

Hawthorne, Margaret. "'That Certain Piece of Furniture': Women in Colonial Louisiana, 1685–1763." *Journal of Mississippi History* 53 (August 1991): 219–27.

Haynes, Robert V. "Historians and the Mississippi Territory." *Journal of Mississippi History* 23 (November 1967): 409–28.

Haynes, Robert V. "James Willing and the Planters of Natchez: The American Revolution Comes to the Southwest." *Journal of Mississippi History* 35 (1975): 1–40.

Haynes, Robert V. *The Mississippi Territory and the Southwest Frontier, 1795–1817.* Lexington: University Press of Kentucky, 2010.

Haynes, Robert V. *The Natchez District and the American Revolution.* Jackson: University Press of Mississippi, 1976.

Heitzmann, Jerry. "The Favre Family." *Mississippi Coast Historical and Genealogical Society* 36 (2000): 63–80.

Heitzmann, Jerry, with Nap L. Cassibry II. *The Favre Family.* Biloxi, Miss.: Coast Historical and Genealogical Society, 1989.

Henige, David. *Historical Evidence and Argument.* Madison: University of Wisconsin Press, 2005.

Henige, David. "If Pigs Could Fly: Timucuan Population and Native American Historical Demography." *Journal of Interdisciplinary History* 16 (1986): 701–20.

Henige, David. *Numbers from Nowhere: The American Indian Contact Population Debate.* Norman: University of Oklahoma Press, 1998.

Herr, Richard. *An Historical Essay on Modern Spain.* Berkeley: University of California Press, 1971.

Herring, Hubert. *A History of Latin America from the Beginnings to the Present.* 2nd ed. New York: Knopf, 1964.

Herring, Todd Ashley. "Natchez, 1795–1830: Life and Death on the Slavery Frontier." Ph.D. diss., Mississippi State University, 2000.

Higginbotham, Jay. *Fort Maurepas: The Birth of Louisiana, 1699–1702.* 2nd ed. Pascagoula, Miss.: Jackson County Historical Records, 1971.

Higginbotham, Jay. *Old Mobile: Fort Louis de la Louisiane, 1702–1711.* 1977. Tuscaloosa: University of Alabama Press, 1991.

Hoffman Paul E. *A New Andalucia and a Way to the Orient: The American Southeast during the Sixteenth Century.* Baton Rouge: Louisiana State University Press, 1990.

Holmes, Jack D. L. "Barton Hannon in the Old Southwest." *Journal of Mississippi History* 44 (February 1982): 69–79.

Holmes, Jack D. L. "Cotton Gins in the Spanish Natchez District, 1795–1800." *Journal of Mississippi History* 31 (August 1969): 154–71.

Holmes, Jack D. L., ed. *Documentos Inéditos para la Historia de la Luisiana, 1792–1810.* Madrid: Turanzos, 1968.

Holmes, Jack D. L. *Gayoso: The Life of a Spanish Governor in the Mississippi Valley, 1789–1799.* 1965. Gloucester, Mass.: Smith, 1968.

Holmes, Jack D. L. "Irish Priests in Spanish Natchez." *Journal of Mississippi History* 29 (August 1967): 169–80.

Holmes, Jack D. L. "Juan de la Villebeuvre: Spain's Commandant of Natchez during the American Revolution." *Journal of Mississippi History* 37 (February 1975): 97–129.

Holmes, Jack D. L. "Notes on the Spanish Fort San Esteban de Tombecbé." *Alabama Review* 18 (October 1965): 281–90.

Holmes, Jack D. L. "Stephen Minor: Natchez Pioneer." *Journal of Mississippi History* 42 (February 1980): 17–26.

Holmes, Jack D. L. "Up the Tombigbee with the Spaniards: Juan de la Villebeuvre and the Treaty of Boucfouca (1793)." *Alabama Historical Quarterly* 40 (Spring and Summer 1978): 51–61.

Holmes, Jack D. L. "William Dunbar's Correspondence on the Southern Boundary of Mississippi, 1798." *Journal of Mississippi History* 27 (1965): 187–90.

Hoole, William Stanley, and Emily Coleman Moore. *Spanish Explorers in the South Eastern United States, 1521–1561.* University, Ala.: Confederate Publishing, n.d.

Houck, Louis. *The Boundaries of the Louisiana Purchase.* 1901. New York: Arno, 1971.

Houck, Louis, ed. *The Spanish Regime in Missouri.* 2 vols. Chicago: Donnelley, 1909.

Howard, Clinton N. *The British Development of West Florida, 1763–1769.* Berkeley: University of California Press, 1947.

Howard, Clinton N. "Colonial Natchez: The Early British Period." *Journal of Mississippi History* 7 (July 1945): 156–70.

Howard, Clinton N. "Early Settlers in British West Florida." *Florida Historical Quarterly* 24 (July 1945): 45–55.

Howell, Elmo. "William Faulkner and the Mississippi Indians." *Georgia Review* 21 (Fall 1967): 386–96.

Hoxie, Frederick E., Ronald Hoffman, and Peter J. Albert, eds. *Native Americans and the Early Republic.* Charlottesville: University of Virginia Press, 1999.

Hudson, Angela Pulley. *Creek Paths and Federal Roads: Indians, Settlers, and Slaves and the Making of the American South.* Chapel Hill: University of North Carolina Press, 2010.

Hudson, Charles M. *Knights of Spain, Warriors of the Sun: Hernando de Soto and the South's Ancient Chiefdoms.* Athens: University of Georgia Press, 1997.

Hudson, Charles M. *The Southeastern Indians.* Knoxville: University of Tennessee Press, 1976.

Hudson, Charles M., Robin A. Beck Jr., Chester B. DePratter, Robbie Ethridge, and John E. Worth. "On Interpreting Cofitachequi." *Ethnohistory* 55 (Summer 2008): 465–90.

Hudson, Charles M., Marvin Smith, David Hally, Richard Polhemus, and Chester De Pratter. "Reply to Boyd and Schroedl." *American Antiquity* 52 (1987): 845–56.

Hudson, Charles M., Thomas J. Pluckhahn, and Robbie Franklyn Ethridge. *Light on the Path: The Anthropology and History of the Southeastern Indians.* Tuscaloosa: University of Alabama Press, 2006.

Hudson, Charles M., and Carmen Chavez Tesser, eds. *The Forgotten Centuries: Indians and Europeans in the American South, 1521–1704.* Athens: University of Georgia Press, 1994.

Hurtado, Albert A. "Parkmanizing the Spanish Borderlands: Bolton, Turner, and the Historians' World." *Western Historical Quarterly* 26 (Summer 1995): 149–67.

Hutchins, Thomas. *An Historical Narrative and Topographical Description of Louisiana and West Florida.* Philadelphia: Aitken, 1784.

Hyde, Lewis. *The Gift: Imagination and the Erotic Life of Property.* New York: Vintage, 1999.

Hyde, Samuel C., Jr. *Pistols and Politics: The Dilemma of Democracy in Louisiana's Florida Parishes, 1810–1809.* Baton Rouge: Louisiana State University Press, 1996.

Iberville, Pierre Le Moyne d'. *Iberville's Gulf Journals.* Trans. and ed. Richebourg Gaillard McWilliams, intro. Tennant McWilliams. Tuscaloosa: University of Alabama Press, 1981.

Inglis, G. Douglas. "Anthony Hutchins: Early Natchez Planter." Master's thesis, University of Southern Mississippi, 1973.

Inglis, G. Douglas. "The Character and Some Characteristics of Spanish Natchez." *Journal of Mississippi History* 66 (February 1994): 17–39.

Inglis, G. Douglas, "Forgotten but Not Lost: Settlers, Families and Communities on the Multi-Ethnic Frontier." Unpublished manuscript, n.d.

Inglis, G. Douglas. "Searching for Free People of Color in Colonial Natchez." *Southern Quarterly* 43 (Winter 2008): 97–112.

Inglis, G. Douglas, and Rodrigo Fernández Carrión. *Colonial Family History in the Lower Mississippi Valley: A Workbook of Methods, Sources and Bibliography.* Gulfport: William Carey College on the Coast, 1998.

Isenberg, Nancy. *Fallen Founder: The Life of Aaron Burr.* New York: Viking, 2007.

Jackson, Jack, Robert S. Weddle, and Winston De Ville. *Mapping the Texas and the Gulf Coast: The Contributions of Saint Denis, Oliván, and Le Maires.* College Station: Texas A&M University Press, 1990.

Jackson, John Brinckerhoff. *Discovering the Vernacular Landscape.* New Haven: Yale University Press, 1984.

James, James Alton. *Oliver Pollock: The Life of an Unknown Patriot.* New York: Appleton-Century, 1937.

John, Elizabeth A. H. "The Riddle of Mapmaker Juan Pedro Walker." In *Essays on the History of North American Discovery and Exploration,* ed. Stanley H. Palmer and Dennis Reinhurtz, 102–32. College Station: Texas A&M University Press, 1988.

Johnson, Cecil. *British West Florida, 1763–1783.* New Haven: Yale University Press, 1943.

Johnson, Cecil. "The Distribution of Land in British West Florida." *Louisiana Historical Quarterly* 16 (1933): 539–53.

Johnson, Cecil. "West Florida Revisited." *Journal of Mississippi History* 28 (May 1966): 121–32.

Johnson, Douglas. *A Concise History of France.* New York: Viking, 1971.

Johnson, Walter. *River of Dark Dreams: Slavery and Empire in the Cotton Kingdom.* Cambridge: Belknap Press of Harvard University Press, 2013.

Jones, Evan T., and Margaret M. Condon. *Cabot and Bristol's Age of Discovery: The Bristol Discovery Voyages, 1480–1508.* Bristol: Bristol University Press, 2016.

Jones, H. G. *Historical Consciousness in the Early Republic: The Origins of State Historical Societies, Museums, and Collections, 1791–1861.* Chapel Hill: North Carolina Society and North Carolina Collection, 1995.

Joutel, Henri. *Joutel's Journal of La Salle's Last Voyage, 1684–7.* Trans. Henry Reed Stiles Albany, N.Y.: McDonough, 1906.

Joutel, Henri. *Joutel's Journal of La Salle's Last Voyage: A Reprint (Page for Page and Line for Line) of the First English translation, London, 1714.* Chicago: Caxton Club, 1896.

Kapp, Paul Hardin, with Todd Sanders. *The Architecture of William Nichols: Building the Antebellum South in North Carolina, Alabama, and Mississippi.* Jackson: University Press of Mississippi, 2015.

Kastor, Peter J. *The Nation's Crucible: The Louisiana Purchase and the Creation of America.* New Haven: Yale University Press, 2004.

Kidwell, Clara Sue. *Choctaws and Missionaries in Mississippi, 1818–1918*. Norman: University of Oklahoma Press, 1995.

Kindelberger, Charles P. *A Financial History of Western Europe*. 2nd ed. New York: Oxford University Press, 1993.

Kinnaird, Lawrence, ed. *Spain in the Mississippi Valley, 1765–1794*. 3 parts. Annual Reports of the American Historical Association, vols. 2–4. Washington, D.C.: US Government Printing Office, 1946–49.

Kinnaird, Lawrence, and Lucia B. Kinnaird. "Nogales: Strategic Post on the Spanish Frontier." *Journal of Mississippi History* 42 (February 1980): 1–16.

Kirkpatrick, F. A. *The Spanish Conquistadores*. 1934. Cleveland: World, 1946.

Klein, Sybil, ed. *Creole: The History and Legacy of Louisiana's Free People of Color*. Baton Rouge: Louisiana State University Press, 2000.

Knapton, Ernest John. *France: An Interpretive History*. New York: Scribner's, 1971.

Kobbé, Gustav. *The New Kobbé's Complete Opera Book*. Ed. and rev. the Earl of Harewood. New York: Putnam, 1976.

Kondert, Reinhart. *Charles Frederick D'Arensbourg and the Germans of Colonial Louisiana*. Lafayette: Center for Louisiana Studies, University of Louisiana at Lafayette, 2008.

Kondert, Reinhart. *The Germans of Colonial Louisiana, 1720–1803*. Stuttgart: Heinz, 1990.

Kupperman, Karen Ordahl. *Indians and English: Facing Off in Early America*. Ithaca: Cornell University Press, 2000.

Kyte, George W. "A Spy on the Western Waters: The Military Intelligence Mission of General Collot." *Mississippi Valley Historical Review* 34 (December 1947): 427–42.

"Land Grants and Other Land Transactions on the Mississippi and Amite Rivers during the English Rule." *Louisiana Historical Quarterly* 12 (October 1929): 630–40.

Lankford, George E. *Looking for Lost Lore: Studies in Folklore, Ethnology, and Iconography*. Tuscaloosa: University of Alabama Press, 2008.

Lankford, George E., comp. and ed. *Native American Legends: Southeastern Legends: Tales from the Natchez, Caddo, Biloxi, Chickasaw, and Other Nations*. Little Rock, Ark.: August House, 1987.

Lauber, Almon Wheeler. *Indian Slavery in Colonial Times within the Present Boundaries of the United States*. Williamstown, Mass.: Corner Press, 1979.

Layton, Brandon. "Indian Country to Slave Country: The Transformation of Natchez during the American Revolution." *Journal of Southern History* 82 (February 2016): 27–58.

Leavelle, Tracy Neal. *The Catholic Calumet: Colonial Conversions in French and Indian North America*. Philadelphia: University of Pennsylvania Press, 2012.

Le Conte, René, and Glenn R. Conrad. "The Germans in Louisiana in the Eighteenth Century." *Louisiana History* 8 (January 1967): 67–84.

Leonard, Irving A. *Books of the Brave: Being an Account of Books and of Men in the Spanish Conquest and Settlement of the Sixteenth-Century New World*. Cambridge: Harvard University Press, 1949.

Leonard, Irving A. "The Spanish Re-Exploration of the Gulf Coast in 1686." *Mississippi Valley Historical Review* 22 (June 1935): 547–57.

Le Page du Pratz, Antoine Simon. *Histoire de la Louisiane, Contenant la Découverte de Ce Vaste Pays; Sa Description Géographique; Un Voyage dans les Terres*. 3 vols. Paris: Lambert, 1758.

Le Page du Pratz, Antoine Simon. *The History of Louisiana or of the Western Parts of Virginia and Carolina: Containing a Description of the Countries That Lie on Both Sides of the*

River Mississippi: With an Account of the Settlements, Inhabitants, Soil, Climate, and Products. 1774. New Orleans: Harmanson, 1947.

Lockhart, James. *The Men of Cajamarca: A Social and Biographical Study of the First Conquerors of Peru*. Austin: University of Texas Press, 1972.

Lockhart, James. *Nahuatl as Written: Lessons in Older Written Nahuatl*. Stanford: Stanford University Press, 2001.

Lockhart, James. *Spanish Peru, 1532–1560: A Social History*. 2nd ed. Madison: University of Wisconsin Press, 1994.

Lockhart, James, ed. *We People Here: Nahuatl Accounts of the Conquest of Mexico*. Vol. 1. Berkeley: University of California Press, 1993.

Lockhart, James, and Stuart B. Schwarz, *Early Latin America: A History of Colonial Spanish America and Brazil*. Cambridge: Cambridge University Press, 1983.

López de Gómara, Francisco. *Cortés: The Life of the Conqueror by His Secretary*. Trans., and ed. Lesley Byrd Simpson. Berkeley: University of California Press, 1966.

Lugan, Bernard. *Histoire de la Louisiane Française*. Paris: Librairie Académique, Perrin, 1994.

Lynch, John. *La España del Siglo XVIII*. 2nd ed. Barcelona: Editorial Crítica, 1999.

Lyon, E. Wilson. *Louisiana in French Diplomacy, 1759–1804*. Norman: University of Oklahoma Press, 1934.

Madley, Benjamin. *An American Genocide: The United States and the California Indian Catastrophe, 1846–1873*. New Haven: Yale University Press, 2016.

Maduell, Charles R., Jr. comp., and ed. *The Census Tables for the French Colony of Louisiana from 1699 through 1732*. Baltimore: Genealogical Publishing, 1972.

Mancall, Peter C. "'The Bewitching Tyranny of Custom': The Social Costs of Indian Drinking in Colonial America." In *American Encounters: Natives and Newcomers from European Contact to Indian Removal, 1500–1850*, ed. Peter C. Mancall and James H. Merrell, 194–215. New York: Routledge, 2000.

Mancall, Peter C. *Deadly Medicine: Indians and Alcohol in Early America*. Ithaca: Cornell University Press, 1997.

Mapp, Paul W. *The Elusive West and the Contest for Empire, 1713–1763*. Chapel Hill: University of North Carolina Press, 2011.

Markham, Clement R., ed. *The Letters of Amerigo Vespucci and Other Documents Illustrative of His Career*. 1894. New York: Cambridge University Press, 2010.

McBee, May Wilson. *The Life and Times of David Smith: Patriot, Pioneer, and Indian Fighter*. Greenwood, Miss.: McBee, 1959.

McBee, May Wilson. *The Natchez Court Records, 1767–1805*. Ann Arbor, Mich.: Edwards, 1953.

McCain, William D. "The Administrations of David Holmes, Governor of Mississippi Territory, 1809–1817." *Journal of Mississippi History* 29 (November 1967): 328–47.

McConnell, Roland C. *Negro Troops of Antebellum Louisiana: A History of the Battalion of Free Men of Color*. Baton Rouge: Louisiana State University Press, 1968.

McDermott, John Francis, ed. *The French in the Mississippi Valley*. Urbana: University of Illinois Press, 1965.

McDermott, John Francis, ed. *Frenchmen and French Ways in the Mississippi Valley*. Urbana: University of Illinois Press, 1969.

McKay, Angus. *Spain in the Middle Ages: From Frontier to Empire, 1000–1500*. New York: St. Martin's, 1977.

McMichael, F. Andrew. *Atlantic Loyalties: Americans in West Florida, 1785–1810*. Athens: University of Georgia Press, 2008.

Medina Rojas, F. de Borja. *José de Ezpeleta, Gobernador de la Mobila, 1780–1781*. Seville: Escuela de Estudios Hispano-Americanos de Sevilla, 1980.

Meinig, Donald W. "The Continuous Shaping of America: A Prospectus for Geographers and Historians." *American Historical Review* 88 (1978): 1186–1205.

Meinig, Donald. W. *The Shaping of America: A Geographical Perspective on 500 Years of History*. Vol. 1, *Atlantic America, 1492–1800*. New Haven: Yale University Press, 1986.

Melville, Herman. *The Confidence-Man: His Masquerade*. London, 1857.

Merrell, James H. *The Indians' New World: Catawbas and Their Neighbors from European Contact through the Era of Removal*. New York: Norton, 1989.

Meyer, Michael C., and William L. Sherman. *The Course of Mexican History*. 4th ed. New York: Oxford University Press, 1991.

Mills, Gary B. *The Forgotten People: Cane River's Creoles of Color*. Rev. ed. by Elizabeth Shown Mills. Baton Rouge: Louisiana State University Press, 2013.

Milne, George Edward. "Bondsmen, Servants, and Slaves: Social Hierarchies in the Heart of Seventeenth-Century North America." *Ethnohistory* 64 (January 2017): 115–39.

Milne, George Edward. *Natchez Country: Indians, Colonists, and the Landscapes of Race in French Louisiana*. Athens: University of Georgia Press, 2015.

Mississippi Department of Archives and History. *Telling Our Stories: Museum of Mississippi History and Mississippi Civil Rights Museum*. Jackson: University Press of Mississippi, 2017.

Moen, Jon. "John Law and the Mississippi Bubble, 1718–1720." *Mississippi History Now* (October 2001). http://www.mshistorynow.mdah.ms.gov/articles/70/john-law-and-the-mississippi-bubble-1718-1720.

Monette, John W. *History of the Discovery and Settlement of the Valley of the Mississippi by the Three Great European Powers, Spain, France, and Great Britain and the Subsequent Occupation, Settlement and Extension of Civil Government by the United States until the Year 1846*. Vol. 1. New York: Harper, 1848.

Montault de Monberaut, Henri. *Mémoire Justificatif: Indian Diplomacy in British West Florida, 1763–1765*. Trans. and intro. Milo B. Howard Jr. and Robert R. Rea. University: University of Alabama Press, 1965.

Moogk, Peter N. *La Nouvelle France: The Making of French Canada—A Cultural History*. East Lansing: Michigan State University Press, 2000.

Moogk, Peter N. "Reluctant Exiles: Emigrants from France in Canada before 1760." *William and Mary Quarterly* 46 (July 1989): 464–505.

Mooney, James. "The Cherokee Ball Play." *American Anthropologist* 3 (1890): 105–32.

Moore, Charles B. "Documentos Menos Conocidos de la Expedición de Hernando de Soto por el Sureste de Nortéamerica." *Revista de Crítica Literaria Latinoamericana* 34, no. 67 (2008): 125–47.

Moore, John Preston. *Revolt in Louisiana: The Spanish Occupation, 1766–1770*. Baton Rouge: Louisiana State University Press, 1976.

Morris, Christopher. *Becoming Southern: The Evolution of a Way of Life, Warren County and Vicksburg, Mississippi, 1770–1860*. New York Oxford: Oxford University Press, 1995.

Mt. Pleasant, Alyssa, Caroline Wigginton, and Kelly Wisecap. "Forum: Materials and Methods in Native American and Indigenous Studies." *William and Mary Quarterly* 75 (April 2018): 207–36.

Nabokov, Peter, ed. *Native American Testimony: A Chronicle of Indian-White Relations from Prophecy to the Present, 1492–2000*. New York: Viking Penguin, 1999.

Napier, John Hawkins. *Lower Pearl River's Piney Woods, Its Land and People.* University: University of Mississippi Center for the Study of Southern Culture, 1985.

Narrett, David. *Adventurism and Empire: The Struggle for Mastery in the Louisiana-Florida Borderlands, 1762–1803.* Chapel Hill: University of North Carolina Press, 2015.

Narrett, David. "Geopolitics and Intrigue: James Wilkinson, the Spanish Borderlands, and Mexican Independence." *William and Mary Quarterly* 69 (January 2012): 101–46.

Narrett, David. "William Panton, British Merchant and Politico: Negotiating Allegiance in the Spanish and Indian Borderlands, 1783–1801." *Florida Historical Quarterly* 96 (Fall 2017): 135–73.

Nasatir, Abraham P. *Spanish War Vessels on the Mississippi, 1792–1796.* New Haven: Yale University Press, 1968.

Nash, Gary B. *Red, White, and Black: The Peoples of Early North America.* 3rd ed. Englewood Cliffs, N.J.: Prentice Hall, 1992.

Nichols, David A. "Land, Republicans, and Indians: Power and Policy in Early National Georgia, 1780–1825." *Georgia Historical Quarterly* 85 (Summer 2001): 199–226.

Nugent, Walter. *Habits of Empire: A History of American Expansion.* New York: Knopf, 2008.

O'Brien, Greg. *Choctaws in a Revolutionary Age, 1750–1830.* Lincoln: University of Nebraska Press, 2002.

O'Brien, Greg. "The Conqueror Meets the Unconquered: Negotiating Cultural Boundaries on the Post-Revolutionary Southern Frontier." *Journal of Southern History* 67 (February 2001): 39–72.

O'Brien, Greg. "Mushulatubbee and Choctaw Removal: Chiefs Confront a Changing World." *Mississippi History Now* (November 2001). http://www.mshistorynow.mdah.ms.gov/articles/12/mushulatubbee-and-choctaw-removal-chiefs-confront-a-changing-world.

O'Brien, Greg, ed. *Pre-Removal Choctaw History: Exploring New Paths.* Norman: University of Oklahoma Press, 2008.

O'Brien, Greg. "'We Are behind You': The Choctaw Occupation of Natchez in 1778." *Journal of Mississippi History* 64 (Summer 2002): 107–24.

O'Gorman, Edmundo. *La Invención de América.* Mexico City: Fondo de Cultura Económica, 1986.

O'Neill, Charles Edwards. *Church and State in French Colonial Louisiana: Policy and Politics to 1732.* New Haven: Yale University Press, 1966.

Onís, Luis de. *Memoria sobre las Negociaciones entre España y los Estados Unidos de América.* 3rd ed. Madrid: Turanzas, 1969.

Onuf, Peter S. *Jefferson's Empire: The Language of American Nationhood.* Charlottesville: University Press of Virginia, 2000.

Osburn, Katherine M. B. *Choctaw Resurgence in Mississippi: Race, Class, and Nation Building in the Jim Crow South, 1830–1977.* Lincoln: University of Nebraska Press, 2014.

Padrón, Ricardo. *The Spacious Word: Cartography, Literature, and Empire in Early Modern Spain.* Chicago: University of Chicago Press, 2004.

Pagden, Anthony. *Lords of All the World: Ideologies of Empire in Spain, Britain, and France, c. 1500–1800.* New Haven: Yale University Press, 1995.

Palmer, R. R., and Joel Colton. *A History of the Modern World.* 8th ed. New York: McGraw Hill, 1995.

Parry, J. H. *The Age of Reconnaissance.* New York: New American Library, Mentor, 1963.

Parry, J. H. *The Establishment of the European Hegemony, 1415–1715.* New York: Harper and Row, 1961.

Pate, James P. "The Fort of the Confederation: The Spanish Fort on the Upper Tombigbee." *Alabama Historical Quarterly* 44 (Fall and Winter 1982): 170–86.

Pate, James P. "LeFlore, Greenwood." *Encyclopedia of Oklahoma History and Culture*, accessed May 13, 2020, https://www.okhistory.org/publications/enc/entry.php?entry=LE008.

Pauketat, Timothy E., and Thomas R. Emerson, eds. *Cahokia: Domination and Ideology in the Mississippian World*. Lincoln: University of Nebraska Press, 1997.

Payton, Annie. "Tougaloo Nine." *Mississippi Encyclopedia*, June 11, 2018. http://mississippiencyclopedia.org/entries/tougaloo-nine/.

Peckham, Howard H. *Pontiac and the Indian Uprising*. Chicago: University of Chicago Press, 1947.

Pénicaut, André. *Fleur de Lys and Calumet: Being the Pénicault Narrative of French Adventure in Louisiana*. Trans and ed. Richebourg Gaillard McWilliams. Tuscaloosa: University of Alabama Press, 1981.

Peterson, Frederick. *Ancient Mexico: An Introduction to the Pre-Hispanic Cultures*. New York: Capricorn, 1962.

Phelps, Dawson A., ed. "Excerpts from the Journal of the Reverend Joseph Bullen, 1799 and 1800." *Journal of Mississippi History* 17 (October 1955): 254–81.

Phelps, Dawson A. "The Vaudreuil Expedition, 1752." *William and Mary Quarterly* 15 (October 1958): 483–93.

Phelps, Matthew. *Memoirs and Adventures of Captain Matthew Phelps, Formerly of Harwington in Connecticut, Now Resident in New Haven in Vermont*. Comp. Anthony Haswell. Bennington, Vt.: Haswell, 1802.

Phillips, Faye. "Writing Louisiana Colonial History in the Mid-Nineteenth Century: Charles Gayarré, Benjamin Franklin French, and the Louisiana Historical Society." *Louisiana History* 49 (Spring, 2008): 163–90.

Phillips, William D., Jr., and Carla Rahn Williams. *The Worlds of Christopher Columbus*. New York: Cambridge University Press, 1992.

Pickett, Albert James. *A History of Alabama and Incidentally of Georgia and Mississippi from the Earliest Period*. 1851. Tuscaloosa, Ala.: Willo, 1962.

Picturing Mississippi, 1817–2017: Land of Plenty, Pain, and Promise. Jackson: Mississippi Museum of Art, 2017.

Piker, Joshua A. "'White and Clean' and Contested: Creek Towns and Trading Paths in the Aftermath of the Seven Years' War." *Ethnohistory* 50 (Spring 2003): 315–47.

Pinnen, Christian. *Complexion of Empire in Natchez: Race and Slavery in the Mississippi Borderlands*. Athens: University of Georgia Press, 2021.

Pinnen, Christian. "Slavery and Empire: The Development of Slavery in the Natchez District, 1720–1820." Ph.D. diss., University of Southern Mississippi, 2012.

Pinnen, Christian. "Slavery, Race, and Freedom on the Spanish Anglo Borderlands." *Latin Americanist* 61 (2017): 551–68.

Pineda, Marika. "Preserving Good Order: John Girault of Natchez Mississippi, 1783–1813." *Journal of Mississippi History* 68 (Winter 2006): 307–45.

Pipe Dreams: Louisiana under the French Company of the Indies, 1717–1731: An Exhibition, June 18–September 15, 2013. New Orleans: Historic New Orleans Collection, 2013.

Polk, Noel, ed. *Natchez before 1830*. Jackson: University Press of Mississippi, 1989.

Powell, Lawrence N. *The Accidental City: Improvising New Orleans*. Cambridge: Harvard University Press, 2012.

Prévost, Abbé. *Histoire du Chevalier de Grieux et de Manon Lescaut*. Ed. J. Sgard. Paris: Flammarion, 2012.

Prévost, Abbé. *Manon Lescaut*. Trans. Angela Scholar. Oxford: Oxford University Press, 2004.

Priestley, Herbert Ingram. *The Luna Papers: Documents Relating to the Expedition of Don Tristán de Luna y Arellano for the Conquest of La Florida in 1559–1561*. Freeport, N.Y.: Books for Libraries Press, 1971.

Pritchard, James. *In Search of Empire: The French in the Americas, 1670–1730*. Cambridge: Cambridge University Press, 2004.

Pruitt, Sarah. "Early Spanish Colony Unearthed in Pensacola." History.com, September 6, 2018. https://www.history.com/news/early-spanish-colony-unearthed-in-downtown-pensacola.

Pusch, Donald. "Jean-Jacques-Blaise d'Abbadie, Director General of Louisiana, 1763–1765." *Louisiana History* 58 (Summer 2017): 263–99.

Quinn, David R. *North America from Earliest Discovery to First Settlements: The Norse Voyages to 1612*. New York: Harper and Row, 1977.

Rasmussen, Hans. "Southern Progressives and the Beginning of Public History in Mississippi." *Journal of Mississippi History* 70 (Summer 2008): 147–77.

Rea, Robert R. *Major Robert Farmar of Mobile*. Tuscaloosa: University of Alabama Press, 1990.

Read, William A. *Louisiana—French*. Baton Rouge: Louisiana State University Press, 1931.

Reeves, Carolyn Keller, ed. *The Choctaws before Removal*. Jackson: University Press of Mississippi, 1985.

Remini, Robert V. *Andrew Jackson and His Indian Wars*. New York: Viking Penguin, 2001.

Remini, Robert V. "Andrew Jackson Takes an Oath of Allegiance to Spain." *Tennessee Historical Quarterly* 54 (Spring 1995): 2–15.

Reséndez, Andrés. *A Land So Strange: The Epic Journey of Cabeza de Vaca*. New York: Basic Books, 2007.

Restall, Matthew. *Seven Myths of the Spanish Conquest*. New York: Oxford University Press, 2013.

Richter, Daniel K. *Facing East from Indian Country: A Native History of Early America*. Cambridge: Harvard University Press, 2001.

Riley, Franklin L. "Extinct Towns and Villages of Mississippi." *Publications of the Mississippi Historical Society* 5 (1902): 311–83.

Riley, Franklin L. "The Life of J. F. H. Claiborne." *Publications of the Mississippi Historical Society* 7 (1903): 217–44.

Riley, Franklin L. "Sir William Dunbar—The Pioneer Scientist of Mississippi." *Publications of the Mississippi Historical Society* 2 (1899): 85–111.

Rolph, Stephanie R. *Resisting Equality: The Citizens' Council, 1954–1989*. Baton Rouge: Louisiana State University Press, 2018.

Romans, Bernard. *A Concise Natural History of East and West Florida*. Vol. 1. 1775. Gretna, La.: Pelican, 1998.

Roper, L. H. *Advancing Empire: English Interests and Overseas Expansion, 1613–1688*. New York: Cambridge University Press, 2017.

Rothman, Adam. *Slave Country: American Expansion and the Origins of the Deep South*. Cambridge: Harvard University Press, 2005.

Rothman, Joshua D. *Flush Times and Fever Dreams: The Story of Capitalism and Slavery in the Age of Jackson*. Athens: University of Georgia Press, 2012.

Rowland, Dunbar. *General Correspondence of Louisiana, 1678–1763.* New Orleans: Polyanthus, 1976.

Rowland, Dunbar, comp. and ed. *Mississippi Provincial Archives, 1763–1766: English Dominion.* Vol. 1. Nashville, Tenn.: Brandon, 1911.

Rowland, Dunbar. "Plantation Life in Mississippi before the War." *Publications of the Mississippi Historical Society* 3 (1900): 85–97.

Rowland, Dunbar. "The Rise and Fall of Negro Rule in Mississippi." *Publications of the Mississippi Historical Society* 2 (1899): 189–99.

Rowland, Dunbar, and Albert Godfrey Sanders, comps., eds., and trans. *Mississippi Provincial Archives: French Dominion.* Vols. 1–3. Jackson: Mississippi Department of Archives and History, 1927, 1929, 1932.

Rowland, Dunbar, Albert Godfrey Sanders, and Patricia Galloway, eds. and trans. *Mississippi Provincial Archives: French Dominion.* Vols. 4–5. Baton Rouge: Louisiana State University Press, 1984.

Rushforth, Brett. *Bonds of Alliance: Indigenous and Atlantic Slaveries in New France.* Chapel Hill: University of North Carolina Press, 2012.

Sabo, George, III. "Rituals of Encounter: Interpreting Native American Views of European Explorers." *Arkansas Historical Quarterly* 51 (Spring 1992): 54–68.

Sadler, Graham. "Jean-Philippe Rameau." In *The New Grove Dictionary of Opera*, ed. Stanley Sadie, 3:1225–34. London: Macmillan, 1992.

Sadler, Graham, and Thomas Christensen. "Jean-Philippe Rameau." In *The New Grove Dictionary of Music and Musicians*, 2nd ed., ed. Stanley Sadie, 20:778–806. London: Macmillan, 2001.

Safier, Neal. "The Confines of Colony: Boundaries, Ethnographic Landscapes, and Imperial Cartography in Iberoamerica." In *The Imperial Map: Cartography and the Mastery of Empire*, ed. James R. Ackerman, 133–84. Chicago: University of Chicago Press, 2009.

Sánchez-Fabrés Mirat, Elena. *Situación Histórica de las Floridas en la Segunda Mitad del Siglo XVIII (1783–1819): Los Problemas de una Region de Frontera.* Madrid: Ministerio de Asuntos Exteriores, Dirección de Relaciones Exteriores, 1977.

Saunt, Claudio. "Go West: Mapping Early American Historiography." *William and Mary Quarterly* 65 (2008): 745–78.

Saunt, Claudio. *A New Order of Things: Property, Power, and the Transformation of the Creek Indians, 1733–1816.* Cambridge: Cambridge University Press, 1999.

Sawyer, Sarah Elizabeth. *Tushpa's Story.* Canton, Tex.: Rock Haven, 2016.

Sayre, Gordon. "Plotting the Natchez Massacre: Le Page du Pratz, Dumont de Montigny, Chateaubriand." *Early American Literature* 37 (2002): 381–413.

Schama, Simon. *Landscape and Memory.* New York: Vintage, 1995.

Scott, Kenneth, ed. "Britain Loses Natchez, 1779: An Unpublished Letter." *Journal of Mississippi History* 26 (February 1964), 45–46.

Seed, Patricia. *Ceremonies of Possession in Europe's Conquest of the New World.* New York: Cambridge University Press, 1995.

Shoemaker, Nancy. "How the Indians Got to Be Red." *American Historical Review* 102 (June 1997): 625–44.

Shoemaker, Nancy. *A Strange Likeness: Becoming Red and White in Eighteenth-Century North America.* New York: Oxford University Press, 2004.

Siebert, Wilbur H. "The Loyalists in West Florida and the Natchez District." *Mississippi Valley Historical Review* 2 (March 1916): 465–83.

Silver, Peter. *Our Savage Neighbors: How Indian War Transformed Early America*. New York: Norton, 2008.

Silver, Timothy, *A New Face on the Countryside: Indians, Colonists, and Slaves in the South Atlantic Forests, 1500–1800*. Cambridge: Cambridge University Press, 1990.

Simpson, Lesley Byrd. *Many Mexicos*. 4th ed. rev. Berkeley: University of California Press, 1971.

Skates, John Ray. *Mississippi's Old Capitol: Biography of a Building*. Jackson: Mississippi Department of Archives and History, 1990.

Sleeper-Smith, Susan. *Indian Women and French Men: Rethinking Cultural Encounter in the Western Great Lakes*. Amherst: University of Massachusetts Press, 2001.

Smith, Adam. *An Inquiry into the Causes of the Wealth of Nations*. Ed. Edwin Cannan. Chicago: University of Chicago Press, 1976.

Smith, F. Todd. *Louisiana and the Gulf South Frontier, 1500–1821*. Baton Rouge: Louisiana State University Press, 2014.

Snyder, Christina. *Slavery in Indian Country: The Changing Face of Captivity in Early America*. Cambridge: Harvard University Press, 2010.

Southerland, Henry DeLeon, Jr., and Jerry Elijah Brown. *The Federal Road through Georgia, the Creek Nation, and Alabama, 1806–1836*. Tuscaloosa: University of Alabama Press, 1989.

Sparks, Randy J. "Mississippi's Apostle of Slavery: James Smylie and the Biblical Defense of Slavery." *Journal of Mississippi History* 51 (May 1989): 89–106.

Sparks, Randy J. *On Jordan's Stormy Banks: Evangelicalism in Mississippi, 1773–1876*. Athens: University of Georgia Press, 1994.

Sparks, Randy J. *Religion in Mississippi*. Jackson: University Press of Mississippi, 2011.

Spear, Jennifer M. *Race, Sex, and Social Order in Early New Orleans*. Baltimore: Johns Hopkins University Press, 2009.

Spiller, Robert E. *The Cycle of American Literature: An Essay in Historical Criticism*. New York: Macmillan, 1956.

Starr, J. Barton. *Tories, Dons, and Rebels: The American Revolution in West Florida*. Gainesville: University Presses of Florida, 1976.

Steigman, Jonathan D. *La Florida del Inca and the Struggle for Social Equality in Colonial Spanish America*. Tuscaloosa: University of Alabama Press, 2005.

Stein, Stanley J., and Barbara H. Stein. *The Colonial Heritage of Latin America: Essays on Economic Dependence in Perspective*. New York: Oxford University Press, 1970.

Steponaitis, Vincas P., ed. *The Natchez District in the Old, Old South*. Chapel Hill: University of North Carolina Press, 1998.

St. Jean, Wendy. "Squirrel King and the Eastern Chickasaw Band." *Journal of Mississippi History* 65 (Winter 2003), 343–54.

Strang, Cameron B. *Frontiers of Science: Imperialism and Natural Knowledge in the Gulf South Borderlands, 1500–1850*. Chapel Hill: University of North Carolina Press, 2018.

Surrey, N. M. Miller, ed. *Calendar of Manuscripts in Paris Archives and Libraries Relating to the History of the Mississippi Valley to 1803*. 2 vols. Washington, D.C.: Carnegie Institution of Washington Department of Historical Research, 1926.

Surrey, N. M. Miller. *The Commerce of Louisiana during the French Régime, 1699–1763*. New York: Columbia University Press, 1916.

Swanton, John R. *The Indians of the Southeastern United States*. Washington, D.C.: Smithsonian Institution Press, 1946.

Swanton, John R. *The Indian Tribes of the Lower Mississippi Valley and Adjacent Coasts of the Gulf of Mexico*. 1911. Mineola, N.Y.: Dover, 1998.

Sydnor, Charles S. *A Gentleman of the Old Natchez Region: Benjamin L. C. Wailes*. Durham: Duke University Press, 1938.

Sydnor, Charles S. "Historical Activities in Mississippi in the Nineteenth Century." *Journal of Southern History* 3 (May 1937): 139–60.

Takaki, Ronald T. *Iron Cages: Race and Culture in Nineteenth-Century America*. Seattle: University of Washington Press, 1979.

Tate, Roger D. "Franklin Riley and the University of Mississippi (1897–1914)." *Journal of Mississippi History* 42 (May 1980): 99–111.

Taylor, Alan. *American Colonies*. New York: Penguin, 2001.

Taylor, Alan. *The Divided Ground: Indians, Settlers, and the Northern Borderland of the American Revolution*. New York: Knopf, 2006.

Taylor, Alan. "Introduction: Expand or Die: The Revolution's New Empire." *William and Mary Quarterly* 74 (October 2017): 619–66.

TePaske, John. "French, Spanish, and English Indian Policy on the Gulf Coast, 1513–1763: A Comparison." In *Spain and Her Rivals on the Gulf Coast*, ed. Ernest F. Dibble and Earle W. Newton, 8–39. Pensacola, Fla.: Historic Pensacola Preservation Board, 1971.

Thomas, Daniel H. *Fort Toulouse: The French Outpost at the Alabamas on the Coosa*. Tuscaloosa: University of Alabama Press, 1989.

Thomas, David Hurst. "A Retrospective Look at *Columbian Consequences*." *American Antiquity* 57 (October 1992): 613–16.

Thomas, Hugh. *Conquest: Montezuma, Cortés, and the Fall of Old Mexico*. New York: Simon and Schuster, 1993.

Thomassy, R. *De La Salle et Ses Relations Inédites de la Découverte du Mississippi: Extrait de la Géologie Practique de la Louisiane*. Paris: Douniel, 1859.

Tocqueville, Alexis de. *Democracy in America*. 2 vols. New York: Vintage, 1960.

Trouillot, Michel-Rolph. *Silencing the Past: Power and the Production of History*. Boston: Beacon, 1995.

Tucker, Robert W., and David C. Hendrickson. *Empire of Liberty: The Statecraft of Thomas Jefferson*. New York: Oxford University Press, 1990.

Turner, Samuel. "Juan Ponce de León and the Discovery of Florida Reconsidered." *Florida Historical Quarterly* 92 (Summer 2013): 1–31.

Usner, Daniel H., Jr. "From African Captivity to American Slavery: The Introduction of Black Laborers to Colonial Louisiana." *Louisiana History* 20 (Winter 1979): 23–48.

Usner, Daniel H., Jr. *Indians, Settlers, and Slaves in a Frontier Exchange Economy: The Lower Mississippi Valley before 1783*. Chapel Hill: University of North Carolina Press, 1992.

Valverde, Nuria, and Antonio Lafuente. "Space Production and Spanish Imperial Geopolitics." In *Science in the Spanish and Portuguese Empires, 1500–1800*, ed. Daniela Bleichman, Paula De Vos, Kristina Huffine, and Kevin Sheehan, 198–215. Stanford, Calif.: Stanford University Press, 2009.

Van Horne, John C. "Andrew Ellicott's Mission to Natchez." *Journal of Mississippi History* 45 (Fall 1983): 160–85.

Vicens Vives, Jaime. *Approaches to the History of Spain*. 2nd ed. Trans. and ed. Joan Connelly Ullman. Berkeley: University of California Press, 1972.

Vickers, Daniel, ed. *A Companion to Colonial America*. Malden, MA: Blackwell, 2006.

Villiers du Terrage, Baron Marc de. *L'Expédition de Cavelier de La Salle dans le Golfe du Mexique, 1684–1687.* Paris: Adrien-Maisonneuve, 1931.

Villiers du Terrage, Baron Marc de. "History of the Foundation of New Orleans (1717–1722)." Trans. Warrington Dawson. *Louisiana Historical Quarterly* 3 (April 1920), 157–251.

Villiers du Terrage, Baron Marc de. *The Last Years of French Louisiana.* Trans. Hosea Phillips, ed. Carl Brasseaux and Glenn R. Conrad. Lafayette: Center for Louisiana Studies, University of Southwestern Louisiana, 1982.

Villiers du Terrage, Baron Marc de. *La Louisiane: Histoire de Son Nom et des Frontières Successives (1681–1819).* Paris: Adrien-Maisonneuve, 1929.

Villoro, Luis. "La Revolución de Independencia." In *Historia general de México,* 2nd ed., 2:303–56. Mexico City: El Colegio de México, 1977.

Wallace, Anthony F. C. *Jefferson and the Indians: The Tragic Fate of the First Americans.* Cambridge: Belknap Press of Harvard University Press, 1999.

Wallace, Anthony F. C. *The Long Bitter Trail: Andrew Jackson and the Indians.* New York: Hill and Wang, 1993.

Wallerstein, Immanuel Maurice. *The Modern World System II: Mercantilism and the Consolidation of the World Economy, 1600–1750.* Berkeley: University of California Press, 2011.

Walton, Shana, ed. *Ethnic Heritage in Mississippi: The Twentieth Century.* Jackson: University Press of Mississippi and the Mississippi Humanities Council, 2012.

Waggoner, May Rush Gwin, ed. *Le Plus Beau Païs du Monde: Completing the Picture of Proprietary Louisiana, 1699–1722.* Lafayette: Center for Louisiana Studies, 2005.

Ward, Joseph P., ed. *European Empires and the American South: Colonial and Environmental Encounters.* Jackson: University Press of Mississippi, 2017.

Washington, George. *The Writings of George Washington.* Ed. John C. Fitzpatrick. Washington, D.C.: US Government Printing Office, 1931–44.

Watson, Jay, Annette Trefzer, and James G. Thomas Jr., eds. *Faulkner and the Native South.* Jackson: University Press of Mississippi, 2019.

Watson, Samuel. "Conquerors, Peacekeepers, or Both? The U.S. Army and West Florida, 1810–1811: A New Perspective." *Florida Historical Quarterly* 92 (Summer 2013): 69–105.

Waselkov, Gregory. *A Conquering Spirit: Fort Mims and the Redstick War of 1813–1814.* Tuscaloosa: University of Alabama Press, 2006.

Weber, David J. *Bárbaros: Spaniards and Their Savages in the Age of the Enlightenment.* New Haven: Yale University Press, 2005.

Weber, David J. *The Spanish Frontier in North America.* New Haven: Yale University Press, 1992.

Webre, Stephen. "The Problem of Indian Slavery in Spanish Louisiana, 1769–1803." *Louisiana History* 25 (Spring 1984): 117–35.

Weddle, Robert S. *Changing Tides: Twilight and Dawn in the Spanish Sea, 1763–1803.* College Station: Texas A&M University Press, 1995.

Weddle, Robert S. *The French Thorn: Rival Explorers in the Spanish Sea, 1682–1762.* College Station: Texas A&M University Press, 1991.

Weddle, Robert S., ed. *La Salle, the Mississippi, and the Gulf: Three Primary Documents.* College Station: Texas A&M University Press, 1987.

Weddle, Robert S. *Spanish Sea: The Gulf of Mexico in North American Discovery, 1500–1685.* College Station: Texas A&M University Press, 1985.

Weddle, Robert S. *Wilderness Manhunt: The Spanish Search for La Salle.* College Station: Texas A&M University Press, 1999.

Weeks, Charles A. "A Choctaw Chief and a Spanish Governor: Franchimastabé and Manuel Gayoso de Lemos." *Mississippi History Now,* May 2018. http://www.mshistorynow.mdah .ms.gov/articles/423/a-choctaw-chief-and-a-spanish-governor-franchimastab%C3%A9 -and-manuel-gayoso-de-lemos.

Weeks, Charles A. "The Encounter: A Time for Celebration?" *Focus on Humanities* (Mississippi Humanities Council), July 1991.

Weeks, Charles A. *The Juárez Myth in Mexico.* Tuscaloosa: University of Alabama Press, 1987.

Weeks, Charles A. *El Mito de Juárez en México.* Trans. Eugenio Sancho Riba. Mexico City: Jus, 1977.

Weeks, Charles A. "Of Rattlesnakes, Wolves, and Tigers: A Harangue at the Chickasaw Bluffs, 1796." *William and Mary Quarterly* 67 (July 2010): 487–518.

Weeks, Charles A. *Paths to a Middle Ground: The Diplomacy of Natchez, Boukfouka, Nogales, and San Fernando de las Barrancas, 1791–1795.* Tuscaloosa: University of Alabama Press, 2005.

Weeks, Charles A. "The Politics of Trade: Delavillebeuvre's 1787 Mission to the Choctaws and His Journal." *Journal of Mississippi History* 65 (Spring 2003): 33–72.

Weeks, Charles A. Review of *Columbian Consequences: Archaeological and Historical Perspectives on the Spanish Borderlands East,* vol. 2, ed. David Hurst Thomas. *Journal of Mississippi History* 53 (May 1991): 159–62.

Weeks, Charles A. "Voices from Mississippi's Past: The Spanish Provincial Records in the Mississippi Department of Archives and History." *Journal of Mississippi History* 61 (Summer 1999): 149–79.

Weeks, William Earl. *Building the Continental Empire: American Expansion from the Revolution to the Civil War.* Chicago: Dee, 1996.

Welch, Kimberly M. *Black Litigants in the Antebellum South.* Chapel Hill: University of North Carolina Press, 2018.

Welch, Paul D. *Moundville's Economy.* Tuscaloosa: University of Alabama Press, 1991.

Wells, Gordon M., comp. "British Land Grants—William Wilton Map of 1774." *Journal of Mississippi History* 28 (May 1966): 152–60.

Wells, Mary Ann. *Native Land: Mississippi, 1540–1798.* Jackson: University Press of Mississippi, 1994.

Wells, Samuel James. "Choctaw Mixed Bloods and the Advent of Removal." Ph.D. diss., University of Southern Mississippi, 1987.

Westfall, Carroll William. *Architecture, Liberty, and Civic Order: Architectural Theories from Vitruvius to Jefferson and Beyond.* London: Routledge, 2016.

Whitaker, Arthur Preston. *The Mississippi Question, 1795–1803: A Study in Trade, Politics, and Diplomacy.* Gloucester, Mass.: Smith, 1962.

Whitaker, Arthur Preston. *The Spanish-American Frontier, 1783–1795: The Westward Movement and the Spanish Retreat in the Mississippi Valley.* Lincoln: University of Nebraska Press, 1927.

White, David Hart. *Vicente Folch, Governor in Spanish Florida, 1787–1811.* Washington, D.C.: University Press of America, 1981.

White, Hayden. *The Content of the Form: Narrative, Discourse and Historical Representation.* Baltimore: Johns Hopkins University Press, 1987.

White, Hayden. *Metahistory: The Historical Imagination in Nineteenth-Century Europe.* Baltimore: Johns Hopkins University Press, 1973.

White, Hayden. *Probing the Limits of Representation.* Berkeley: University of California Press, 1992.

White, Sophie. "Massacre, Mardi Gras, and Torture in Early New Orleans." *William and Mary Quarterly* 70 (July 2013): 497–538.

White, Richard. *The Roots of Dependency: Subsistence, Environment, and Social Change among the Choctaws, Pawnees, and Navajos.* Lincoln: University of Nebraska Press, 1983.

Williams, Frederick D. "The Career of J. F. H. Claiborne, States' Rights Unionist." Ph.D. diss., Indiana University, 1953.

Williamson, Joel. *William Faulkner and Southern History.* New York: Oxford University Press, 1993.

Wilson, Charles Reagan. *Baptized in Blood: The Religion of the Lost Cause, 1865–1920.* Athens: University of Georgia Press, 1980.

Wilson, Samuel M. *Hispaniola: Caribbean Chiefdoms in the Age of Columbus.* Tuscaloosa: University of Alabama Press, 1990.

Wilson, Samuel M. *The Indigenous People of the Caribbean.* Gainesville: University of Florida Press, 1997.

Winsor, Justin. *The Mississippi Basin: The Struggle in America between England and France, 1697–1763.* Boston: Houghton, Mifflin, 1895.

Winston, E. T. *The Story of Pontotoc: Part 1, The Chickasaws.* Pontotoc, Miss.: Progress, 1931.

Wolf, John B. *The Emergence of the Great Powers, 1685–1715.* New York: Harper and Row, 1951.

Wood, Peter H., "La Salle: Discovery of a Lost Explorer." *American Historical Review* 89 (April 1984): 294–323.

Worcester, Donald E. *Brazil: From Colony to World Power.* New York: Scribner's, 1973.

Wright, J. Leitch, Jr. *William Augustus Bowles: Director General of the Creek Nation.* Athens: University of Georgia Press, 1967.

Wright, Ronald. *Stolen Continents: Conquest and Resistance in the Americas.* London: Phoenix, 1992.

Zitomersky, Joseph. *French Americans—Native Americans in Eighteenth-Century French Colonial Louisiana: A Population Geography of the Illinois Indians, 1670s–1760s* with *B. Supplement: The Form and Function of French-Native Settlement Relations in Early Eighteenth-Century Louisiana.* Lund, Sweden: Lund University Press, 1994.

INDEX

ABOUT THE AUTHORS

Courtesy Charles A. Weeks

Charles Weeks holds degrees from Dartmouth College, University of Michigan, and Indiana University. He helped develop and teach a program of humane letters or humanities in St. Andrew's Episcopal School in Jackson, Mississippi.

Credit: Robby Followell

Christian Pinnen is an associate professor of history at Mississippi College. His research and teaching focuses on the history of race, slavery, and the law in the American colonial borderlands.